Then Sings My Soul

MUSIC IN AMERICAN LIFE

A list of books in the series appears
at the end of this book.

Then Sings My Soul

The Culture of Southern Gospel Music

DOUGLAS HARRISON

University of Illinois Press

URBANA, CHICAGO, AND SPRINGFIELD

Permission to reprint certain song lyrics is noted as applicable
in the notes.

Portions of chapter 1 and a few short sections of the introduction
appeared in "Why Southern Gospel Music Matters," *Religion and
American Culture* 18, no. 1 (2008): 27–58. © 2008 The Center for
the Study of Religion and American Culture. Published by the
University of California Press.

A version of chapter 4 with a somewhat different focus appeared
in "Gaither Homecomings, College Football Reunions, and the
Consecration of Cultural History," *Journal of Religion and Popular
Culture* 22, no. 1 (2010): http://www.usask.ca/relst/jrpc/art22(3)-
homecomings.html. Permission to reprint portions of this essay
granted by the editor.

Portions of chapter 5 were first published in "Southern Gospel
Sissies: Evangelical Music, Queer Spirituality, and the Plays of
Del Shores," *Journal of Men, Masculinities, and Spirituality* 3, no.
2 (2009): 121–43. Permission to reprint portions of this essay
granted by the editorial board of the journal.

Library of Congress Cataloging-in-Publication Data
Harrison, Douglas, 1975–
Then sings my soul : the culture of southern gospel music /
Douglas Harrison.
p. cm. — (Music in American life)
Includes bibliographical references and index.
ISBN 978-0-252-03697-2 (hardcover : alk. paper) —
ISBN 978-0-252-07857-6 (pbk. : alk. paper) —
ISBN 978-0-252-09409-5 (e-book)
1. Gospel music—Southern States—History and criticism.
2. Popular culture—Religious aspects. I. Title.
ML3187.H39   2012
782.25'408909075—dc23   2011045145

For MSQ, and in memory of MVH

Contents

Acknowledgments

In some ways, I have been preparing to write this book all my life. Consequently, there is a lifetime's worth of influence, indebtedness, gratitude, and generosity to acknowledge. I learned to love music in the rural Baptist churches of my childhood and was lucky to have musical parents who encouraged my early interest in music generally and the piano particularly. Maxine Sanders, whose classic Baptist-church-lady style of playing galvanized my fascination with the gospel sound, helped my father teach me basic chord structures on the piano when I was a young boy. As I progressed at the keyboard, my mother and grandmother invited me to accompany them when they sang so-called specials (that is, solos) at church. In this, I learned how not to step on someone else's best lines—an invaluable lesson in music and life. More deeply, providing improvised piano accompaniment for my family at church taught me at a young age to rely on my own expressive instincts, to "let the spirit move," as we would say back home, and trust that the right notes will follow. I will always be grateful for this early immersion in the art and instruction of Protestant evangelical sacred music.

Alan Freeman and Diana Hill both took an uncommon interest in my musical education as a teenager and provided years' worth of applied tutorials in music theory and piano pedagogy during the time I played piano for a regional gospel quartet in southern Missouri in my late teens and early twenties. Perhaps more than anything else, my musical sensibility is indebted to the countless gospel singers whose music so often seemed to be saying something for and about and to me that was both immediately recognizable yet also somehow revelatory.

Intellectual debts are wide and deep, but I would be remiss not to acknowledge the influence, example, and friendship of Robert Milder as a teacher and adviser in the study of American literature and culture. Philip Goff has provided unflagging support for this project since its inception. Rebecca Totaro, Meredith Neuman, Stephen Shearon, Carl Urion, Jay Twomey, Judith Linville, Jessica Lott, Joe Wisdom, David Thurmaier, Ryan Harper, Matthew Myers, Katherine Hale, and Margaret Hambrick read all or significant portions of the book at various stages and provided insightful feedback and encouragement. I am particularly grateful for the generosity of time and attention Rebecca Totaro gave in reading and responding to the project as it developed. She has been a ready sounding board for ideas, a candid critic, a deft mentor, and a close confidante through this process. I also benefited immensely from conversations with Stephen Shearon about the shape-note culture of southern gospel and gospel music history more generally and with Carl Urion about questions of genre and style in North American Christian music. Students in both my undergraduate and graduate seminars on gospel music and American literature became fellow travelers with me during the year in which most of the book was written. Reading and responding to the work of Crystal Matey, Karen Gravlin, Jamie Gillhespy, Elizabeth Weatherford, and Sarah Burt were particularly valuable to my own thinking about questions of race, sexuality, celebrity, and politics in gospel music.

The Center for Popular Music at Middle Tennessee State University was an unmatched resource for shape-note songbooks and related artifacts. I am grateful for the resourcefulness and good humor of Grover Baker and the entire center staff for helping me put my hands on the right material in a timely fashion. Research at the center was generously funded by a grant from the Department of Language and Literature in the College of Arts and Sciences at Florida Gulf Coast University; I am particularly thankful for the support that Myra Mendible and Donna Price Henry provided for this work. I am also grateful for the Gaylord Music Library at Washington University in St. Louis—both its collection and its quiet subterranean workspace. Kristine DeWelde, Joe Cudjoe, James Goff, Coray Ames Hoffner, Karron Skog, Leeann Adams, Mark Bradshaw Busbee, and Norman Linville all met my requests for information, assistance, or other forms of support with patience and generosity.

At the University of Illinois Press, Judy McCulloch showed early interest in my work, for which I remain grateful. The press's external reviewers who read both the book proposal and the manuscript supplied what for me has been an embarrassment of scholarly riches that immeasurably clarified my thinking and refined my writing. Most of all, Laurie Matheson has been the kind of editor with whom every author hopes to work. Her insightful advice, keen editorial eye, and finely calibrated judgment have improved the book at every stage.

Most fans and professionals in southern gospel music know me not as a scholar but as a blogger, and I owe a special thanks to the many readers of averyfineline.com. Their patronage and regular feedback (even and especially at its most antagonistic) have grounded me and helped keep my thinking about southern gospel from floating off into the ether of academic abstraction. From among these thousands of readers, I am particularly indebted to Dean Adkins and Norm Graham for their historical knowledge of the music and for providing generous access to their personal archives (and memories) of southern gospel music and memorabilia. My thanks go as well to scores of industry professionals whom I would like to—but shall not—name (in the world of southern gospel, one's professional reputation would not always necessarily be burnished by association with a project of this kind). Though unnamable, they know who they are, and I wish to convey my deep appreciation to them for the generous, reliable, and indispensable supply of news and information about the southern gospel industry that they send my way.

Finally, I am unboundedly thankful for the long-suffering graciousness of Matthew Myers. He has been a reassuring light of ever-present love and encouragement amid the inconveniences, disruptions, and occasionally mighty upheavals that this book introduced into our lives. If, as the old gospel song famously says, I wouldn't take nothin' for my journey now, it is not least of all because I have had the best company along with me for the ride.

Introduction

A Native Informant's
Report from the Field

In July 2000, *New York Times* writer R. W. Apple Jr. went to Nashville to write about his experience there in a travel piece for the newspaper. For the scholar of culture, the report is perhaps most interesting for a moment of acute discomfort Apple had while attending a performance at the Grand Ole Opry. He and his travel companion, he wrote, "realized what aliens we were in this culture when the crowd lustily cheered an explicitly sexist, rabidly homophobic, stunningly anti-government ditty called 'We Want America Back.'"[1] Apple was hearing what was at the time a chart-topping song performed by the Steeles, a southern gospel family who made a name for themselves in the late 1990s as quasi-sociopolitical singing activists. The group popularized other songs besides "We Want America Back," but it was this jeremiad set to music—about reclaiming a once godly nation from the destructive grip of sin—that landed the Steeles on the Opry stage. Released in 1996, the song capitalized on widespread conservative Christian displeasure over the country's perceived turn toward godless impunity during the Clinton years.

Apple's description of the song was not factually inaccurate, but in his inimitably arch way, he succumbed to the trap of intentionally outrageous rhetoric from the Christian Right. As Susan Harding has shown, this rhetoric operates by seizing on criticism from half-comprehending critics like Apple and treating it as an attack from unbelieving outsiders bent on destroying Christianity.[2] A few weeks after Apple's column appeared in print, I was at the National Quartet Convention (NQC) in Louisville, Kentucky. During one of the packed-out evening concerts that anchor the event, Jeff Steele, the family patriarch, took the stage and proudly cited criticism of the group and their song in the *Times,* which is a galvanizing symbol of East Coast atheism to American fundamentalists, as evidence that the forces of darkness were attacking the advancing army of Christian righteousness in a battle for the soul of the country. The crowd—in this case, upwards of twenty thousand, roughly five times the capacity of the Opry—cheered lustily.

Apple might be forgiven the lapse, for he made a mistake common to many humanist intellectuals and academics: treating conservative evangelical values and culture as a curious artifact from some socially recalcitrant land that time forgot. Southern gospel is arguably "America's most enduring yet obscure musical subculture," but it is a part of America—evangelical, fiercely fundamentalist, intensely pietistic, intellectually literal minded—in which many academics are at best visiting scholars, at worst intellectual tourists of the R. W. Apple variety.[3] To complicate things even more, for at least eighty years in both the academic and the popular imagination, *gospel singing* has always already been "the favored term for what working-class black congregations [do]," often to the exclusion of white traditions.[4] When nonblack gospel has been the primary focus of scholarly attention, it has typically emphasized gospel first of northern, urban extraction long associated with hymns of the so-called Sunday-school movement in the mid–nineteenth century, and later the evangelistic music typified by Ira Sankey, who was Dwight Moody's music director during the last quarter of the nineteenth century, and Homer Rodeheaver, Billy Sunday's music man from 1910 to 1930.[5] Southern sacred music has both shaped and been shaped by these phases of white gospel's broader development (as well as the later white gospel music of the Billy Graham era). Nevertheless, sustained scholarly attention has come late and infrequently to professional white gospel music with a southern accent.[6]

The term *southern gospel* was not used to describe this music until the 1970s and did not gain widespread use until the 1980s. Before then the music was simply known to its practitioners and fans as *gospel,* a "vague and inadequate" term that has historically encompassed a wide and shifting range of sacred music within Anglo-European and African American Protestantism in North America.[7] In its broadest sense, today's "southern gospel" includes a variety of musical expressions constituting the Protestant evangelical musical universe of the South. Southern gospel in its modern, professional form—the primary focus of this book—descends from a broad-based, post–Civil War recreational culture built around singing schools and community (or "convention") singings popular among poor and working-class whites throughout the South and Midwest.[8] This more participatory style of music gave birth to today's professional southern gospel music industry, even as the singing school movement and singing conventions were displaced from the dominant position in southern gospel by ascendant modes of professionalized music making beginning in the 1930s.

Critics of country music and scholars of southern culture occasionally make incursions into this territory. But for the most part, these forays are typically conducted on the way to somewhere else.[9] Southern gospel was what Elvis Presley really wanted to sing. Its biggest names have performed at the White House, have sung live on the *Today* show, and regularly appear on American evangelicalism's most influential stages—among them Jerry Falwell's Thomas Road Baptist Church, Pat Robertson's 700 Club, the Trinity Broadcast Network, the First Baptist Church of Atlanta, and national gatherings of the Southern Baptist Convention.[10] In 2004 the genre's most successful impresario, Bill Gaither, and his Homecoming Friends concert tour outranked Elton John, Fleetwood Mac, and Rod Stewart for ticket sales worldwide.[11] Nonetheless, despite these facts, southern gospel remains largely unexamined by scholars and critics of culture. Until recently, the only sustained treatments of the subject were nonacademic and, as James Goff says, "sketchy at best and . . . lacked a broad perspective."[12] Indeed, it was not until the 2002 publication of Goff's own *Close Harmony* that a comprehensive scholarly history of the genre existed.[13]

Then Sings My Soul provides the first book-length critical engagement of modern, professional southern gospel music and culture. In the chapters that follow, I propose a fundamental realignment of the scholarly approach to contemporary southern gospel's historical emergence and to the scholarly understanding of the music's function as a modern cultural phenomenon. At its heart, this study argues that the interaction of lyrics, music, and religious experience in southern gospel functions as a way for evangelicals to cultivate the social tools and emotional intelligence necessary for modern living. Through southern gospel, evangelicals develop the capacity to think and act as modern pluralists or situational relativists when necessary, while retaining their identification with antimodern religious traditions that notionally believe in timeless, unchanging absolutes. Southern gospel is typically treated as emblematic of a single "rhetoric"—one that serves to "devalue the earthly lives of believers" and shift their focus to a heavenly afterlife as compensation for hardships in this world.[14] In contrast, I propose southern gospel to be best understood as a network of interconnected rhetorics and signifying practices. Evangelicals use this music not to diminish experience in this world but to understand better Protestant theological doctrines and to create meaning from the vicissitudes of conservative Christian life.

This aspect of the music's cultural function emerged from the shaping pressures of the Reconstruction-era South. There, the music took on its modern form and was infused with an abiding concern for tensions between orthodox doctrine and unorthodox experience.[15] Though partisans often locate the music's origins in the early twentieth century, the shaping forces that define modern southern gospel actually originated at least a generation earlier, as I show. In the decades after the Civil War, community singing schools and all-day singings flourished across the South and Midwest due in large part to the popularity of shape-note music education, which taught people to read music by associating a unique shape with each note on the do-re-mi musical scale. This shape (or shaped) notation music, distinct from the earlier four-note method used in *Sacred Harp* singing, became a distinguishing trait of southern evangelical music in the nineteenth century. Fierce battles between the so-called round heads (those promoting the use of traditional notation) and square toes (shape-note advocates) over music pedagogy[16] became a proxy fight for larger cultural divides that were opening up between subsistence farmers and their descendants from the pious, rural countryside and the rapidly industrializing, educationally advanced, and increasingly ecumenical urban centers of America.

An entire culture of social distinction and aesthetic accomplishment proliferated around the seven-shape notational system in the final decades of the nineteenth century. Mastering the music and its unique theoretical system became an accessible way for southerners to assert aesthetic mastery over their world. For people whose identity was rapidly fragmenting after the Civil War and whose agrarian ways of life were increasingly being displaced by emergent industrialism, reestablishing a coherent sense of self through unique indigenous forms of popular culture was particularly important. The cultural innovations of southern shape-note music helped offset the encroachments of modernity, even as the sentimental and nostalgic lyrical content of the music preserved traditional religious ideals and memorialized earlier modes of pious pastoralism. In effect, the form of white gospel that became identified with the postbellum South anticipated a type of popular culture that Michael Kammen identifies in the interwar years of the twentieth century and describes as "nostalgic modernism"—what Stuart Patterson calls the "juxtaposition of the past and present in order to construct meaningful narratives about shifting cultural identities."[17]

Though I trace professional southern gospel forward from its postbellum roots in songbook publishing, shape-note music schools, and singing conventions, this book is not a comprehensive study of these phenomena or their musical and cultural development. I am primarily interested in the

do   re   mi   fa   so   la   ti   do

A seven-shape notional scale on a vertical staff. Both shape-note and round-note systems use lines and spaces, but those able to read shape notation could get by without them. (Courtesy Matthew S. Myers.)

southern shape-note tradition for what it has contributed to the gestalt of professional southern gospel today.[18] "Southern gospel," in its widest sense, encompasses the professional side of the music as well as the world of convention singings, singing schools, and a carefully cultivated corpus of "convention songs" that are still being written today in the (mostly) old-time way. This less professionalized subculture of convention singing defines southern gospel music for many people, and it deserves much more scholarly attention than it has yet received. But for most people today, and for my purposes in the pages that follow, "southern gospel" denotes an overlapping, commercialized national network of musical products, professionals, and their fans, commonly referred to as "the industry." Many of the people associated with this industry claim traditional founders in the southern singing schools and white quartet traditions of the late nineteenth and early twentieth centuries, while embracing a dizzying variety of musical styles and sounds that share few common formal features. For this reason, my definition of "southern gospel" de-emphasizes the definitional value of musical style in favor of an emphasis on patterns of cultural experience and affiliation. Today, southern gospel is most powerfully defined by common historical, economic, social, and cultural connections among professionals and fans to a constellation of corporate and professional organizations that anchor the creation, consumption, and commemoration of the music. These organizations include the Southern Gospel Music Association, *Singing News* magazine, the National Quartet Convention, the Southern Gospel Music Hall of Fame, and the Gaither Homecoming Friends phenomenon, as well as a cluster of record and distribution labels. Here and throughout, I use the term *southern gospel* to indicate the music and culture of those people who choose to associate themselves with this tradition and these entities in some fashion.

Contemporary southern gospel retains the dualistic quality inherent in all forms of nostalgic modernism, layering the music with strata of psychosocial complexity. A song such as "Lord Build Me a Cabin in the Corner of Gloryland" might initially seem to be mainly about reinforcing orthodox evangelical diminutions of this life: "I don't care for the fine mansions on earth's sinkin' sand," the first verse declares, in favor of even the most modest home in heaven.[19] Here, it would seem, is another boilerplate ditty from Apple's culturally alien hinterlands. Considered in the psychosocial milieu of the 1950s and 1960s, however, when the Blackwood Brothers quartet popularized the song, the lyrics mount a subtler defense of pan-southern aesthetics and ways of life that were being exported, but also attenuated, by the great postwar migration of white southerners to northern, midwestern, and southwestern states. In the context of suburban tract homes replacing the modern homestead for transplanted southerners, music that evokes the homesteader's cabin—a powerful symbol of agrarian ways of life and their rapidly receding values—calls into being a nostalgic home to return to in the imagination. At the same time, the song implicitly comments on midcentury class conflicts, asserting the superiority of southern values and rural aesthetics over those of the secularist consumer culture represented by "fine mansions." Though they were part of the growing American middle class typically assumed to be striving for a mansion of their own in this life, deracinated suburban southerners distinguished themselves from the worldly acquisitiveness of the petit bourgeois by aligning themselves with religious music that set them apart. Though living in the world, they are not, as the writer of Acts describes it, *of* the world: all the faithful Christian really wants is a cabin in the corner of Gloryland.

This sentiment is not conveyed mournfully, or with bitterness, not even bittersweetness, at least not in the Blackwoods' rendition from 1965. The song is arranged in a midtempo style. The vocalists sing in homophonic harmony, with musical phrases anchored mainly on the downbeat, creating a feeling of uniformity and reverence befitting an address to the divine. Behind and around the vocalists, the piano soars and sails, lilts and rolls, weaving in and out of the vocals in pirouettes of arpeggiated runs and ornamental fills that often threaten to upstage the singers. The effect is a respectful playfulness, both commemorating a rural evangelical ethos of rustic piety and flashily celebrating the vernacular music culture of southern gospel that descends from that rusticity.

This song captures the way southern gospel symbolically reunites a coalition of evangelical strivers affiliated with southern Protestantism in the Calvinist tradition—and continues to do so.[20] Beyond the everyday world of southern gospel itself, nowhere is the ongoing psychodynamic value of the music more evident than in literary works that draw imaginative energy from this music. I draw on key texts from this subset of American literature in the chapters to come, but I note here that these works amplify a set of concerns

The Blackwood Brothers quartet in the early 1960s.
Members are, *sitting,* Wally Varner; *seated,* J. D. Sumner;
standing, left to right, Cecil Blackwood, Bill Shaw, James
Blackwood. (From the collection of Dean Adkins. Used
by permission of the Blackwood Brothers quartet.)

that often remain largely hidden but are deeply embedded in the music's
psychosocial DNA. In 2007, just a few miles down the road from the university where I work in Southwest Florida, a small community theater staged
Four Part Thunder, an original play by a playwright from southern Illinois
about an East Coast pop-music critic who finds common ground with her
estranged grandfather only after learning that he used to be a quartet man
back in southern gospel's midcentury heyday.[21] The music's unique sound
and history have an emulsifying effect on intergenerational differences. In

the play's depiction, southern gospel exerts a unifying force upon family bonds that are portrayed as under pressure from the depersonalizing forces of late-capitalist American life. In this light, southern gospel's seemingly conventional restatement of what David Fillingim calls fundamentalism's "message of world rejection" reveals itself as scaffolding for a much more complex reconceptualization of postmodern evangelical identities in flux.[22]

This reimagining calls to mind Benedict Anderson's concept of imagined communities. For Anderson, networks of social affiliation and communal bonds are constructed not around the increasingly unstable terms of geography or nationality but through cultural processes that link people in shared intellectual and imaginative activities (newspapers are one of Anderson's key examples). As imaginative constructs, these communities achieve a degree of psychosocial coherence missing from ordinary life fractured by the too-muchness of modernity. Along these lines, this book explores southern gospel as a means of negotiating evangelicalism's tensions by reimagining them. The result is a musical mode of expression in which millions—and I count myself among them—find the right key in which their souls can sing.[23]

The Popular Music of American Christianity

Broadly defined, southern gospel songs fall into four general types. There are songs of celebration (including novelty tunes like the enormously popular Kingsmen quartet hit from the 1980s, "Excuses," in which singers mimic—and mock—common excuses that people give for not going to church), as well as more commonplace toe-tappers and other upbeat feel-good songs meant to entertain within the Christian context of praise to God; patriotic and political songs; songs of supplication (any invocation of God's power, help, comfort, or forgiveness); and songs of surrender, which espouse lyrical statements of unworthiness, unmerited favor, or resolutions to abandon the self to God's mercy and direction. By far the latter two types of songs predominate, and any given song can easily cross the permeable borders among these categories, as "Lord Build Me a Cabin" suggests. Across all song styles and types, a tension persists between the music's function as an instrument of conversion and as a vehicle of aesthetic satisfaction. As I demonstrate in the chapters that follow, this tension is submerged beneath the music's role as a tool for recreation, ministry, and supplication in orthodox evangelical terms. At a deeper psychosocial level, the music grants people access to a version of what Raymond Williams first called "structures of feeling" through which to interpret and negotiate the paradoxes of cultural change.[24]

While southern gospel engages modern methods of identity formation, it does so in a way that outwardly reinforces the antimodern worldview of evangelical fundamentalism. This dynamic poses a unique set of interpretive challenges for the scholar of religious culture. To an academic outsider (and depending on what factors one emphasizes), southern gospel may appear as the contemporary expression of a very old and fundamental roots tradition; a stylistic mishmash of borrowing from Reformed church hymnody, country, pop, bluegrass, and even jazz and classical music; or a derivative of more highly regarded and stylistically coherent sacred-music traditions. Culturally, the overt and fervent piety of southern gospel fan culture and performance styles may also give the impression to the uninitiated that southern gospel is a mere musical adjunct to (and is best understood within the context of) more familiar religious practices such as traditional congregational worship experiences.

Indeed, the fact that southern gospel resonates with a large segment of contemporary evangelicals may suggest that this music is a generic soundtrack for all varieties of conservative evangelical Protestant theology, a cultural or an artistic extension of evangelical church culture and history. But even though evangelical Christians from divergent theological traditions can enjoy and identify with the same southern gospel song, that identification takes hold despite—not primarily because of—evangelical church membership. Local Protestant congregations define the individual primarily as part of a specific theological and denominational history or as part of the self-contained social networks created by nondenominational suburban megachurches. In each case, religious identity emerges from the individual's willing acceptance of the denominational creed or the officially sanctioned doctrines and normative practices of the local congregation. In order to receive comfort and support of a church community, the churchgoing individual usually has to submit to the social, liturgical, and theological conventions of the larger body of believers. Southern gospel music, however, with its emphasis on the individual Christian's ordinary struggle in a world of woe, has been the form of evangelical popular culture that most stridently encourages people to construct a religious identity through an individualized musical experience. A Southern Baptist and a Pentecostal enjoy the same song not because of its sufficient theological vagueness but because each listener has given the song an individualized meaning.

This individualization in part reflects the influences of gospel-music publishers. Publication of the sacred music of Anglo-European Protestantism in America stretches back at least as far as the mid–eighteenth century.[25] But as Edward Ayers notes, southern gospel's cross-denominational appeal grew out of a specifically southern branch of gospel-music publishing that began to take root in the 1870s and continued into the early twentieth century: "Publishers strove to please a diverse audience, [meaning] they combined songs with divergent theological emphases."[26] Ecumenism sells better than sectarianism, and it helped the music fit in a variety of recreational settings where gospel songs were popular.[27] Other influences were less direct. Bill C. Malone notes that at the same time, around 1900, "a great stream of religious songs, fed by the big-city revivals of the era, flowed into American popular culture," seeping into the rural religious culture of the South and Midwest, where southern gospel music was beginning to crystallize.[28] All these strands of ordinary self-interest and less-than-sacred influence were woven into gospel music from the first and helped strengthen what William Lynwood Montell describes as "the democratic Christian ideals" of Anglo-Protestantism.[29]

Like evangelical theology, southern gospel receives special emphasis in the South but is popular throughout American society, geographically and socioeconomically. What is difficult to identify is who listens to and buys southern gospel. My research into demographics of southern gospel indicates that fans tend to be middle-aged, working- and middle-class Christians who identify mainly as some variety of Baptist or Pentecostal, reside in suburban parts of the South and Midwest, are educated (bachelor's degrees or some college), marginally more male than female, largely self-identified as straight, and, perhaps needless to say, overwhelmingly white.[30] These statistics suggest that A. D. Horsley is justified in calling southern gospel "the popular music of American Christianity,"[31] distinct from any particular sectarian or congregational affiliation or church-music tradition.

Church music—hymns and their contemporary descendants, the praise and worship chorus—has historically served as a vehicle for adoration and praise and is, as one mid-twentieth-century southern gospel music executive insightfully put it, "more or less written on God and his attributes, not on man."[32] In contrast, southern gospel is a form of Christian music whose songs have historically dealt with what that same executive described as "the human experience of [Christian] life." Thus, "Brethren, We Have Met to Worship," a song that calls the faithful to meet, worship, "and adore the Lord our God," functions as a hymn, while "Too Much to Gain to Lose," a song about all the "many miles," "the many trails," "the many tears" that remind the spiritual pilgrim she has too much to gain in eternity to give up and lose out on heaven now, is a southern gospel song—"written in a folksy manner and from that angle."[33] All these factors contribute to southern gospel's broad appeal within and well beyond the South: "People of all evangelical Protestant denominations can come together and sing or listen to gospel music and not experience the tug of doctrinal divisions."[34] Southern gospel music thrives across a wide span of conservative Protestantism by relocating the locus of authority from church hierarchy and tradition to the individual in his or her interaction with the gospel in song.

No Music for Old Methods: Methodology and Academic Borders

My method for accessing and understanding southern gospel's cultural function pays careful attention to what participants at all levels of the music's production and consumption say about their own understanding of the music, and how they say it. For almost a decade now, I have maintained a blog devoted to criticism and commentary about southern gospel music and culture at averyfineline.com. From the first, I have made a point to encourage a wide-ranging, free-flowing online conversation about southern gospel. I think this commitment to an open exchange of ideas helps account for my site's having become a convergence point for a range of voices and perspectives. Within the world of southern gospel, averyfineline is well known as the place to go for a thoroughgoing conversation about the music and its mores. Readers include both orthodox fans and professionals who regularly and vociferously dissent from my secular humanist approach to the music and its culture, as well as those voices and perspectives that have found no other meaningful outlet for this type of conversation in the epistemologically cloistered world of southern gospel. Throughout the research for and writing of this book, averyfineline has been an organic encyclopedia of everything from the most obscure historical trivia to the complex cultural crosscurrents that run beneath the surface of evangelical consensus about the "correct" meaning of the music.

The chapters that follow reflect my experience of being immersed in southern gospel culture as a blogging fan and critic, as well as on published comments online and in print, and on my own encounters with the rhetoric emerging from live performance. I also draw on information I have gathered in interviews and from relationships I have established with industry insiders over my years following and researching the music. Finally, I draw on qualitative data collected in a large-scale survey I conducted in the research phase of this project to document some commonly held attitudes and beliefs in southern gospel culture, and to do so with more certainty than my own hunches allow.[35] Taken together with song lyrics, these data points constitute a significant portion of the source material I rely on to understand the individualized meanings that privately build up beneath the surface of consensus.

Because this process of meaning making built into the music is my primary focus, I have let mainstream southern gospel tastes guide my selection of songs and other phenomena, even when that leads me to music that does not originate within southern gospel itself but has been adopted or absorbed by the culture. This absorption principle is aptly illustrated by the song from which my title is taken: "Then Sings My Soul." Gospel music fans and many others will immediately recognize the opening lines from the chorus of the famous anthem "How Great Thou Art," sung by almost every southern gospel group at one point or another. Though technically a folk hymn[36] first made famous on the Billy Graham revival circuit, "How Great Thou Art" has nevertheless been wholeheartedly adopted by mainstream southern gospel and its fans as one of their own, to the point that it is the first song listed on the cover of *The World's Greatest Southern Gospel Songs*.[37] This tendency to incorporate and re-voice complementary songs, similar styles, and receptive patterns of human experience has been a key factor in my selection of music and other evidentiary materials. They have been chosen for their value as a window into the southern-gospel psyche, even when they may not be "authentically" southern gospel in origin. This approach reflects a more general tendency to put southern gospel at the center of my scholarly frame, focusing less on what its development means in terms of music history and more on what southern gospel's emergence can tell us about its particular cultural function.

Even as I rely on text-based sources of evidence in my analysis, I do so with an awareness of the inherent risks of scholarship about absolutist religious culture that focuses on textual evidence exclusively. Indeed, our understanding of insular religious subcultures like southern gospel has not always been well served by scholarship that lopsidedly privileges textual records, artifacts, or productions. As Jane Tompkins has noted, modern humanist scholars are often suspicious of didactic art and literature that explicitly try to influence the lives of audiences.[38] This suspicion can lead to scholarly studies of evangelistic religious cultures that are inadvertently dismissive or gratuitously cutting. When it comes to evangelical artistic and literary productions, scholarship often adopts the same conflictual stance so common in imaginative works of conservative Christianity. As if internalizing the religious separatist's antagonistic view of the other, Barbara Rossing, for example, begins her study of eschatology in conservative Christianity by announcing that the "the rapture is a racket." Such barely suppressed contempt is not solely the province of scholars looking in on evangelicalism from the outside. Evangelical historian Mark Noll has written perhaps the most sustained critique of evangelical anti-intellectualism, arguing that "the scandal of the evangelical mind is that there is not much of an evangelical mind" at all. Christian painter Franky Schaeffer is no less blunt, titling his book on contemporary Christians and the arts "Addicted to Mediocrity." Focused primarily on the textual record or literal meanings of the artifactual output from within evangelicalism, these approaches invariably arrive at some version of Noll's own conclusion that contemporary evangelicalism is engaged in the "vigorous prosecution of the wrong kind of intellectual life."[39]

Ethnographers have attempted to correct the sort of biases at work in these interpretive approaches by letting people speak for themselves. This approach decenters the scholar's interpretive paradigm in favor of focusing on the subjects of scholarship themselves. As Jeff Todd Titon notes in his study of rural southern Freewill Baptists, "What seemed plainly in the word of a text to me [as a scholar] was not necessarily the meaning the church members derived from it. The meaning was contexted by their lives, not mine. Early on, I realized I must rely on the church members' own remarks about their language in religious practice." In foregrounding the scholar's role as a participant-observer, ethnography situates what people say about their lives in the richly documented context of the scholar's embedded experience within that world. Ideally, this arrangement diminishes the risk that scholarship will superimpose academic theories or interpretations onto observed phenomena in ways that do fundamental violence to the reality of lived experience. Titon explains it this way: "This is not to say I accepted everything they had to say at face value, but to underscore that I had to know what they thought they believed and how they thought it motivated their actions before I could understand their language in religious practice in terms of its affective power when performed in the church community."[40] Of course, when an ethnographer's object of study is a culture in which the ethnographer has independent personal experience, the task of remaining true to the experience of a culture or tradition is both more and less complicated: an insider's knowledge of customs and idioms closes the gap that often separates researcher and researched. But deeply personal connections to the world being submitted to scholarly scrutiny can also make it difficult to maintain proper distance. The scholar, in effect, becomes both analyst and analysand.

I come to the study of southern gospel music through lived experience. I grew up a conservative Southern Baptist immersed in the depth and complexity of evangelical life that is often lost in denunciations of evangelicalism's wrong ways of thinking. Consequently, my work has benefited from ethnographic methodologies that refocus scholarly attention on the value of closely documenting the primary data of religious experience. Moreover, as a diehard southern gospel fan all my life—"diesel sniffers," we are called, inasmuch as our unwavering devotion to the music evokes the image of fans trailing after the diesel-powered motor coaches in which artists travel—I am particularly indebted to autoethnography for empowering scholars to mobilize personal experiences too long deprecated by humanist scholarship.

At the same time, I am by training and sensibility a literary and cultural critic attuned not just to the language people use to describe their experience but also to the way that language can belie what is really going on. This is particularly true in conservative evangelicalism, where what people say is often engineered, whether consciously or not, to reinforce fundamentalism's teleological worldview, especially when private experience presents a challenge to orthodox doctrine. The antimodern worldview of conservative evangelicalism that predominates in southern gospel fuels suspicion of entendre and interpretive ambiguity in language and resists intellectualized reflection on the subtexts of experience. When it comes to Christian music, the orthodox approach downplays judgment of artistic merit: "We must carefully avoid judging the music or the artist performing it," a prominent Christian music producer has written about how to succeed in Christian music. "Judgment is Someone [*sic*] else's job. Our job is to pray for and love all artists." In this view, all music is good if it makes a joyful noise to the Lord. Indeed, I have come to think of this philosophy of religious music as Joyful Noise-ism, and it illustrates a basic truth in the study of evangelical life: what evangelicals say about themselves in their religious practice and spiritual experience can be at times, as Titon discovered, "shallow or simply wrong"—but no less complex or less worthy of scholarly deciphering.[41]

It is perhaps a mildly bemusing irony that this book's methodology draws eclectically and pragmatically from a constellation of related disciplines that have—for the most part—shown very little interest in engaging southern gospel primarily on its own terms. The longer it has gone unexplored, the wider the gulf has grown between modern, pluralistic, secular American society so well represented in academe and the proudly primitive world that encompasses southern gospel. Though I am convinced the scholarly neglect of southern gospel in part signifies doubts about its fitness as a topic for academic study, I think an equally important reason for this neglect is much more benign: academics do not always know what to make of sacred music that derives from folk traditions but is not folk music, reflects underclass sensibilities but is not itself the product of a minority culture, and cultivates a vernacular separateness from mainstream American popular culture yet strives to imitate its styles and to succeed on its terms. In other words, southern gospel exists in a kind of academic blind spot.

Matters are only further complicated by the self-effacing economic modes in which contemporary southern gospel operates. As large suburban mega-churches have become the center of evangelicalism in the popular American imagination, evangelicalism's much smaller, rural, and less aesthetically sophisticated congregations have receded from mainstream view even as they have increasingly become the place where the live concert, the foundation of the southern gospel economy, thrives most regularly. These concerts go largely unnoticed outside the subculture of southern gospel not just because they possess a certain untranslatable quality but also because they are economically all but invisible. Instead of charging admission, the majority of these concerts collect a "freewill love offering," during which audiences are asked to give whatever amount they feel "led by the Lord" to contribute. Freewill love offerings are central to the image of the southern gospel concert as a ministerial—rather than a profit-seeking—activity. But because it is not uncommon for freewill offerings barely to cover travel expenses for the artist (to say nothing about the cost of promoting and producing concerts), product sales at the tables performers set up at concerts are performers' primary source of revenue. Few groups submit these so-called table sales to reporting agencies such as SoundScan, whose data are important indicators to the wider world of writers and researchers of a musical genre's scope and scale. (This is also true of most radio airplay in southern gospel.)[42] Thus, table sales and freewill love offerings effectively mask any reliable measure of the southern gospel economy.

Economic invisibility is also true for larger concerts that charge admission. Even ticketed events that attract thousands of people rarely, if ever, are reported to any accounting agency, as would be standard practice at far smaller ticketed events in secular musical genres and many other genres of Christian entertainment (the Bill and Gloria Gaither Homecoming Friends tour and merchandising are exceptions to this general rule). Consequently, there is no systematic way to register these events' scale or economic impact. Indeed, save for those retail sales of products that pass through recording companies' distribution channels, the southern gospel industry could be described as a loosely affiliated network of small businesses (event promotion, radio, concert production, artist-entrepreneurs) whose links remain minimally articulated and informally maintained.

The tendency for the southern gospel economy to de-emphasize its own economic operations reflects the constant tension in the Christian music world between "ministry" and "entertainment." In the case of southern gospel, the evangelical emphasis on Christian separateness from the world at large intensifies this tension. And this tension, in turn, accounts for the development of an economic infrastructure—freewill offerings, informally retailed "table products," self-effacing ticket sales, untracked radio airplay— that seeks to minimize the profit motive as secondary or inconsequential while encouraging audiences to see their financial investments in the music as participation in an entertaining form of Christian evangelism. In addition to structuring the psychosocial experience for gospel music consumers, these vernacular economic networks present formidable obstacles to the uninitiated student of the music seeking to understand southern gospel from the outside.

In short, southern gospel scrambles the conventional coordinates that academics use to navigate unexplored (sub)cultures. A novel in the *Left Behind* series or a Rick Warren sermon may be readable to scholarly outsiders in ways that southern gospel is not because fundamentalist fiction and evangelical sermons make use of rhetorical frameworks and conform to textual conventions that are academically familiar and interpretable to scholars, even if the evangelical worldview is foreign.[43] In contrast, southern gospel is much less rhetorically coherent and accessible. The performance and consumption of the music fuse the conventional aims of live entertainment with evangelicalism's teleological discourse of conversion and exhortation. This fusion forms a single but polyvalent cultural phenomenon encompassing several rhetorics: the rhetoric of musical lyrics, the rhetoric (or semiotics) of live performance, and the rhetoric of the music's fans and their consumer culture. Understanding these dynamics requires an approach as multidimensional as the culture itself: the documentarian's eye for idiom and vernacularisms, the literary critic's close reading of text and subtext, the cultural critic's appreciation for cultural artifacts as "model[s] of the self performed" and "brought tangibly into existence," and the (new) musicologist's willingness to take popular music seriously as a "cultural product," while also realizing that the formal characteristics of music help construct its meaning.[44] I do not claim to be all these things, or that a project of this sort does not risk approbation for its methodological eclecticism. But the song goes on, as an old Bill Gaither tune has it, and in a way that demands an academic accounting that no single scholarly method alone provides.

In listening to that song and in trying to take it and its "cultural priorities" seriously, to borrow Susan McClary's term, I have found the tools of specialists in fields adjacent to my own to be indispensable in my efforts to understand the polyvalence of southern gospel's signifying practices and the multidimensionality of its cultural function.[45] Thus, when I approach a gospel song about how "this world is not my home, I'm just passing through," I see in it not just a musical restatement of the basic Protestant evangelical worldview but the lyrical currency of a dense cultural exchange.[46] In this transaction, fans are invited to form a mutually ennobling spiritual alliance with performers that celebrates Christian commitment and memorializes struggle in this life by embracing the blandishments of the next.

Then Sings My Soul

As both a participant-fan in the world of southern gospel music and a scholar trained in the study of the literature and psychology of American religious experience, I am in the fairly unique position of being both a gospel-music insider and outsider. I grew up as what the playwright Del Shores has called a "Southern Baptist sissy": in my case, a deeply closeted preacher's kid who could not get enough of southern gospel music, whether listening to it, singing it, playing it on the piano in church, or performing it onstage with others (including four years as the pianist for a largely forgotten regional quartet in southern Missouri). My theological commitments to orthodox evangelicalism did not fare well amid the rapid intellectual expansion of an undergraduate liberal arts education, and they collapsed altogether in the process of coming out in my early twenties. Evangelicalism as a paradigm for self-understanding is now nearly half a lifetime away for me. Though I write from the perspective of a participant in the world of southern gospel, I explicitly position my perspective outside the theological a priori assumptions that are commonly associated with this community. Yet southern gospel has always been and continues to be just about the only constant in my life that resonates as deeply with me now—an openly gay, secular humanist academic—as it did to me as an adolescent evangelical publicly professing my dedication to a life in Southern Baptist ministry. To some extent, southern gospel functions as a nostalgic touchstone for what I have come to think of as a previous life to which I could never return (or want to), but with which I still wish to remain meaningfully connected. More deeply, though, my experience with the music transcends nostalgia alone. Southern gospel makes a lived reality for me of what I think McClary means when she describes music as a "living code" that "undergoes continual renegotiations as new and extant meanings are accepted."[47]

In effect, my own experience has come to serve as a microcosm of the larger dynamic the book explores. Moreover, it is only fitting that deeply personal concerns should inform my professional work here, given the emphasis I place throughout the book on the private origins of popular culture. Still, my decision to pursue an academic monograph about southern gospel culture has not been without its attendant anxieties, particularly a concern that my choice of topic or approach may be misinterpreted as an apologia for postmodern fundamentalism. I have no hesitation in criticizing fundamentalist evangelical tendencies toward moral self-indulgence and ideologically self-serving habits of thought and action. Here is probably a good place to note that dismissive though he was, R. W. Apple had a point about that song, "We Want America Back." It is aggressively crude and uncomfortable to listen to, especially in the song's long polemical monologue that begins by suggesting that public school children should be armed by law to defend their right to pray in school. A little later on, nonheterosexuals are implicitly likened to dogs.[48] All too eager to perpetuate the myth of the persecuted Christian majority, the song—like so much of the religious Right—obstinately refuses to acknowledge that contemporary evangelicalism is almost always complicit in the sociopolitical conflicts that conservative Christians bemoan.

But even while I am abundantly skeptical of fundamentalist culture and the kinds of excesses represented by "We Want America Back," I am fundamentally sympathetic to southern gospel and its appeal. Even in extreme cases, the rhetorics of southern gospel are ideologically and lyrically driven by a unifying concern with the conduct of life in a context of human struggle. Calling forth that struggle in song—even if it has to be manufactured or imagined—gives it a value that is produced in the musical performance and experience. Drawing on experiential data from ordinary postmodern life, southern gospel music lyrically dramatizes those data and gives the newly improved experience back to its listeners, who can then repurpose the emotional content of the music in their own lives. This dynamic constitutes a "way of life," as Raymond Williams uses the phrase in his discussion of modern culture, "a mode of interpreting . . . common experience, and, in this new interpretation, changing it."[49] This is the cultural function of southern gospel, and my sense of its value as a scholarly object of study derives not just from my observation as a researcher but my own encounters with the music over a lifetime of experience.

There are no readily accessible paradigms, either in evangelicalism or in most realms of academe, for explaining my rather queer kind of interest in the popular culture of antimodern Protestantism in America, no familiar models for understanding why a homosexual nonbeliever is writing an unpolemical book that argues for the surreptitiously modern sensibility of a musical tradition whose contemporary exponents regularly denounce modernity in general and homosexuality in particular. On its face, it does not immediately make much sense, I admit. I have written elsewhere about trying (and thankfully failing) to hide the fact of my personal and academic interest in southern gospel when I first began writing publicly about the music and its culture online.[50] The anxiety surrounding my initially secret life as a southern gospel blogger was symptomatic of the professional premium often placed on depersonalized inquiry in much of the humanities. Here, Harold Bloom speaks, as he so often does, for the high-literary perspective when he defines humanist scholarship as the "search for a difficult pleasure" in the masterworks of Western culture, works whose greatness is always already assumed to transcend the merely personal or the purely parochial. For his part, Bloom goes on to offer a robust case for the value of subjective experience in the scholar's work. But that has not prevented a good deal of friction from building up between neoformalism and cultural studies. In these debates, popular culture studies is often seen as a "waste of thought on objects that were not made for it" and that "threaten to degrade the value of intellectual life in general and the value of humanities in particular."[51]

Such disputes are perhaps nowhere more prevalent than in English departments, where I live my professional life, but this attitude is well represented in the study of theology, religion, and music as well. Heidi Epstein has astutely noted the tendency of scholarship about religion and music "to harness the system of Western tonality, with its prerequisite of final harmonic resolutions, to defend an unequivocal"—and often hegemonic—"good by erasing loss and negation."[52] At some basic level, this sort of academic outlook promotes ignorance—ignorance of most human cultures beneath the "worthy" objects of scholarly study in general and, in the case of southern gospel music, ignorance of a part of the world that most Americans deal with in one way or another almost every day, whether they realize it or not. Yet the study of popular music has become professionally nonsuicidal in musicology just since the mid-1990s—thanks to the so-called new musicologists, who challenged conventional assumptions about the insuperable value of transcendent art music.[53] In this we see one way the academic study of music can artificially cut the scholar off from public access to the vital private energies that not only motivate but also often clarify scholarly study.

This clarifying effect of the personal has, in any event, been my experience. This project only started making real sense to me when I began to embrace, rather than efface, the personal motivations behind my work. It is no coincidence that this academic truth has played itself out perhaps nowhere more powerfully in academe than in queer studies. Indeed, my experience researching and writing about southern gospel has a good deal in common with that of many other queer academics, who often learn to capitalize on the inescapable fact that, as Judith (now Jake) Halberstam observes, "there are selves behind projects and those selves are deeply invested in discovering how to articulate desires and genders"—and, I might add, spiritual sensibilities—"we have been told make no sense." Sometimes censure takes the form of explicit obstacles placed in front of unorthodox inquiries; there are powerful parallels between historical biases against the wrong kind of scholarship in academe and the sorts of rejection so many queer people have experienced from mainstream evangelicalism. At least my somewhat self-embattled effort to claim with pride my own scholarly interest in southern gospel has often reminded me more than I care to admit of coming out from within conservative Christianity. I am grateful that I have enjoyed the unilateral support of my peers at Florida Gulf Coast University, where I have worked during the majority of the research and writing of this monograph. Nevertheless, academe regularly places unconventional swerves toward autobiography on the short side of an academic ledger that values high over low, the difficult pleasure over the "simple pleasure with difficult explanations."[54]

This book is not exclusively a work of queer theory or criticism. But it may fairly be said to reflect a queer methodology, which is, as Halberstam puts it, "a scavenger methodology," one that uses "different methods to collect and produce information on subjects" and forms of experience "that have been deliberately or accidently excluded from traditional studies." It would not be wrong, then, to hear an echo of my own identity and history in the personal experience called to mind by the book's title—*Then Sings My Soul*. This book is, of course, a scholarly work first and foremost, and I have taken pains not to "merely replace objectivity with the evidence of experience" in order to "resuscitate argumentative credibility," or to let personal history stand in for others' thoughts or feelings. But as a "native informant," to borrow John Champagne's term," I draw regularly on personal experience—in some cases explicitly but more often as an underlying guide to analysis—wherever it seems appropriate or apt.[55]

* * *

As with my own identity, this book emerges at the intersection of the scholarly and the sacred. My approach imagines both an audience of humanist scholars and students of humanities from a cluster of overlapping disciplines and fields, as well as nonspecialist readers with an interest in southern gospel specifically, Christian entertainment generally, or simply a better understanding of a form of music and American life that sometimes seems to be present almost everywhere yet goes virtually unrecognized in mainstream America. Addressing these various audiences, the book is designed to accommodate different approaches. After setting out the main lines of my argument in chapter 1, the remaining chapters are arranged in more or less chronological order, a structure that allows me to challenge settled narratives about southern gospel's history and to reimagine the music's modern development from the Civil War to contemporary postmodernity. At the same time, each chapter is also loosely organized around a figure, theme, or topic that can be taken out of order as necessity dictates or the spirit moves.

Chapter 1 provides an extended inquiry into the psychodynamics of southern gospel. Here, I identify a reciprocal process of sentimental exchange in the music that sustains a surreptitious modernity within a fundamentalist culture. This dynamic operates just beneath the surface of consensus about the music and about evangelicalism as a structure of belief. Methodologically, the chapter draws on literary critical readings of song lyrics in relation to analysis of live performance and the music's fan culture. This approach reveals that the experience of southern gospel music invites (indeed, it requires) personal interpretation and application of a given song's theology, but in a way that does not disrupt southern gospel's ecumenical unity and the appearance of ideological like-mindedness. I show how the music allows the individual to confront feelings of doubt, insecurity, fear, isolation, and general spiritual discontent—even or especially when these feelings might contradict orthodox doctrine—without ever putting the individual in direct, public conflict with orthodoxy. Ultimately, this chapter demonstrates how a shaky but workable pluralism takes hold within evangelical fundamentalism.

With this conceptual framework in place, chapter 2 traces the emergence of modern southern gospel forward from its Reconstruction roots. I am particularly attentive here to the abiding influence of the songbook publisher, songwriter, romantic poet, and melancholic Civil War veteran Aldine S. Kieffer. As the more creative half of the Ruebush-Kieffer songbook publishing empire, Kieffer played an inimitable role in the industrialization of southern gospel at a pivotal moment when shape-note music education was transitioning from a paraprofessional recreation to a commercialized economy based on songbooks and increasingly professionalized music teachers and singers. In the process, I make the first comprehensive case in extant scholarship for Kieffer as the most important originator of modern southern gospel discourse, an archetypal figure whose work in early southern gospel infuses the music with a lasting concern for tensions between the self and society that arise from sociocultural upheaval in the postbellum South.

Chapter 3 takes issue with the widely held and uncritically accepted belief in the southern gospel imagination that James D. Vaughan, an early-twentieth-century disciple of Ruebush-Kieffer, is the "founder" of today's southern gospel. In challenging his status, I trace an alternative history of southern gospel in the twentieth century that reinterprets the meaning of Vaughn as a cultural icon. This alternative account emphasizes the music's synchronous interaction with broader shifts in American life beyond the narrow confines of what are often thought to be southern gospel's insular borders. The most visible evidence of these shifts is the emergence of the term *southern gospel* itself in the last half of the twentieth century. Over time, this term came to describe the white evangelical music of southern extraction that had in the first half simply been known as "gospel." But this nomenclatural adjustment is only the most visible and relatively belated development in a century-long resacrilization of evangelical fundamentalist popular culture in America. *Southern gospel* as a descriptive term emerged as a token of the tradition's cultural displacement from the center of influence in Christian entertainment—and mainstream American culture more generally. Taken together, these two chapters form a historiography of professional southern gospel that reimagines its prehistory as a musical tradition and its importance as a cultural phenomenon of evangelicalism.

The book's final chapters offer case studies of the music and its culture as they have developed in the contemporary, postmodern era—in this case, roughly since the rise of the term *southern gospel*. In chapter 4, I provide the first comprehensive academic treatment of Bill Gaither and the Bill and Gloria Gaither Homecoming Friends concert tour and video series. The chapter explores the private origins of Bill Gaither's public oeuvre. The focus here is on the way Gaither's life and music crystallize a set of widespread anxieties and ambitions among the generations of cold war, postmodern evangelicals who follow his music. The chapter identifies the strategic manner in which Gaither Homecomings repurpose the habits of early-twentieth-century singing-convention style in southern gospel. I conclude by demonstrating how these updated patterns of expression refract the music's long-standing function as a pressure regulator between tradition and modernity in postmodern America.

Finally, in chapter 5, I try to bring together the different facets of southern gospel's surreptitious modernity as developed in the book, consolidating them in the experience of nonheterosexuals in gospel music. For at least a generation, the fact of queer contributions to the music at all levels has operated as an open secret in southern gospel. Fundamentalism's absolute prohibition on homosexuality makes acceptance of their contributions impossible, of course. Nevertheless, the psychodynamic structure of the music invites nonconformists to identify with southern gospel's emphasis on the sojourning soul's solitary struggle to find spiritual peace in this dry and barren land. This chapter examines the gay-gospel paradox as a microcosm of fundamentalism's conflict with the postmodern world. This conflict encapsulates a broader contest for cultural authority. In this context, evangelicalism's uncompromising opposition to homosexuality vies with the sense of self-affirmation that many gay "sinners" experience through southern gospel. I know whereof I argue. Relying on a personal voice informed by my own complicated queer identification with the music and its culture, I attempt a redemption of the southern gospel sissy. In him the music merges a network of desires—for transcending the binarist definitions of identity, for affirmation, for the salvation of acceptance without the surrender of self—that are only intensified by the difficulty of ever fully realizing them for more than a few majestic, fleeting moments within gospel music's ineffable harmony.

This final chapter is the book's most direct engagement with my own experience as a gay man in gospel music. But the book in its entirety functions as a sustained effort to explain both to myself and for others all the variant affections that southern gospel inspires—not least of all my own—to make sense of and, ultimately, to legitimize them. I noted earlier that this book challenges the old distortions that proceed from academe's often antagonistic relationship with fundamentalist religious cultures by tracing forward the surreptitious modernity of southern gospel. It seems equally important to say that the book also attempts to speak reciprocally to orthodox evangelical audiences, to unsettle their not-always-unjustified view of academic analysis of religious subcultures as a cold-blooded dissection of an etherized patient. In addition to the other functions served by the visible presence of my personal investments in the pages that follow, they are my effort to demonstrate the urgency and immediacy of what is at stake in this study for me both personally and professionally. They are my effort, as it were, to put some skin in the game.

To approach southern gospel music this way—as a set of polyvalent rhetorics that speak to private as well public experience, orthodox doctrine and unorthodox experience—accomplishes three things. First, it goes beyond what southern gospel insiders intend to say to one another about themselves and their faith through this music. The aim here is to disambiguate the internal logic of the music, exploring why it says what it does and in what ways it does so—in Clifford Geertz's terms, to offer an intellectual "construction of other people's construction of what they and their compatriots are up to."[56] Second, it is to see southern gospel as a distinct set of cultural

nialist worldview that predominates in southern gospel culture. In "I'll Fly Away," the lyrical trope is a common one: notionally gazing heavenward in anticipation of eternal paradise, the song predicates its celebration of the afterlife on a shared belief in the sorrow and suffering the Christian endures during the struggles and strife of life on earth.

But southern gospel lyrics only tell part of the story. If the experience of country music often starts in the car, with the radio, as Cecilia Tichi suggests, then the experience of southern gospel starts in the pew, the auditorium seat, the folding chair of the county fair. Live performance remains the basic ingredient of experience in southern gospel. Absent this context of performance and the surrounding culture that the music both shapes and is shaped by, lyrics have very little to tell us about the larger affective and experiential dynamics through which the music achieves its full force as an instrument of contemporary evangelical culture. "I'll Fly Away" lyrically exemplifies the focus in southern gospel music on what David Fillingim has called "a message of world rejection" in a religious vernacular historically associated with southern, rural, conservative Christianity.[3] Yet the song does so using a catchy melody and a clappable rhythm that are organized around ascending chord progressions and high, expansive intervals. These musical elements combine across the length of the chorus to suggest the very experience of transcendent spiritual flight even amid life on this earth. The song's toe-tapping, feel-good style pits the lyric's notional rejection of this world against an infectious, irresistible, and uplifting musical buoyancy that affectively undercuts the rhetorical emphasis on earthly life as existential incarceration that opens the second verse: "Like a bird from prison bars have flown. . . ." In fact, it might not be too much to say that at its best, the song turns prison life into a musical paradise.

By itself, then, scholarly analysis focused primarily on the textual artifacts of southern gospel takes insufficient account of vital, nonverbal elements at work in the music. The singing of lyrics, the way vocalists interpret songs (including their body language and the timbre and dynamic level of their singing voices), the spontaneity of the artist and audience in the live performance, and, perhaps most important, a song's tune and arrangement—all of these elements interact dynamically and contingently in the musical moment to create a powerful paralanguage to which participants make reference when they explain their connection to southern gospel. Asked as part of my research to talk about a song or musical experience that had made an impression on his life, one fan put it this way: "'I've Come too Far to Turn Back,' [by] the Hoppers. An oldie but goodie, their remake of this song will give you chill bumps when Connie Hopper launches into an a cappella encore. The skill of each performer . . . combined with the spiritual aspect is an experience like no other. What is wonderful is that words cannot always describe what you're feeling, but nonetheless the experience is all too real for you." Another fan wrote: "I recall sitting at work performing menial tasks (nearly twenty years ago, mind you) while listening to the arrangements of one particular producer, and feeling the tears pouring from my eyes—not because of the lyrics, but rather the sheer emotion of the soaring contrapuntal lines. I realized later that the same music, divorced from the lyrics, in and of itself was powerful enough to create a feeling in my heart without actually having changed my heart."[4] These comments are typical in referring to the multimodality of feeling the music generates, suggesting that southern gospel is far more than a musicalized restatement of orthodox doctrine. For these people and others like them, the experience of southern gospel acts as a musical vessel passed back and forth between audience and artist. Into this vessel, listeners can (and, if they are to take anything relevant away from the experience, must) pour individualized meanings. In the "I'll Fly Away" example, this might mean responding to the music with personal associations, memories, feelings, and beliefs elicited by the song's general description of a heavenly flight from the prison of life in this world. Shaded with personalized responses, southern gospel becomes the music of the individual and the collective body, simultaneously. The experience of southern gospel music invites—indeed, it requires—personal interpretation and application of a given song's theology or outlook, but in a way that does not disrupt southern gospel's ecumenical unity and the appearance of ideological like-mindedness.

By necessity and design, this interplay produces a far more unstable, fluid religious identity than lyrics alone might suggest. In southern gospel, the role of both performer and fan constantly shifts and realigns with the individual and collective fluctuations of feeling and rhetoric that the music creates. In the live setting, performers' artistic choices—about song selection and showmanship, about how to bend the emotional curve of a song, about how to encore a song that is well received, or whether to slow down the pace of the program with personal testimonies or religious memories—evolve with the audience's collective response to the music in a reciprocal process of sentimental exchange that fans often describe as spiritual experiences. Performers and fans alike frequently become (or appear to be) overtaken by emotion: humor, sadness, grief, humility, thankfulness, inspiration. It is often difficult to distinguish between the authentic and inauthentic, which drives a common assumption within and beyond southern gospel that the entire exchange is so much manufactured religious melodrama in which

emotionally manipulative performers mesmerize the religiously gullible.
Doubtless this critique hits bedrock at times, both in the seats and on the
stage, but as an explanatory framework, it is unhelpfully reductive. Not least
of all, this view fails to recognize that dissembling or otherwise performing
religious piety expresses an authentic, if displaced, feeling of some kind.
More deeply, for most southern gospel fans and performers, gospel music
seems to trample the intellect and stampede straight to the heart, the soul,
the spirit to an extent other music does not and in ways that often manifest
themselves in thick arcs of melodramatic pietism. This is not so much proof
of the inauthenticity of southern gospel music or, alternatively, evidence of
a single, homogenous evangelical attitude or mind-set. Rather, it is a point
of entry into an inquiry about the cultural function of sentiment and music
in the world of southern gospel.

By stressing the multiple levels on which southern gospel creates meaning, this chapter takes up just such an inquiry. I reimagine southern gospel
music as a polyvalent "structure of feeling," to borrow Raymond Williams's
framework for exploring "meanings and values as they are actively lived and
felt." Southern gospel structures of feeling reinforce orthodox worldviews
even as they sustain an array of unorthodox ideas and emotions beneath
the visible surface of orthodoxy described by lyrics. This approach should
not be understood to mean that lyrics do not matter. The southern gospel
fans and professionals I have encountered in my research overwhelmingly
identify lyrical content as the single most important defining characteristic
of the music. A clear majority of those point to "biblical" or "scripturally
sound" lyrics as constitutive factors in determining what makes the music
"good" in their estimation. Nevertheless, these same people also associate
their own most meaningful southern gospel experiences not with a particular
song lyric or lyrical conceit but with the memory of some great upwelling
of religious affect occasioned by a favorite song or a beloved performer.
As one person I asked aptly put it, "There is a certain chord structure and
'feeling' that is the foundation of the traditional 'four-part traditional male
Quartet' Music that I love." Another person responded, "A good gospel song
connects emotionally." A third person reinforced this notion: "It [a good
song] gives me an honest emotional response."[5] The emphasis in southern
gospel culture on the self-authenticating truth of religious affections aroused
by the music—which includes but is not limited to lyrics—means that a
song's seemingly simplistic rhetorical surface belies a much more richly
textured and highly contoured topography of spiritual experience at the
heart of the music's cultural function. Contextualized within this network

of constantly shifting sentiment and feeling, southern gospel lyrics come into proper focus as the linguistic dimension of a densely layered cultural discourse. Evangelicals rely on this discourse to manage the friction that forms around conflicts between absolutist evangelical culture and mainstream secular American pluralism.

Dealing with Difference

Since at least the time of the Puritans' arrival in the New World, Christianity in the Calvinist tradition has struggled to balance theoretically absolute doctrines governing Christian living with the human need for some individual agency and freedom. It has been one function of evangelical culture to manage this tension. The seventeenth-century Puritan narratives of melodramatic captivity and tearful restoration, the pietistic emotionalism of the Great Awakening that swept New England in the eighteenth century, the sentimental novels of religious moralism by women writers of the nineteenth century—each of these discourses tried to make felt connections between uneven human experience and absolute religious doctrine.[6] The texts that emerged from these discourses allowed people to feel there was some room for self-determination in a world theologically understood to be divinely preordained from the foundations of time.

Southern gospel attempts to address this paradox by using music to engage modern methods of identity formation, but in a way that outwardly reinforces the antimodern worldview of evangelical fundamentalism. Relying on the conventions of musical theater (role playing, impersonation, and the use of songs to engage metaphorically deeper questions of identity and personality), the experience of southern gospel allows people to express and indulge a range of states of mind, feeling, and expressions of feelings in the "safe" context of Christian musical drama. Some of the more emotionally intense of these responses may well contradict orthodox evangelical doctrine, which teaches that feelings of forsakenness are signs of insufficient faith or the work of sin and Satan. Certainly, the long-standing popularity of a song like "Till the Storm Passes By" seems connected to its evocation of the real threat posed by quiescence and despair in the life of ordinary evangelicals. The song begins:

> In the dark of the midnight
> Have I oft hid my face
> While the storms howl above me
> And there's no hiding place.[7]

But the risk that evoking feelings of darkness and spiritual isolation will lead to apostasy or other unorthodox conclusions is blunted by the context of theological certainty in which southern gospel publicly unfolds. The song's concluding cry to the divine—"Keep me safe / till the storm passes by"—functions less as an invocation and more as a guarantee of salvific protection voiced in the form of a plea that tacitly acknowledges the self's insufficiency without God's help. Spiritual insecurity is a precondition for salvation. To sing or experience the song is to secure the spiritual safe passage it describes and so give teleological value to negative feelings. Just as the saints are held fast in God's hand while the storm passes by, the song passes over underlying questions about the origins of suffering—especially suffering among the saints—and other negative experiences in the world. Suffering has value for what it conveys about humanity without God. As for the origins of suffering, another old song explains it this way: "We'll understand it better by and by."[8]

Evangelicalism is defined by the dynamics to which these songs allude: pushing through the conflicts of everyday experience to an assured salvation. Recognition of the sinner's failure is in some ways the point, and southern gospel is not the only place where these narratives of struggle and recovery play out within evangelicalism. As I write, the once mighty megachurch minister Ted Haggard, who fell from grace into drug addiction, philandering, paying for sex, and the "sin" of homosexuality, is quite publicly trying to rehabilitate his image among evangelicals while also reaching out in some limited ways to nonheterosexual Christians, and he is doing all this independently of southern gospel's structures of feeling. Obviously, southern gospel is not alone in speaking to the tension between the spirit and flesh. Nevertheless, southern gospel's way of managing that tension has been integrally shaped by the struggle among generations of poor and working-class evangelical whites to retain a connection to religious tradition, value, and meaning while simultaneously making sense of themselves in a modern world that seems to have little place for them. So while Ted Haggard is undergoing some version of this struggle, he is doing so with far less supple and nuanced tools than southern gospel could provide for negotiating, in this case, the path between meth-induced sex with a gay hooker and a partially reconstructed megachurch evangelist. Someone in Haggard's position primarily has at his disposal the hard but brittle rhetoric of evangelical assurance as it descends to our moment in the sermonic discourse of postmodern pietistic heart religion. In this realm of evangelicalism, there are very few ways to make sense of someone like Haggard—or help Haggard make sense of himself—and his claim both to have been forgiven for his sin of homosexuality and to be called by God to welcome homosexuals into his newly formed church (though some restrictions do apply).[9] Meanwhile, southern gospel music thrives as naturally in conventionally pietistic settings as it does in gay bars with drag queens impersonating southern gospel divas. People use both evangelistic preaching and gospel singing to make sense of postmodern identity. But unlike many other spheres of evangelicalism that formulaically or superficially call forth failings and suffering only to deny their power in the name of transcendent redemption, southern gospel treats individual negative feelings as invaluable units of spiritual identity to be affirmed and even celebrated.

The orthodox interpretations of suffering and the problem of evil offered by songs such as "Till the Storm Passes By" and "We'll Understand It Better By and By" do not prohibit individuals from arriving at their own private and theologically idiosyncratic conclusions. Southern gospel possesses a somewhat moldable center encased in the hard shell of orthodoxy. Within this paradigm one can safely confront individualized feelings of doubt, insecurity, fear, isolation, and general spiritual discontent, assured of an ultimate resolution of these concerns in a way that neither forces one to disown private feelings nor puts one in public conflict with evangelicalism. Consider the second verse of a song titled "Oh That Wonderful Promise," recorded by the Perrys:

> He [Christ] will defend the poor and needy
> And that is me, oh that is me
> When I am weak, he giveth power
> And just any moment he'll be here with the help I need.[10]

Southern gospel lyrics imagine a variety of situations from Christian life and dramatize a range of topics germane to Protestant faith. But in general, southern gospel songs operate much like this Perrys lyric: singing about or alluding to some form of separation—be it alienation and disaffiliation from God, longings to go "home" to heaven, or, in this case, destitution (being "poor and needy," whether physically, materially, or spiritually)— that is ultimately resolved not only by divine assistance but also by the song's resolution into harmonic symmetry that is the aesthetic foundation of southern gospel music.

Southern gospel songs typically follow a standard verse-chorus-verse-chorus-chorus structure. But there is a variety of augmentations to this pattern that combine to build harmonic and emotional tension. Chief among these are musical tags and bridges. A bridge is usually a four- or eight-bar interlude between the penultimate chorus and the conclusion of the song.

Lyrically, bridges comment on what has come before and anticipate the song's ending. Musically, bridges are often set in higher registers than the rest of the song (usually a perfect fourth above the main melody) and create a sense of expectation and suspense by using unresolved harmonies or ending in modulations to higher keys. Tags create similar emotional effects but are usually shorter bits of the chorus's conclusion that are repeated at the end of the song. During the endings of the best southern gospel songs, the ensemble voices reach higher and higher, clashing against each other dissonantly before returning in a staggered fashion to harmonic consonance prolonged at first in a straight tone—voices without vibrato, a vocal effect that builds intensity with its directness—then ultimately rounded out in a warmer, more expansive vibrato. On the album *Alive: Deep in the Heart of Texas,* the southern gospel group the Cathedrals recorded a classic example of a white gospel ending during the song "Oh, What a Savior." The song tumbles toward its final climax, first gently, then more intensely, then fantastically, powerfully—the voices in the three highest registers rising, reaching, the bass-guitar line falling, thumping steadily, syncopated against the bass singer's voice as it attacks the descending bass notes, until finally the harmonic resolution sets in and the crowd dissolves into assorted screaming, hand clapping, and shouting hallelujah.

"Oh, What a Savior" vividly illustrates the power of southern gospel part singing, typically referred to as the quartet style. This style of singing dates from the postbellum period of American history when singing conventions that prized soaring tenors and plunging bass voices became popular at shape-note community singings and singing schools. The classic quartet style features homophonic verses, in which harmonically voiced parts move in the same rhythm. Choruses are typically rendered contrapuntally. Each part sings tonally and rhythmically unique lines that rejoin one another in the final bars of the refrain. Quartets often reprise this style today, singing either classic quartet songs from the early to mid–twentieth century (such as "I'll Fly Away") or new songs written in this older style (such as "Oh That Wonderful Promise"). But the quartet style survives more commonly in what are typically known as staggered endings, in which each vocal part lands on its consonant position in the tonic of the chord at a different time than the other voices—as in the Cathedrals' rendition of "Oh, What a Savior." Technically, the quartet style is vocally demanding, requiring counterpoint skills, an ear for blending one's voice in the ensemble, and a developed intuition for proper tone placement, especially during the final moments of songs when multiple parts are often suspended against one another in dissonant chords. Psychosocially, this style—particularly the

The Cathedral quartet, 1994. Members are, *front row, left to right,* Glen Payne, George Younce, Scott Fowler; *back row, left to right,* Roger Bennett, Ernie Haase. (From the collection of Dean Adkins; courtesy of Ernie Haase, Gina Erosky, and Todd Payne.)

staggered endings of classic quartet music—implicitly encourages singing communities to understand differences and conflict as dissonances always about to be resolved into consonant harmonies.

For southern gospel insiders, this ultimate return of harmonic symmetry is a familiar and deeply satisfying triumph of musical consonance and beauty over chaos and incongruence. The dissonance-to-consonance harmonic movement accessibly metaphorizes the "extreme 'rightness' and 'wrongness'" of conservative Christian theology.[11] The lyrics and music call into being a contradictory or dissonant situation in one breath (*I am poor and needy but he will defend me . . . I am weak but he giveth power*) in order to resolve and undo it in another: "any moment he'll be here with the help I need." The song's ending is always ultimately consonant, God's sovereignty and faithfulness to his children always finally (re)affirmed in the deeply personal terms of spiritual self-embattlement. So consonance triumphs over dissonance only insofar as the former relies upon and emerges directly out of the latter. As the music holds orthodoxy in tension with the idiosyncratic contours of often unorthodox experience, a surreptitious but workable form of psychosocial pluralism takes hold within fundamentalist culture.

"Gospel" Aesthetics and Emotional Belief

Both the southern gospel sound and its psychodynamics are in some ways "strikingly similar to contemporary Afro-American quartet" music. White and black gospel have a long history of stylistic exchange and mutual influence, and each of these "gospels" supports aesthetic expressions of Christian ideals in musical pageantry. Indeed, the black gospel influence is so pervasive that many early white gospel recordings might easily be mistaken for black music.[12] Yet despite this legacy of influence across racial lines, many southern gospel performers and fans understand the term *gospel* quite differently from what it typically signifies when applied to the black gospel tradition, with its emphasis on deeply felt soulfulness and spiritual improvisation. Among white evangelicals, "gospel" is most commonly viewed as a musical tool for Christian conversion and "ministry," meant to be experienced (all evidence to the contrary) as what might best be described as the musical equivalent of the "plain-style" Protestant sermons pioneered by seventeenth-century Puritans: artless and spiritually deductive. One southern gospel fan told me that a good song is a "witness for Jesus our Savior and touches the heart of one maybe going through something difficult with encouragement or a song that leads a lost person with conviction to become a Christian."[13]

This notion of "gospel" music is not unique to the southern gospel tradition, but it emphasizes the ministerial and an evangelizing dimension of gospel in a way that helps clarify the relationship between southern gospel and black gospel. The latter "embrace[s] a performance tradition that seeks to forge a communal response to assaults on black integrity." In the performance and reception of black gospel, built around an Afrocentric call-and-response style, "leader and community define one another in relation to the shared historical understandings encoded in the songs and the form of their expression."[14] Black gospel song lyrics tend to be rhetorically recursive professions of God's never-failing mercy and salvation that uphold the spiritual journeyer—for instance:

> Can't nobody,
> Can't nobody.
> No. No. Nobody.
> Can't nobody
> Do me like Jesus.[15]

The specific emotional or spiritual content of these lyrics is constructed anew with each performance by the individual performer's interpretation of them and the audience's collective response to them. Performance styles regularly highlight a soloist who emerges from among a choir to improvise vocally while the chorus provides harmonic backup. By emphasizing the power of the individual (the soloist) within the community (the congregation of audience and singers) to assert the self idiosyncratically (the solo improvisation) and still find a place within the collective identity of the larger group (the chorus), the music and semiotics of the black gospel tradition highlight the historical bonds of social solidarity and the centrality of multivocal professions of faith and fellowship in resisting "the cultural domination involved in the performance tradition" typical of Euro-American aesthetics. Craig Werner sees important psychosocial and aesthetic implications in this style. "The continual testing of artistic perception against audience response, immersed in the flow of time," is part of a larger movement toward the cultivation of artistic byplay and polyphonic discourse in Afro-modernism that he has dubbed "the gospel impulse."[16]

Applied to the southern gospel tradition, Werner's concept helps draw attention to what is psychosocially at stake in religious music, but the types of individual and collective narratives of spiritual experience characteristic of southern gospel performances complicate the notion of a single Afrocentric "gospel impulse" and reveal the scholarly impoverishment that proceeds from "gospel" construed primarily as a phenomenon of the African American experience. When a southern gospel fan recalls how the "messages in SGM touch the soul" in a way that "depends on [my] current struggles or situations," he is testifying to the propensity of participants in all varieties of gospel music to dwell in the possibilities of spiritual subjectivity and the idiosyncrasy of individual religious experience.[17] Yet he does not seem to mean that the song ameliorates suffering by absorbing individuals into a community of fellow strugglers, as is more common in black gospel. Rather, the culture of southern gospel—like the music itself—forms around an experiential theology of the saint's solitary self-embattlement. Southern gospel unites people, not on the basis of the Christian community's ability to alleviate that struggle, but in the acknowledgment that all God's children are called to bear their crosses alone.[18]

This emphasis on the solitary struggler helps explain why choirs and choruses are far less common in southern gospel than in black gospel. Instead, small groups of three or four vocalists—often dressed in matching suits or other coordinated costumes—sing in close harmony about the alluring mysteries of the soul's striving after (and, without God's help, failing to receive) grace and salvation. And whereas the artistic intensity and emotional center of black gospel tend to be the improvisational middle of the song, in which soloists spontaneously construct a vocal counterpoint to the chorus's main melodic theme, southern gospel hinges on the achievement of harmonic and symbolic consonance of the song's ending. It is not coincidental that southern gospel's lyrical didacticism and visual and harmonic symmetry echo the didactic and absolutist culture of evangelism out of which the music emerges.

It is difficult to overstate how intensely southern gospel audiences identify with the "preaching of the gospel" in song. For southern gospel fans and performers, no other form of Christian entertainment can rival this music's commitment to evangelism. In asking fans and performers what specifically southern gospel's ministerial function entails, I received plenty of answers that cited the salvific power of gospel music to convert unbelievers and its rejuvenating effect on the backslidden. But nearly everyone I asked said that ministry in song primarily means not saving the lost, but supporting and encouraging Christians in times of struggle. Moreover, the association of southern gospel with spiritual striving is linked to an equally strong view of the music as a surreptitious method through which to work out personalized understandings of orthodox doctrine and culture: a supermajority of fans and professionals says that gospel music means different things to most people; a majority says that some of the reasons they listen to or work in southern gospel music are not what other people might necessarily imagine.[19]

These responses suggest that alongside Werner's "[black] gospel impulse" and its function as an idiom for psychosocial reconstitution of oppressed minorities, there are other interpretive processes at work in gospel. Chief among these is the southern gospel paradox of overtly affirming orthodoxy while covertly validating unorthodox feelings and experiences. This emphasis suggests that instead of one "gospel impulse," we might more helpfully approach gospel music as a domain of aesthetic and semiotic variables. In this view, each variable combines and recombines in a shifting matrix called "gospel music." In the process, gospel performs various types of spiritual and political labor simultaneously, depending upon the racial, socioeconomic, psychosocial, and historical contexts in which the music is embedded.

Absolutist religious discourses cannot, of course, acknowledge the compromises that orthodoxy must make to remain relevant across time. But this fact only increases the value of expressive systems like southern gospel that effectively model pluralistic modes of identity and interaction in an absolutist idiom. What we might call the absolutist's pluralism that emerges in southern gospel must necessarily work subtly, as in "God on the Mountain," first performed by the McKameys. The song won the 1989 *Singing News* Fan Award for Song of the Year and remains popular today:

Life is easy, when you're up on the mountain.
You've got faith like you've never known.
But then things change and you're down in the valley.
Don't lose faith, you are never alone.

For the God of the mountain is still God in the valley.
When things go wrong, he'll make them right.
The God of the good times is still God in the bad times.
The God of the day is still God of the night.[20]

What is striking here is the ceremonial exchange of sentiment formalized in this music—most notably in the parallel structures and imagery. Each line of the chorus is a self-contained unit of thought that moves between extremes: God of the mountain/God in the valley; things go wrong/he'll make them right; God of the good times/God in the bad times; God of the day/God of the night. The parallelism redefines negative experience as but one point in a continuum of existence over which God presides with all authority and beneficence. In listening to these songs about the believer upheld in trials and tribulation by the hand of God, audiences are implicitly invited to identify with the religious experience and feeling the lyric portrays, without actually experiencing the suffering and hardship the lyric describes. At the same time that this invitation is being made to the audience, the artist is able to inhabit briefly—to dramatize musically—the spiritual life imagined in song, a life in which all reversals and suffering, every setback and failure, have meaning within a providential framework. This is more than just so much "rhetoric of assurance."[21] The singer becomes both prophet of the spiritual triumph sung about and proof of belief's efficacy. One believes, in the southern gospel vision of the world, because one survives the torpor and despair of ordinary life to sing about God's faithfulness to the weak and weary in times in times of trial.

Tracy Dartt, who wrote "God on the Mountain," seems to have had something like this in mind when he conceived the song's central image: "nothing grows on tops of mountain," he has said of the idea from which the song emerged. "It's all rock and ice and snow. The growth is always down in the valley." There is a certain oddness here, to be sure. Taken literally, Dartt's lyrics suggest that the valley is spiritually hollow, that the mountaintop is rich with reward. Yet Dartt himself understands the summit as dead compared to the lowlands. I read this type of oddity as evidence of how southern gospel creates an affective context in which to affirm faith by revaluing negative experience. In this evangelicals are espousing a version of what

I. A. Richards calls "emotional belief," the habit of ascribing truth-value to concepts felt through aesthetic encounters with artistic constructs rather than through lived experience. This form of belief, as Robert Milder notes, "arises from and fulfills a psychological need without . . . making claims on practical behavior."[22] One need only recall from one's past—or simply imagine—a psychospiritual crisis similar to the one described in southern gospel music in order to claim for oneself the personal assurance promised in the song's resolution: a reconciliation not only of the local crisis but also of the prevailing tension between orthodoxy and experience. Belief emerges from the upwelling of sentimental feeling in the musical experience. *Faith* becomes a term to describe the individual's ability to hold in productive tension the way things should be with the way they actually are.

This explanation of the music and its culture is not solely or even primarily the provenance of academic analysis. It is first and foremost a working philosophy of the music espoused by people involved in the southern gospel industry. In the course of a conversation about southern gospel and its place within evangelicalism, one prominent southern gospel leader, speaking to me within earshot of the National Quartet Convention main stage, put it this way: "If I got up on that stage tonight and said 'this is the most ecumenical group [of fans and artists] in Protestantism,' half of them would probably shoot me because half of them don't believe in ecumenism. But if they just talked to the people around them they'd see they're from every kind of Protestant denomination you can find. Now if you don't believe in something but yet you participate in it unknowingly but nobody's mad [about it] . . ."[23] The bemused chuckle that this thought trailed off into aptly captures the paradox of southern gospel's psychodynamics: the music and its culture thrive on a religious and cultural pluralism that many—perhaps most—southern gospel fans and artists would, if pressed, claim to repudiate as doctrinally unsound and personal anathema. Most of these people would not be consciously prevaricating. Southern gospel sustains such a ubiquity of cognitive, ideological, and theological dissonances, I would suggest, because it does not demand that participants square religion and rationality. The music resolves such discontinuities within the monotheistic logic of God's sovereign will. Assured in the ultimate righteousness of this sovereignty, participants can safely cultivate the sociocultural resources necessary for functional citizenship in a free society. Consequently, a Southern Baptist (who believes in the perseverance of the saints) can be seated alongside a General Baptist (who is probably an Arminian) at a gospel concert without imperiling anybody's soul or starting a fight. Southern gospel is the sound of "every kind of Protestant denomination you can find" being right all at once.

The Politics of Southern Gospel

Southern gospel's emphasis on consecrating faith and affirming ideological values by religious affect is particularly vulnerable to the manipulations of artful rhetoric, the seductions of good showmanship, and religious or ideological self-delusion. This is particularly the case in southern gospel songs that treat political themes. The performance of these types of songs relies on emotional belief to perpetuate the myth of a persecuted Christian majority, defiantly celebrating evangelical fundamentalism's rejection of and by secular society. In this vein, an anthem popularized by the Gold City quartet begins by imaging how outsiders view key aspects of Protestant biblical literalism. "Some," according to the lyrics, disbelieve the Virgin birth, doubt the veracity of miracles that scripture attributes to Christ, deprecate his divinity as mere human goodness, and scoff at the notion of a bodily resurrection. "Skeptics rise," the verse concludes, "to speak their lies."[24] Having imaginatively arrayed this host of skeptical straw men against the founding tenets of evangelical fundamentalism, the song triumphantly announces in the chorus, "Truth is marching on." At its emotional center, the song borrows the refrain from "Battle Hymn of the Republic" in a fashion that explicitly militarizes the conservative Christian rejection of modern freethinking and aligns the triumph of the biblical-literalist worldview with the march of spiritual freedom and scriptural truth.

The political polemic is a common subset of southern gospel songs. The Steeles had great success in the late 1990s with "We Want America Back," which warns the country to return to God or face certain ruin. This followed the Nelons' 1993 hit, "We've Got to Get America Back to God."[25] Gold City's "Truth Is Marching On" works in ways similar to these other songs: it encourages audiences to convince themselves emotionally, in the experience of the song's imagination of pervasive anti-Christian bias in the world, that evangelicals suffer real pain through (for them) purely symbolic actions. Courts banning the display of the Ten Commandments in government buildings and prohibiting formally sanctioned prayer in public schools are two common points of focus in southern gospel music of a political nature, as are same-sex marriage and abortion. John Dougan overstates things considerably in claiming that "current performers seem to *uniformly* embrace" this type of politicized rhetoric, but it is by no means uncommon, either.[26] In nearly two decades of attending the National Quartet Convention, I cannot recall a year when at least one prominent artist did not engage in some kind of political polemic from the convention's main stage. Often at NQC during the 1990s, the Inspirations, an all-male group with a rustic look and sound and an enormous following in the southern uplands, performed an antiabortion song, "Cry for the Children," that goes far beyond "Truth Is Marching On" in its stridency and coarseness.[27] Just after the events of September 11, 2001, artists were fond of introducing songs about the everlasting truth of Christ's Crucifixion as a culturally supremacist rebuke of radical Islamic terrorism. Since the election of Barack Obama to the presidency, the political rhetoric from southern gospel artists has expanded to include the imagined infiltration of Islamism into seats of political power in American life. In 2009 the singing Greenes used one of their NQC concerts to promote the sale of a customized T-shirt premised on an assertion by family patriarch Tony Greene that Obama had officially declared America no longer a Christian nation (Obama is widely believed in right-wing circles to be a barely closeted Muslim/socialist/communist).[28] In this kind of irrational and feverish political environment, standard expressions of right-wing political positions go over doubly well. The same year the Greenes were selling their T-shirts at NQC, Brian Free and his quartet, Assurance, used a twenty-year-old antiabortion song to close out their twenty-minute set of otherwise ordinary southern gospel songs. While the rest of their rather musically tepid performance received an average response from the audience, the antiabortion tune received a boisterous standing ovation—one of the most robust of the evening, though the song was sung no differently from their others.

To point out that conservatives and, in many cases, conservative Christians enjoy a great deal of access and power in government, culture, and society at all levels is both to miss and to make the point simultaneously. Obviously, these songs misrepresent sociopolitical reality: at the time of this writing, gay marriage, for instance, is legal in only six states (plus the District of Columbia), and the federal Defense of Marriage Act prohibits gay marriage nationwide. Meanwhile, more than two dozen states have their own laws explicitly forbidding such unions. To consider this state of affairs constituting Christianity under attack speaks to the volatility of evangelical identity and its reliance on narratives of conflict, crisis, and persecution that are constructed and maintained through the kind of cultural exchanges embodied in politicized southern gospel. When the idea of a unified, evangelical America appears to be challenged by historical or cultural shifts, politically oriented southern gospel songs are one way to reassert the image of a more perfect Christian union. One is reminded in all this of Kenneth Burke's description of literature and art as "strategies for selecting enemies and allies, for socializing losses, for warding off evil eye, for purification, propitiation, and de-sanctification, consolation and vengeance, admonition and exhortation, implicit commands or instructions of one sort or another."[29]

Andrew Sullivan has argued that the influence of Christian fundamentalism on conservative politics in America generally and among the Republican Party (and now the Tea Party) particularly has given rise to an age of "Christianism."[30] Sullivan uses this term to describe Christianity that is committed to the legislation of restrictive moral codes in the name of protecting religious freedom for Christians who believe themselves to be under assault by modernity. Extending this line of thought, we might similarly speak of southern gospelism to describe the dominant form of conservative Protestant musical expression and entertainment dedicated to constructing a dominionist evangelical identity in open spiritual conflict with secularism, humanism, and other forces of modernity thought to be obstructing the advancement of Christendom. Participation in the performance, sale, and spread of this music becomes a way for people to feel they are realizing in tangible ways the conservative evangelical aspiration for separateness from the secular world, without requiring evangelicals to give up the prerogatives of their status in secular, late-capitalist American democracy. More deeply, musical condemnations of secularism and moral decline create a vitally important role for fundamentalist evangelicals in contemporary American life. Through southern gospel jeremiads, evangelicalism's lifeways and values are repurposed as bulwarks against the morally and socially destructive blandishments of postmodern relativism.

The politically polemical strain of southern gospel songs brings in sharp relief a dynamic that holds true in less extreme realms of southern gospel experience. In effect, southern gospel songs call into being the reality they imagine—God's faithful remnant subject to daily slings and arrows of adversity and trial—and resolve the attendant tension within the logic of ultimate harmonic consonance. Politically inflected songs tend to focus on ideological triumphalism, whereas songs of personal struggle contain a greater emotional complexity. But in both song forms, the singer's performance acts as an occasion for audiences to consider themselves similarly beset and persecuted, similarly believing, similarly triumphing. In terms Burke uses to explain the cultural function of literature, southern gospel similarly works as a "device for arousing and fulfilling expectations in an audience." To sing or listen to music about overcoming temptation, doubt, fear, or other forms of sin and strife is to overcome these obstacles. When audiences respond to the chorus of "Sheltered in the Arms of God," which defies "the storm clouds" of negative experience to "rage high / The dark clouds rise / They don't worry me / For I'm sheltered safe / within the arms of God," they are not just rehearsing the formulas of evangelical orthodoxy.[31] They are also fulfilling a religious destiny—through uneven upswings and downturns troped as the storms of life—by recognizing it in the performance of the song.

Transformative Suffering

According to artists and fans, southern gospel music gives them access to what is experienced as contact with some form of divine grace or other supernatural force. Often southern gospel fans and performers will talk of "glory bumps" or a feeling of the presence of the Lord or of an "anointing" of the Holy Spirit or of redemption pouring down from heaven. Of the hundreds of fans and professionals I asked, more than a third specifically identified "that feeling of chills that seem to come out of nowhere" as evidence of the music's ministerial efficacy. But in my experience, these moments beggar all attempts at description, vernacular or otherwise. In such instances, live performance distills sensation to a kind of experiential essence, burns away the superfluous, and filters out the ancillary, secondary impressions and responses—leaving a wordless feeling that, in its purest form, exists at the ethereal level of intuitions sharpened by metaphysical intensity and encounters with beauty. When artists perform with real "authority," as Emerson used the term to indicate a way of communicating that "can pour light as a flood through the soul," lines of force and feeling running through an audience can be consolidated suddenly and inexplicably into an overwhelming immensity of sentiment. Something as simple as a song's up-tempo rhythm can create an irresistible enthusiasm that spreads unbeckoned through a crowd, giving expression to what I have often thought is best described as a collective urge to run somewhere. Followed by a slower, more meditative song—a ballad, perhaps, that reflects on the struggle for ordinary people of faith to live up to the unattainable ideals of orthodox theology or to remain within the favor of an omnipotent God whose presence comes and goes by a sovereign logic of its own—moments of enthusiasm can morph seamlessly into emotionally intense explorations of spiritual alienation and separation, feelings perhaps not unlike what Emily Dickinson described as a "sumptuous destitution."[32]

The move in southern gospel music from religious enthusiasm to cultivated despair (and vice versa) exemplifies "two behavioral extremes" emerging from within fundamentalist evangelical religious experience.[33] Such extremes reflect the paradox at the heart of contemporary freewill evangelicalism: God divinely ordains whom he will and will not save *and* holds human beings eternally accountable for "choosing" a predetermined outcome. Southern gospel acknowledges the incommensurability of this proposition not by attempting to explain it (it must simply be accepted) but by emotionally revaluing the extreme feelings that fundamentalism can give rise to: from despairing uncertainty and spiritual worthlessness to what the writer of the book of Peter in the New Testament (and an old hymn as well) refers to as "joy unspeakable and full of glory." Consequently, the unmerited favor of Christ's crucified redemption is often illustrated in southern gospel by songs that take the Calvinist logic of God's sovereign, boundless love and humanity's total depravity to its extreme, as in the song "That I Could Still Go Free," which begins:

> Lock me up in a prison
> And throw away the key.
> Take away the vision
> From these eyes that now can see.
> Deprive me of the food I eat
> And even bind my hands and my feet.
> For as long as I know Jesus
> Then I can still go free.

The singer is not actually imprisoned without any human hope of release, not actually blinded or starved, nor bound hand and foot. But because the same divine redemption that is believed to be able to rescue someone languishing in this manner can also save people in less extreme conditions, the singer and audience can claim for themselves the joy of salvation in extremis that has always defined Christianity: from Paul and Silas singing in prison to the iconic imagery of salvation from blindness in "Amazing Grace." The metaphor sharpens the lines between lost and saved, especially for those evangelicals whose salvation experience was largely interiorized and not accompanied by any radical change in lifestyle or behavior. The chorus develops this notion more fully:

> That I could still go free
> What kind of man would reach down his hand and do this for me,
> Unworthy to live and not fit to kill.
> Yet a man on the cross put me in His will
> And said that I could still go free.[34]

The first verse operates by a metaphorical conceit, which says in effect, even if I *were to be* blind, bound, and starving in prison, I would still be able to go free through Jesus. Notice how the chorus takes that conceit from the verse's conclusion and recasts it into a personal reflection on the singing sinner's own salvation experience and the conditions under which it was possible to actually go free through Christ at the moment of salvation—in the chorus's words, "that I could still go free" (*could* here is not used in the conditional sense of "I might be able under different circumstances," but rather idiomatically, as in "that I was able to go free"). Whenever I have experienced the transition between the first verse and chorus of this song in live performance, I have always had the impression of someone being interrupted midmetaphor by an unsought insight about his own spiritual condition that leads to another more ruminative line of thought in the chorus. A metaphorical abstraction about a spiritual what-if in the verse gives way to literal contemplation in the chorus of one's own enfleshed soul and its unmerited salvation. In the process, the imprisonment metaphor imperceptibly dissolves, so that the verse's figurative trope becomes literally, spiritually self-actualizing in the chorus. The singer's spiritual status in the chorus is no longer *like* the physical condition conceptualized in the verse. They are, in the song's logic, the same: debased, worthless, without human hope or help, saved, as the book of Hebrews (and a song by the Speer Family) has it, to the uttermost only by the divine dispensation of "His will."

Both Kenny Hinson, who originally performed the song in the 1970s with his family of singers, and Mike Bowling, who revived performances of the song a few years ago with the Crabb Family, render many of the song's best lines using a countrified type of throat singing that usually involves delivering key lyrical phrases in a guttural, growly overtone. This technique creates an intense mood of pathos. The lyrics seem to emerge from somewhere deep within the singer—literally from the back of his throat and figuratively from the depths of the soul—reinforcing the song's emphasis on the enormity of redemptive salvation. It is as if the song taps some nearly unspeakable immensity of feeling that might at any moment exceed the lyrics' linguistic limits and spill over into cries of pain and shouts of joy. Indeed, when I heard the song at the NQC in 2005, the response to it included just such shouts and cries from the audience. In this way, artists perform and fans identify with the role of the persecuted and abject Christian, a role dispensationalists and (pre)millennialists believe is an essential counterpoint to redeemed life on earth, all the while knowing that the suffering and abjection will be swept away by God's mighty hand in a compensatory flash of divine mercy and justice. They know, that is, how the song will end: *I can still go free.* Evangelicalism's conflicts with an antagonistic modern world and the carnal temptations of the soul's lower self are occasions for God to renew his covenant with his people. To be on guard against encroachments of worldliness or one's own deterioration of love for God (and to sing about it) is to be always on the brink of another triumph over the enemy, another victory over sin.

By His Wounds

The psychodynamics of evangelical conversion and the resultant habits of religious living provide a useful context for understanding the prevalence of lyrics preoccupied with violent debasement of the spirit and the flesh, as well as the persistence of lyrical imagery about the blood of Christ on Calvary. "I will glory in the cross," says the chorus of a famous Dottie Rambo song of the same name.

> Lest his suffering all be in vain
> I will weep no more for the cross that he bore
> I will glory in the cross.[35]

In 2010 the Bowling Family singers released a single echoing Rambo's hit, this new song titled "I Still Glory in the Cross." The song's chorus declares:

> I still glory in the cross [. . .]
> For I would still be lost
> had it not been for the old rugged tree.[36]

A 1988 song recorded live by the Greenes is even more explicit in evoking crucifixion:

> When I knelt [at the cross], the blood fell
> Sin lost the battle, the Lamb had prevailed.
> What made all hell tremble rang heaven's bells
> When I knelt, the blood fell.[37]

Abjection in images of the self prostrate before the crucified Christ, unwarranted mercy poured out in the atoning blood of "the Lamb," sin vanquished—the more melodramatic and highly sentimentalized the evocation of suffering, the more intense the feelings of relief and joy, gratitude and grace that flood the saved soul: "heaven's bells" peal for the sinner redeemed. This holds true not only in the conversion experience but also in consequent moments of recalling and reinhabiting a state of grace through religious music.

For outsiders, the sustained linkages among violence, sanguinity, and salvation in southern gospel can bespeak a disturbingly premodern Christian cosmology, a gruesome form of the "fleshly religiosity" that Jonathan

Edwards warned against amid the emotional extremism of the Great Awakening in eighteenth-century New England. But it is more helpful, I think,
to understand violent imagery and expressions in southern gospel music
in the context of broader habits of mind and imagination from which the
music emerges. Bertram Wyatt-Brown has identified not only a propensity toward aggression and violence in the southern imaginary, but also a
tandem tendency toward exaggeration and boastfulness, a "love of round
numbers, a fondness for stating a thing in the largest terms." Some version
of this notion can be traced back at least as far as Walter Hines Page's 1909
novel, *A Southerner*. The novel's reformist protagonist, Nicholas Worth,
finds in his native South "an exaggerated manner and a tendency to sweeping generalizations" working in concert with "the undue development" of
the "emotional nature."[38] Once manifested in brawling and duels, these
larger-than-life modes of thinking, feeling, and behavior are rerouted in
postmodern times into, among other places, songs about violent bondage
to sin and the blood-bought redemption of a crucified Christ.

This need to explore the visceral release and resolution of negative feelings suggests that southern gospel music is important not only for the conclusion it reaches about God's omnipotence and mercy, which is always
already absolute, but also for what it permits on the way to that conclusion:
a stylized and often profoundly evocative exploration of feelings of helplessness, incapacity, fallibility, and despair. In "Through the Fire," an acclaimed
song written and recorded by the Crabb Family, there is something quasi-
Miltonic in making the experience of sin and evil an opportunity "to justify
the ways of God to men" in the vernacular:[39]

> He never promised that the cross would not get heavy
> And the hill would not be hard to climb.
> He never offered our victories without fighting
> But He said help would always come in time.
> Just remember when you're standing in the valley of decision
> And the adversary says give in, just hold on, our Lord will show up.
> And He will take you through the fire again.[40]

Beneath the theological idiom and the religious image of trials by fire, a
sophisticated psychodrama is being played out here, one that is centered
on feelings of abandonment and internal conflict. The lyrical hook to the
song ("He will take you through the fire") depends on a vivid rendering of
the "fire" itself, the periodic experience of especially difficult or challenging circumstances that often end in personal failure and can be overcome
only through divine help. Notice that five of the chorus's seven lines are

devoted to describing the struggle, while only two are concerned with divine relief. Fillingim argues that southern gospel music depicts the trials and tribulations of Christian living as part of "a conceptual universe in which, psychologically, suffering does not matter, and therefore, might as well be nonexistent."[41] But the description of suffering in southern gospel music seems at least as important as the conclusion, in this case, that "He will take you through the fire again." Private doubt and uncertainty, fears and depressions about suffering and misfortune are publicly revalued as the Christian's cross to bear, not because "suffering does not matter" in southern gospel music but *because these feelings matter so much*.

The Soundtrack of Evangelical Exceptionalism

The preoccupation in southern gospel music with the self-defining experience of suffering, temptations, trials, and other threats to religious belief recalls the role of humiliation in traditional Calvinist conversion most powerfully articulated by seventeenth-century Puritan divine Thomas Shepard: preceded by conviction of sin and compunction for sin, humiliation strips the heart of any belief in the human capacity to save itself. Thus humiliated, the contrite sinner is prepared, as scripture puts it, to deny himself, take up his cross, and follow Christ (Matt. 16:24). Within this framework, "both deliverances and trials become measures of fulfillment, and to the covenanted disclose what others can never perceive," as Perry Miller writes. "For a dedicated people, seeking the Lord on a day of humiliation thus becomes a redefinition of the common purpose; a thanksgiving is a reaffirmation of it."[42]

In its struggle to remain relevant in an increasingly individualistic world, contemporary evangelicalism has made adjustments to Puritans' archetypal morphology of conversion. Most significantly, the modern path to salvation today emphasizes the role of the human will in choosing to accept God's free gift of salvation (to early Puritans, free will was dangerous heresy). But the centrality of negative feelings in southern gospel music suggests that the contemporary evangelical model of religious conversion, though it may speak to the need for individual agency in choosing to accept or reject salvation, fails to account adequately for the full range of the modern spiritual existence. Contemporary evangelical Protestantism officially looks heavenward, locating the meaning of redemption in God's free gift of grace that one must willingly accept (or not). But the persistent drift in everyday evangelical life toward forms of expression and modes of experience that emphasize the frisson of the imperiled soul points in another direction, inward, to the spiritual value of private conflicts and tensions in defining the contours of conservative Protestant religious living. For millions of evangelicals today, their identity as a covenanted elect emerges from within the ongoing struggle to manage and resolve spiritual disquietude through the experience of southern gospel music.

This mode of expression, this use of cultural practice to manage the tension between sentiment and faith, the experientially fluctuant and the doctrinally absolute, is more than just a compensation for the paradoxes of evangelicalism. The individual structures of religious feeling and thought that emerge from within southern gospel cohere into postmodern patterns of psychology characteristic of the "I-in-process" that Sacvan Bercovitch first located in seventeenth-century American heart religion among the Puritans. This ever-evolving spiritual identity is defined by "daily, hourly losses [that] threaten what ought to be a foregone resolution" to surrender the self to the Almighty. Memorializing these trials and tribulations in sacred song functions as the modern equivalent of what the Puritans considered "evidence that God hath chosen us, entered into covenant with us and taken us to be his [in a way] the world ha[s] not witnessed since Christ culled the Apostles out of it."[43] In this context, southern gospel serves as a private means of religious identity formation, but it also acts as a public discourse in which many evangelicals reaffirm their exceptionalist identity by collectively consecrating the strife of daily living without surrendering cause for optimism.[44]

This process must necessarily reckon with the experience of insufficiency and powerlessness, of spiritual neediness. Yet so much of mainstream evangelicalism today embraces a version of what William James calls a "religion of healthy-mindedness" intently focused on self-help and the power of positive thinking. The most prominent figures in contemporary evangelicalism are exponents of some version of this philosophy: Joyce Meyer preaches about helping you "win the battle in your mind." Rick Warren extols the virtues of "the purpose driven life." And Joel Osteen's thousand-watt smile telegraphs his high-beam focus on helping you "activate your faith, achieve your dreams, and increase God's favor" in your life.[45]

Despite their religious enthusiasm, there is a certain emotional shallowness to these approaches that largely denies the authenticity of negative feelings by describing them as manifestations of sin or evidence of the forces of darkness trying to keep you down. In contrast, southern gospel music encourages much freer play of religious affect and authenticates the felt reality of spiritual vicissitudes. When southern gospel fans speak, as they often do, about southern gospel going deep into the soul in a way that traditional sermons and preaching cannot, they are acknowledging that the music allows evangelicals to develop personally meaningfully responses to problems of faith and Christian living in the modern world without forcing them to disaffiliate themselves from evangelical orthodoxy or their own experience. Southern gospel music transforms orthodox ideas and ordinary speech into a form of vernacular poetry, a melodic lyricism that makes negative emotions and experience acceptable to express in a religious culture that has very few meaningful ways of dealing with these things in the lives of the redeemed. Bathed in the bright lights of the stage, arrayed in the poetry of musical lyrics, brought to life in the magical moment of live performance, the doctrines of Protestant evangelical theology and the narrow commitments of conservative ideology become affectively accessible. They become experientially real. In a word, they are *felt* through southern gospel music in the soul-soaring mystery of a sensate self, simultaneously transformed and transcended.

2. Nostalgia, Modernity, and the Reconstruction Roots of Southern Gospel

By the time Lee surrendered to Grant at Appomattox Court House in early April 1865, Aldine S. Kieffer had been a Confederate prisoner of war at Fort Delaware for almost a year.[1] For ordinary Confederate conscripts, Lee's surrender was a humiliating defeat. For most POWs, it was also also effectively an additional sentence of anywhere from a few weeks to several months. Throughout April and into May, the U.S. government focused on capturing the Confederacy's military leadership and liberating Union POWs from southern prisons.[2] Releasing Confederate prisoners was not a high priority. Yet Kieffer, a twenty-four-year-old farm boy from central Missouri by way of the Shenandoah Valley, received a pardon and his walking papers just ten days after Appomattox.[3] In absence of verifiable explanations for this uncommon good fortune, family lore proliferated. One story suggests that Kieffer's pardon resulted from an appeal to the White House by his brother-in-law and close friend, Ephraim Ruebush, whom Kieffer met when the two taught music together and worked in the music-printing company owned by Kieffer's grandfather before the war.[4] Another story has Kieffer's mother personally requesting that Lincoln pardon her son days before the president was shot so that Kieffer could resume his work as a music teacher and help rebuild the southern uplands. For his part, Kieffer was largely silent later in life about the ordeal and his release. In a series of autobiographical sketches he published in 1890 about the postwar beginnings of his music career, he wrote of captivity and release only that "I have no words to express my feelings, but leave the reader to guess."[5]

Whatever the circumstances leading up to Kieffer's release, we do know that Ruebush was waiting for Kieffer when he walked out of prison—which must have seemed to Kieffer a remarkable testament to their friendship, considering that he believed Ruebush had fought for the North in the war.[6] After spending his first days of freedom with his sister and brother-in-law in Morgan County, West Virginia, Kieffer arrived in mid-May at his family's home in the heart of the Shenandoah Valley. Kieffer recalled the experience of his return this way:

> We arrived at Mountain Valley [Va.] (now Singers Glen) on the 12th of May, 1865. The old printing office, the old homestead, the old farm gate, the fences, all had put on the habiliments of woe, but the forest, the stream, the mountain peak, and the cerulean skies, seemed like dear companions. The war was over—what was to be done? A ruined country, poverty stricken people, and no currency! What could be done? Where should I begin life anew? Or how could I? But I reflected that I had been a soldier; that I was still a young man, and then I began looking about for something to do.[7]

As a species of postbellum stock taking, the scene contains many of the psychosocial dynamics that would fuel the rise of the New South: most palpably, feelings of "woe"—about the devastation of homesteads, the destruction of businesses, and the damage to the land—lifted out of despair by a diminished but indomitable spirit of survival rooted in the mythos of a rejuvenating, pastoral homeland.[8] At least as striking, however, as Kieffer's conclusion that he must make a way for himself by drawing on his youth and military experience are the mixed feelings with which he decides to start "looking about for something to do." As decisions go, this one does not so much ring with the authority of resolution as echo his mournful cry: *What was to be done? . . . What could be done? . . . Where should I begin life anew? Or how could I?*

Indeed, variations on the idea of *doing something* with himself, and what precisely that should be, recur throughout his descriptions of his experience in those early days of life after the war. "I began looking about for something to do," he recalled of himself a few weeks into his return home. Several months later after trying (and failing) at farming, he writes that "[I] bethought me of something else" to do.[9] That something for Kieffer ultimately turned out to be gospel music—composing it, publishing it, singing it, and teaching others to sing and teach it—in a way and to an extent that has not yet been fully explored. Within a year of the war's end, Kieffer, Ruebush, and other family members had repaired his grandfather Joseph Funk's printing press and used it to publish a gospel tunebook under the imprint of "Ruebush & Kieffer." In 1870 Kieffer helped launch a revamped version of the periodical his grandfather had published before the war under

Aldine S. Kieffer, 1881.
(From author's collection.)

the name the *Southern Musical Advocate and Singer's Friend*. Kieffer called this new publication the *Musical Million*, a name that suggests the scope and scale of Kieffer's dawning ambition and the possibilities he imagined for his work in gospel music. In 1872 Ruebush and Kieffer formalized their publishing partnership, incorporating the Ruebush-Kieffer Co., with Kieffer overseeing the company's creative and editorial enterprises, while Ruebush mainly managed the financial side of the business. In 1874 Ruebush and Kieffer opened the first singing school for music teachers in the South, the Virginia Normal Music School. By 1877 Ruebush-Kieffer had sold more than a half-million copies of its most popular songbook, *The Temple Star*.[10]

This achievement was more than materially enriching or personally re-habilitating for a "young man" unmoored by the psychospiritual upheavals of war, though it was both of these things too and all the more impressive for taking place during the social and economic depression that gripped the South throughout the Reconstruction era and into the final decades of the century. It is not too much to say Kieffer's songbooks became a kind of cultural and spiritual currency passed from hand to hand among postwar white southerners and their descendants. His songs and the style of southern sacred music they came to typify offered people a powerful language in which to express complicated feelings of fear and faith, to voice a nostalgic longing for what had been lost, and to work toward a better life here in this world by singing of their pietistic hopes for a brighter day hereafter. In little more than a decade after meeting up with Ephraim Ruebush outside the Fort Delaware prison, Kieffer emerges as the most influential songwriter, publisher, and advocate for the earliest modern form of commercialized southern gospel.

At the time and for generations to come, this music's most distinguishing feature was its reliance on a system of music notation that used seven shape notes (sometimes called patent notes) instead of round notes (both shape-note and round-note systems use lines and spaces, but those able to read shape notation could get by without them). Each shape note corresponds to one of the seven separate pitches in the Western major scale. The lines-and-spaces approach assigns a pitch to each note based on its position on the musical staff, the key signature that applies at any given time, and accidentals, which alter the pitch, usually by a half-step. Contrastingly, students in the shape-note tradition may learn all that, but, in addition, they learn seven shapes associated with each of the seven scale degrees—do, re, mi, fa, sol, la, and ti—that substitute for the oval noteheads of standard notation.

Shape-notation music was not a southern invention. Four-shape notation emerged in the early nineteenth century and spread widely across the early Republic.[11] But the seven-shape notation conceived by Jesse Aiken and popularized by Ruebush-Kieffer, among others, became associated with the gospel music that flourished in the rural areas and small towns of the South and Midwest, especially among whites. The primary motivations behind the emergence of the seven-note system were to improve the quality of congregational music making by teaching as many people as possible how to sight-read (and train a few well enough to lead music) and to fill a void in recreational music making for musically inclined Christians. In the process, southern shape-note music provided moral instruction to at least three generations of postbellum rural, working-class, and poor evangelicals who acquired an education in theology and cultural norms in the process of learning music. Indeed, in the years after the Civil War, white gospel in the South was as well known for the fervency of its partisans' commitment to the seven-shape notational system of music education as a means of social

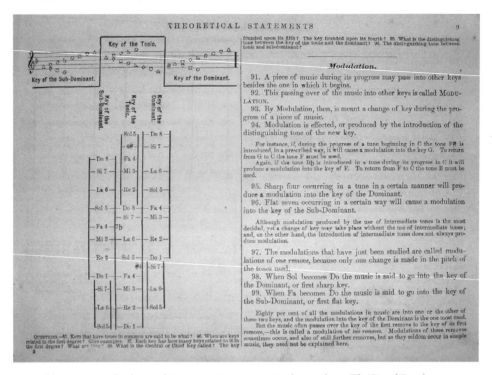

Chart on tonal relationships in section on music theory from *The Royal Procla-mation*, a Ruebush-Kieffer shape-note songbook published in 1886. Around the turn of the twentieth century, the music-theory sections of shape-note songbooks fell away and were published separately. (From author's collection.)

reform as it was for its seven quirky little shapes.[12] At a basic level, the so-cializing element in southern shape-note music reflects the model of music "as a tool for refining the taste and judgment of the body politic [and] for advancing civilized values in moral and aesthetic domains" first established in Boston by Lowell Mason.[13] However, the sacred music Ruebush-Kieffer came to typify promoted a distinctly southern brand of moral instruction that in many ways pushed back against the values and mores of the very urban centers where the music-as-moral-tutor model originally appeared. In Kief-fer's words, southern white gospel meant "the masses against the classes."[14]

Most fans and professionals within contemporary southern gospel music have little or no awareness of Kieffer. When he is acknowledged, Kieffer is usually seen as an influential figure in the southern shape-note singing-school movement. In these accounts, he is described as having helped professionalize the instruction of the music and commercialize early white gospel in the New South. Even then his contributions are typically treated as part of southern gospel music's prehistory in the nineteenth century.[15] This view has been particularly dominant since the appearance of James Goff's *Close Harmony,* in which modern southern gospel is depicted as being pioneered by pious prayer warriors of the new twentieth century who transformed southern shape-note music into "the music of much of America." In a rare departure from this approach, musicologist Stephen Shearon has suggested that Kieffer is "perhaps the single most important figure in the birth of Southern gospel music," but up to now, there has been no sustained case made for such an interpretation of Kieffer's influence on modern southern gospel.[16]

This chapter takes seriously the notion of Kieffer as founding figure in southern white gospel and explores the implications of this view for our understanding of the music's cultural function that continues into our own time. Kieffer began his postwar career in music fairly soon after his release from prison, yet his emergence as a visionary initiator of the modern southern gospel tradition, as we shall see, was not at all an inevitable outcome of his casting about for something to do after the war, any more than it was immediately obvious to Kieffer that he should relaunch and expand his grandfather's music business. The question Kieffer was confronting in May 1865 was less "what shall I do and become?" and more "can my life and work in the world still matter?" In this context, gospel music became Kieffer's life's work not because it allowed him to achieve great things (though it did that, too) but because it gave him a way to confront questions of material and spiritual survival forced upon him in the crucible of war and Reconstruction.

Constructing meaningful narratives about shifting cultural identities through new indigenous forms of popular cultural expression was particularly important for southerners in Reconstruction. Agrarian ways of life were increasingly being displaced by emergent industrialism in the years after the Civil War, and so agrarian identity was rapidly fragmenting. Southern white gospel as a cultural innovation helped offset the encroachments of modernity by aligning a large segment of evangelicals with the present age of progress, even as the sentimental and nostalgic lyrical content of the music preserved traditional religious ideals and memorialized earlier modes of religious pastoralism. Traced forward from the crisis of identity and calling that befalls Kieffer during that woeful survey of the land and his life, white gospel music from the South emerges as a set of cultural practices born of struggle and infused with a dual concern for preserving traditional values and practices while also absorbing the psychosocial upheaval of modern life.

Repurposing Pastoralism

Kieffer did not immediately go inside his grandfather's printing shop when he returned to Singers Glen, as he explained in this excerpt from the 1890 autobiographical essays:

> After a few days' rest, I walked into the old printing office. All was silent . . . silent as the grave save the flapping of startled bats' wings, or a wink from the eyes of the bird of wisdom. I turned away in sadness, Joseph Funk [Kieffer's grandfather], the founder of that printing office, was no more [Funk died in late December 1864]. . . . [T]he old printing office had gone down, as many another did in our Sunny South. This to me was the saddest defeat of all. Sick at heart, I left the old printing office and bethought me of something else.
>
> It was not many days until Mr. Ruebush, my only brother, L. R. Rieffer [sic], and myself undertook to do farm work, such as making hay, reaping grain, and other farm labor. I even undertook a contract to split rails, which is but half-finished unto this day.[17]

As it was for thousands of veterans in the summer of 1865, farming for Kieffer presented itself as both a consolation and a last resort. For one thing, there simply were no other jobs available. For another, war had "respected no rigid delineation between home and battlefront."[18] Killing and dying had intruded into the lives and homes of millions of Americans on a previously unknown scale, not only altering attitudes about death but also destabilizing people's confidence in the individual's ability to reclaim the self, the spirit, and the soul from the myriad ravages of war. Kieffer's postwar experience registers the pervasive effect of this shift in self-perception and behavior, his doleful assessment of the family homestead externalizing his own mordancy. Though he approaches the printing office with hopes of finding it in something close to working condition, the silence Kieffer encounters there portends for him not postwar peace and quiet to be filled with the potential for progress and prosperity but the sepulcher and "sadness."

His reaction was undoubtedly tinged by grief for what had been lost: property, wealth, opportunity, and material and sentimental connections to his childhood and grandfather, who filled the gap left by the 1847 death of Kieffer's father (who died after swimming across the Missouri River on a bet).[19] Yet insofar as he seems to have approached the printing-office door hoping to escape the uncertainty and upheaval of the present—*What was to be done? . . . What could be done?*—by stepping back into the pastoral peacefulness of the past, the dejection with which he turns and leaves and heads for the field to pick up the plow bespeaks a certain kind of unslakable sadness for what cannot be recovered, a feeling beyond grief and mourning that Freud designated with the term *melancholia*. In this context, farming was not just the next-best—and only obvious—choice for an able-bodied male from the Shenandoah Valley with access to arable land. It also became a more realistic means of escaping the present by reclaiming the past, or trying to anyway.

Whatever his expectations, it was almost immediately clear that Kieffer was not cut out for farming, as he self-deprecatingly suggests with the image of the fence rails remaining unsplit after nearly thirty years. This failure probably was inevitable. Most veterans returned from war in 1865 well after the planting season had passed in the South,[20] and in Kieffer's case particularly, there was the added complication of what his friend William Blake called certain "fatal defects of his character," namely, "irresolution and lack of application." Kieffer was melancholic, possibly depressive, and, increasingly with age, fanatical about shape-note teaching and singing. In any event, the young romantic in Kieffer—who despised Shakespeare but was widely read in the classics of romanticism, including Byron, Wordsworth, Coleridge, and Tennyson—might well have initially imagined that farming would mean a sublime communion with the companionable countryside: "the forest, the stream, the mountain peak, and the cerulean skies" that had seemed to welcome him home after the ordeal of soldiering, imprisonment, and military defeat. This sentimental attitude toward the Shenandoah Valley dates back to Kieffer's childhood, when he moved with his mother from Missouri to Singers Glen after his father's death. Recalling the first glimpses of what his child eyes saw as something close to an Eden of beauty and abundance, he later wrote: "To me it seemed a sort of earthly paradise. The large orchards surrounding the house, the rich fields of clover, the grand old oaks which clad the hills, the schoolhouse with its playground shaded by huge churry [sic] trees whose temptingly luscious fruit was then beginning to blush, together with the spring whose crystal waters not only refreshed the school-children, but likewise a fertile meadow in which the lowing herd found ample room and the long lines of mounts in the west, all gave me infinite pleasure."[21] Failing at farming represented nothing short of a failure of precisely this sort of antebellum pastoral romanticism to address the concerns of life in the postbellum world. This failure forced Kieffer to acknowledge the futility of melancholic nostalgia untempered by a vision of himself in a better future that he could help build.

By August 1865, he was back to earning "a living by teaching singing schools in the country churches" as he had done while working for his grandfather before the war.[22] At this Kieffer proved a natural, and he spent the rest of his career championing shape-note music education in the South and building an infrastructure that persists to this day in the various forms, institutions, and practices of modern southern gospel music. Historical accounts of Kieffer's emergence invariably ignore or quickly pass over this agricultural interlude, emphasizing instead the pivotal contribution Kieffer came to make as a music educator and publisher to the social and economic rehabilitation of the New South.[23] Nevertheless, how people behave in moments of crisis reveals a great deal about the unseen historical realities and dynamics submerged beneath the choices they make and the movements in which they participate. The path Kieffer took immediately after the war—trying and failing to rebuild the family farm before taking up a career in shape-note music—reminds us that southern white gospel was indeed among the social, political, cultural, and aesthetic developments that collectively came to define the New South. But this music and its culture matter at least as much historically for their fundamental role in helping pious whites reshape their identities and interpret the vicissitudes of experience during a period of great turmoil and strife, without surrendering their sense of holding fast to the faith of their fathers.

Through white gospel, Kieffer maintained a deeply southern connection to the part of the South he knew and loved, and modeled a way for others to do so themselves, not by farming the land, but by using the pastoral landscape as an imaginative resource to catalyze the creation of gospel songs and energize the experience of southern religious culture. These songs draw heavily on scenes of the "twilight shadows" that "gently fall upon the cottage lawn," or evocations of the "dark valley and shadow of death" beyond which "bloometh an evergreen shore," and urgent pleas to

> fly from the fields of sin,
> Fly for thy life, to-day,
> Fly to our Father's house,
> Enter the narrow way.[24]

These images were not just abstractly constructed products of the imagination but also reflections of the historical moment: the concern with the "Father's house," for instance, surfaces at a moment when mountain homes of rough-hewn logs and stone built by the homesteading forefathers of the Shenandoah Valley were being replaced by more modern structures of milled lumber.[25] At the same time, southern subsistence farming was squeezed out in the transformations brought about by modern industrial technology and federal stimulus for mass agriculture. The salient point, then, in emphasizing Kieffer's abandonment of farming in favor of music, is not that agrarian values and lifeways were rendered inoperative by the war and the fervor for reform that followed. Rather, those values ceased to be linked to, or meaningfully lived through, traditional farm life. Instead they received a new, modern shape in the ascendant technologies and modes of intellectual, creative labor that replaced subsistence farming in the postbellum South.

Insofar as Kieffer abandoned farming and took up music education and publishing after the war, it is not inaccurate to say that he worked "from the foundation provided by the antebellum tunebooks" of his grandfather's era.[26] Kieffer did so, however, with a substantially new image and understanding of himself. If this change was necessitated by the upheavals and pressures of postwar life, it was made possible by gospel music's ability to fuse into productive tension a sentimental longing for a bygone way of life *and* a progressive ambition to perform work in the world with positive, lasting consequences for the future. There is perhaps no better example of this fusion and its psychosocial function than the 1872 formation of the Ruebush-Kieffer Co. At least in the early days of their work together, Kieffer considered Ruebush far more than a business partner. Recalling the first night he spent at the Ruebushes' house after being released from prison, Kieffer later wrote: "It was only thirty-six hours until we reached his home, and a warm welcome and a kiss from my sister made me realize that the war was over. On the night of our arrival I slept with a Yankee Captain [Ruebush], but our communication was like that of brothers, and as kindly as that of Jonathan and David."[27] Even allowing for the conventions of male friendship in Victorian America, this is a vividly intimate image, all the more so for Kieffer's providing no comment on what, if anything, passed between the two about the years he thought they had spent fighting as enemies during the war. Maybe what was said was too personal to impart. Or, more likely, perhaps there was nothing to be said. Recovery and survival for many ordinary southerners to a large extent meant learning to live with irreconcilable tensions and unresolved paradoxes, such as a Yankee officer and a Rebel soldier sharing the same bed in brotherly amity just days after the Civil War ended. Ruebush had the magnanimity and moral clarity of winning on his side. For Kieffer, as for many southerners like him, the world had to be remade without the benefit of a priori notions of right and wrong.

In comparing his relationship with Ruebush to that of Jonathan and David, whose friendship withstood the homicidal rage of King Saul and exemplified the capacity of brotherly love to overcome the enmities of war and factionalism, Kieffer seems to want to believe in the reconciling power of platonic brotherhood after a conflict of biblical proportions. As a formal confirmation of that brotherhood, the Ruebush-Kieffer corporate alliance the voluntary nature of Christian conversion creeping into an increasingly Arminianized Protestantism in the wake of the Enlightenment's valorization of human reason.[30]

Beyond these general trends in American Protestantism, southern music culture was transformed during the abolition and Civil War eras by a culmination of several dynamics particular to the greater South. Leading up to the war, the rapid industrialization of America largely left the South behind. By 1850 the South could claim "one third of the nation's population but only one-tenth the nation's manufacturing capability." The outbreak of the Civil War and the formation of the Confederacy brought focus and purpose to the theretofore widespread but diffused resentments that ran throughout southern life and reflected the socioeconomic imbalances between the South and the rest of the country. Confederate nationalism was held together by the unifying effect of rebellion, an identity that, among other things, "required its own songs . . . that could symbolize and motivate a new nation." At the same time, secession conveniently nullified federal copyright laws. As a result, contemporary American music was freely borrowed for the purposes of southern identity reformation. In this way, southern music put its own imprint on American popular song styles that responded to the psychosocial crisis of war.[31]

By the final years of the conflict, the southern music industry had collapsed, and no great amount of pro-Confederacy music was produced. Still, the cultural memory of popular music responding to a prolonged crisis of identity—and doing so in overtly religious terms—remained. The deeply religious dimension of postwar southern shape-note music was reinforced by a series of revivals that swept through Confederate camps, first in early 1863 and then again in the winters of 1863–1864 and 1864–1865. Alongside the old memories of antebellum camp-meeting revivals as scenes of festive music making, war-camp revivals permanently infused musical lyrics about spiritual salvation with sociopolitical concerns.[32] The revivalist fixation with God and Satan struggling for man's eternal soul closely paralleled both the martial rhetoric of the South fighting Northern tyranny and the widespread sense among soldiers that an apocalyptic war between God in heaven and the forces of hell had been unleashed on earth.[33]

In addition to providing some little distraction from the squalid and pestilential conditions of war camps, musical moments reliably make for some of the most evocative scenes of uncommon humanity that show up in letters and remembrances from the Civil War. Kieffer himself wrote about his brigade's band serenading the Yankees, who were encamped along the Rappahannock

River in 1862. Kieffer and his fellow musicians attacked the enemy "not with shot and shell, but by blowing them up with brass and horns."

> Our bands reached the water's edge and began the serenade by playing "Hail Columbia" and "The Star-Spangled Banner." This aroused a kindly feeling in the hearts of the Yankee bandsmen, who were soon on the riverbank opposite us, and the tones of "Dixie's Land" and "Bonnie Blue Flag" floated across the river to greet us. Officers in uniforms and men in the ranks forgot all laws of the military code to such an extent as to pass through the picket lines until both armies were facing each other, not with weapons of war, but with human hearts full of love and sympathy and filled with a desire for peace.[34]

Amid a mighty civil war, music was a way for combatants to cultivate "kindly feeling" between foes whose old enmities could be converted into "hearts full of love" with the capacity for peaceful coexistence. Kieffer concludes this story with (for him) rare understatement: "The incident recited speaks loudly of the influence of music upon our natures." Kieffer's experience as a prisoner at Fort Delaware only reinforced his war-forged faith in the transformative, salvific power of music: "Music not only relieved the monotony of prison life, but was, doubtless, the means by which my life was preserved by keeping my mind, heart, and soul from eating away at themselves."[35]

All these psychosocial dynamics converged in the shape-note music education and reform movement that emerged immediately after the war and hastened the success of the sacred music publishing industry during Reconstruction. Well before the Civil War, as Steven Cornelius has shown, Americans were accustomed to taking local themes in music and making broader sociocultural applications.[36] Wartime experiences of music's redeeming slivers of humanity from itself in the face of mass death and dying only deepened and widened the role of musical arts and education in efforts to rebuild the South after the war. Kieffer and other veterans like him naturally brought home with them the connection fortified during fighting between music and the deeper currents of existence, and these experiences were inevitably woven into the fabric of postwar life and culture. While the popularity of shape-note music died out after the war in northern, urban culture,[37] shape notes notably survived and thrived in the South and other parts of rural America. This situation inflected the treatment of common American musical themes with a particularly indigenous quality reflected in the shape-note musical literature produced after the war. Meanwhile, the rise of singing schools associated with flourishing shape-note publishers helped spawn a generation of amateur musical poets, many of whom naturally drifted toward common themes of family and faith in their compositions.

In these writers' songs, lingering resentments, anxieties, hopes, and fears about the South and its fate echo through refrains about salvation and freedom from life in this vale of tears. "By-and-by, when this life is ended," Kieffer wrote in "The Savior Calls,"

> You shall dwell on high;
> Share his love in the many mansions
> Far beyond the sky.

Another Kieffer song, "By the Gate They'll Meet Us," repurposes home-coming scenes at the farmstead gate as a metaphor for heavenly reunions:

> By the gate they'll meet us,
> 'eNeath [*sic*] the golden sky,
> Meet us at the portal,
> Meet us by-and-by.[38]

This music's sentimental mixing of domestic and religious themes effec-tively repurposed habits of feeling and thinking from before and during the war—separation, loss, reparation, and reunion—and revoiced them in innovative, new musical and lyrical terms that helped both the producers and the consumers of this music align themselves with progress, while also retaining a connection with reassuringly familiar patterns of affect and expression.

This reconciliation dynamic—between Yank and Reb, present and past, progress and nostalgia, freedom and bondage, profit and piety—became an enduring feature of southern white gospel that visibly played itself out in the structure and aims of postbellum shape-note gospel songbooks. The majority of the space in these books was filled by old and new songs full of sentimental and nostalgic lyrics. However, the early pages of the songbooks also contained a set of "theoretical statements" on the principles of vocal music in the seven-shape notational tradition. These minitextbooks (usually six to twelve pages) represented the latest developments in shape-note music theory and pedagogy, which emphasized the right foundations of religious singing and, by extension, the development of the spiritual sensibilities voiced in sacred song. By preceding the songs themselves, this instructional material overlaid the music with the progressive, reformist ambitions of the shape-note movement.

Yet just as Kieffer and Ruebush's friendship masks the very paradoxes it managed, the music they published is regularly far more complicated than the lyrics to the music would suggest when studied in isolation, a dynamic succinctly illustrated by one of Kieffer's most famous compositions, "Grave

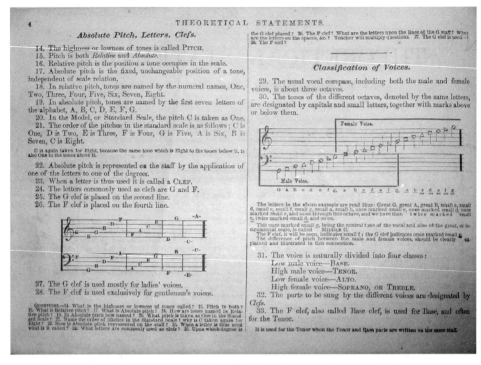

Instructional page in section on music theory from *The Royal Proclamation*. (From author's collection.)

on the Green Hillside." The song describes a "little grave on the green hillside that lies to the morning sun" and calls to mind "the shore of the far-off land" that "we" will reach someday "thro' a grave" of our own on the same "green hill side."[39] The lyrics' intense sentimentality leaves the impression that the song is a relic of an antebellum fixation with death, a holdover from the premodern South just a few notches above the maudlin doggerel that Emmeline Grangerford produces in *Huckleberry Finn* after every death in her rural southern village. Yet this premodern lyric is scored to music of considerable insight: Kieffer's score breaks with the style of music found in popular southern tunebooks of the day, such as *Sacred Harp* and *Southern Harmony*, even as the song incorporates a variety of other antebellum American sacred and secular musical trends. At the same time, the song innovatively anticipates melodic and harmonic developments that would come to define twentieth-century white gospel.[40] These musical innovations made "Grave on the Green Hillside"—like much southern white gospel from this era—as much a part of the modern moment as of the pastoral past.

Herein lies the paradox of pietistic, populist progressivism in the New South: advocates of the postbellum shape-note singing movement saw white gospel as a modern means of teaching a new generation of white evangelicals the "foundation of physical, moral, and mental habits" on which the South would be rebuilt.[41] But these values, originating in and through the music, were often referenced back to the cultural ideals of antebellum agrarianism: hard work, moral rectitude, and intense piety. In the context of rapid and destabilizing change, white gospel songbooks became an early evangelical technology for managing the disorienting effects of modernization through a continuous stream of new shape-note tunes, a dynamic that persists in what remains of shape-note publishing today. As one modern-day leader in shape-note music put it, "Newness is just part of the tradition."[42]

While editors and publishers emphasized the religious value of gospel music, the music in their songbooks was actually more widely applicable to everyday life. The form, in other words, fitted the function. Most songbooks were divided into several categories designed for multiple purposes, not all of them religious, and followed the basic format of the antebellum tunebooks of Joseph Funk's era. These older books typically included sections on the rudiments of music theory, congregational tunes, songs for social gatherings, and familiar anthems. Ruebush-Kieffer organized their books similarly: there are sections for rudiments, singing-school tunes (typically traditional secular songs and ditties), congregational tunes, Sunday-school and early gospel-style songs, and anthems. Around the turn of the century, many gospel songbooks began including responsive readings written for a variety of customary religious and social occasions. Consequently, the books were useful in secular settings as well as for personal devotions, congregational worship, and church choirs. At about this time, rudiments fell away and were published separately, and the books changed from oblong format to small octavo format, while also changing from a separate staff for each voice part to the grand staff, which was easier to read when playing a keyboard instrument. Whereas the old tunebooks were intended to meet everyone's needs and be used for many years, the newer books were published for increasingly niche markets and demands and accordingly changed more often.[43]

In addition to religious tunes, many songs—especially the original compositions—ranged freely over social and political issues. A single songbook in 1896 contains songs that address a network of concerns related to the fragmentation of modern life: "Twas Rum That Spoiled My Boy" treats the scourge of alcoholism, with a composer's instruction that the song be sung "with pathos." "Down in the Licensed Saloon"—the title answering the question in the first verse: "Where is my wand'ring boy tonight?"—musicalizes

Oblong shape-note songbook published by Ruebush-Kieffer in 1886. The oblong format was standard practice in the shape-note publishing world until around the turn of the century. (From author's collection.)

Small octavo shape-note songbook published by Ruebush-Kieffer ca. 1900. The switch to the small octavo format in shape-note songbooks coincided with another change, from printing music on a separate staff for each voice part to use of the grand staff, which was easier to read when playing a keyboard instrument. (From the collections of the Center for Popular Music, Middle Tennessee State University.)

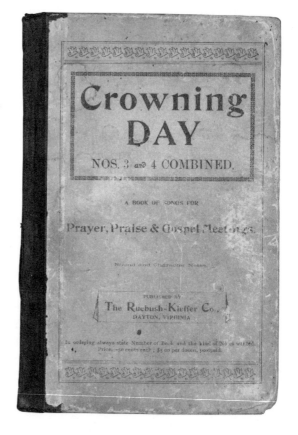

the Temperance movement attack on the normalization of alcohol consumption. "Can a Boy Forget His Mother?" sentimentally speaks to the (lack of) cohesion of the family unit. Meanwhile, "Vote as You Pray," written "for temperance meetings," as an epigraph states, but clearly exportable to other ballot issues, musically conceptualizes the merger of religion and politics.[44]

Measured by the degree to which people heeded these songs' brand of social advice and moral instruction, they would have to be judged overall as a failure. Scholars from W. J. Cash to Wyatt-Brown and Ted Ownby have variously shown the social struggle against these problems.[45] However, underlying the notionally prescriptive aims of these songs is a more basic compensatory function that persists independent of how closely these behavioral prescriptions were followed. Giving musical treatment to the most pressing issues of rural life in the New South, these songs both acknowledged the genuine problems of people who felt as if they were being passed over by the progress of mainstream America and attempted to manage those dilemmas by enclosing them within sentimental discourse of nostalgia ("can a boy forget his mother?"), piety ("vote as you pray"), and pastoralism ("my wand'ring boy" implicitly evoking the image of the lost sheep).

Though sentimental discourse has often been understood by scholars to function mainly as a subversive assertion of female agency in nineteenth-century America, more recent scholarship on sentimentality has come to see it as a subtler language of feeling that builds up around "complex, unstable, and contingent relationships of power," a description that could easily be applied to the shifting dynamics within postbellum southern white culture. As J. Wayne Flynt has shown in his study of "Dixie's forgotten people," poor and working-class whites in the South during Reconstruction and beyond had little more connection to the ruling political class than newly emancipated blacks. Yet the two groups never joined forces politically or musically. Don Cusic has noted that black lives and music were "virtually ignored" by the white gospel world, at least officially, until well into the twentieth century. Among these "invisible" white southerners, as Flynt has called them, feelings of being left out and behind ran high, and this disconnection of the poor and working-class folk from the mainstream power structure resulted in the rerouting of sociopolitical concerns through vernacular forms of indigenous culture. In this way, the proliferation of sentimental discourse in gospel songs about political, moral, and social issues as seen through the lens of rural evangelical pietism functions in part as a prefiguration in evangelical, artistic terms of the "nostalgic ideology" that Laura Lovett has located at work during the Populist and Progressive eras of American history—an ideology that drew on the past as a way to modernize private speed. At the time of their first appearing, however, these songs were vivid evocations of spiritual struggle dramatized in terms that were palpably recognizable to toiling and laboring classes. Rebuilding and expanding freight lines after the Civil War were two main targets of Reconstruction spending by the federal government.[49] By the late 1890s, when "Life's Railway to Heaven" had already emerged as a popular gospel tune, a thriving network of rail lines reconnecting the South to the rest of the country had become a vital source of employment for unskilled laboring whites. The songwriter, Charlie Tillman, had these workers explicitly in mind, dedicating the song "to the railroad men," whose workaday lives and ordinary tribulations are lyrically reimagined as a saint's labor infused with eternal significances.

Well into the first half of the twentieth century, white gospel in the southern tradition continued to help reposition evangelical ideas and beliefs in relation to the changing cultural landscape of modernity. The 1938 Albert E. Brumley tune "Turn Your Radio On," written at the height of radio's influence, conflates wireless audio transmission with the spread of the Christian gospel:

> Turn your radio on and listen to the music in the air
> Turn your radio on and glory share
> Turn your lights down low and listen to the Master's radio
> Get in touch with God and turn your radio on.[50]

Written in the same year as Orson Welles's *War of the Worlds* hoax, "Turn Your Radio On" reimagines radio as an instrument of evangelical culture. Likening the Holy Spirit to radio waves implicitly contests secularism's claim on emerging mass-market technologies, reaffirming the relevance of monotheistic pietism in imagery born of the modern moment, but in the idiom of nostalgic piety. Taken together, "Turn Your Radio On" and "Life's Railway to Heaven" exemplify how southern gospel music has long addressed the contemporary concerns of white laboring classes even as the music itself often provided a way out of that toilsome life for writers such as Tillman and Brumley.[51]

"Without Music, I Had No Dreams"

As shape-note music education provided both instruction in the art of music making and the practice of modern life, the many textures and facets of shape-note songbooks combined to form a kind of contemporary conduct manual for a new breed of southern evangelicals emerging at the turn of the twentieth century. The covers of these songbooks often reinforce this notion: though in general, songbook covers tend toward standard religious or pastoral iconography, covers that include images or illustrations of people almost always depict females or children (or both) in a pious home or church setting—this despite the fact that men were almost exclusively the producers, creators, and business leaders of the gospel-publishing business. These idyllic cover images of straight-and-narrow living literally enclosed the music within a context of moral idealization. While these books were often used in church "Singing Classes, Sunday schools, and all societies of Religious Endeavors," as a songbook from the early 1890s put it, the music's widespread appeal was purposefully transdenominational: "All songs of doctrinal differences have been rejected," an 1895 preface declares, "so that all denominations can use this book, adopting it as theirs."[52]

Though partly this cross-denominational appeal was smart marketing, ecumenical lyrics also helped negotiate the stratification of class and status amid the rapid industrialization of American urban centers from around 1880 onward.[53] Particularly in the South, this trend created what Chad Seales describes as "a new economic landscape 'cultivated' by a class of upwardly mobile white Protestants."[54] For these people, denominational affiliation through church membership became a means of differentiating themselves from lower-class whites. Increasingly inflected with class conflicts, sectarian religious culture came to be seen by many poor and working-class whites as another betrayal of the New South's promise. Thus, even as they advertised themselves as useful for church functions, white gospel songbooks from the South or that were culturally southern aggressively distinguished between congregational church culture and the values and experiences (both spiritual and recreational) available through white gospel music. "If we do not sing with the spirit and with the understanding," one gospel editor wrote in a preface examining the comparative merits of gospel and church music, "our singing is merely mechanical, consequently HEARTLESS, and of no value to singers or to hearers." He continues:

> Every song should be read carefully before singing it, and special attention should be given to pronouncing each word distinctly, so that the words may be heard by all the congregation. As a rule, church choirs are an abomination in the sight of the Lord. They are only efficient in the worship of God when they are used as leaders of the congregation. If those, and those only, are saved, who sing in the church choirs FOR THE GLORY OF GOD ALONE, the Lord will not have to build many additional mansions. They generally whisper, write notes, turn over the leaves in the song book, and play the fool generally. No extra charge for this discovery, for making it now.[55]

The Modern Singer,
published by James
D. Vaughan Music
Publishers in 1917 and
typical of the pious de-
piction of women and
children on those song-
book covers that did
not consist of religious
artwork, scenery, or
iconography. (From the
collections of the Cen-
ter for Popular Music,
Middle Tennessee State
University.)

Here, church choral music is described as inimical to effective singing. Choirs muddle the lyrics and undercut meaningful evangelism in song, and chorus members join church choirs for social stature and other self-aggrandizing reasons, not for the "GLORY OF GOD" and the advancement of the kingdom. Attacking the most prominent feature of denominational sacred song not very implicitly dismisses fin de siècle church music as an impious perversion of true heart religion to be found in gospel singing.

Not all songbook editors were as rhetorically self-possessed, but most of them shared the same commitment to the populist, participatory musical experience articulated here. Set against the more elite, performative style of congregational choral music (the robes, the elevated choir loft, the special choral arrangements), shape-note music education aimed to empower the masses through music literacy. In order for the shape-note movement to accomplish its pedagogical and ethical aims, people had to come together regularly at singing conventions associated with normal schools and less formal all-day sings—a particular favorite among young people of the 1880s and 1890s[56]—to practice and improve themselves, both musically and morally. To upwardly mobile and culturally ascendant urban whites, the lachrymose sentimentality and sharp nostalgic bent of the music at these gatherings of "the masses" smacked of a recidivistic slide into unreconstructed customs of the Old South. And so the two cultural spheres increasingly drifted apart without every fully disconnecting from—and never failing to recognize— one another. In the process, culturally ascendant and socially marginal whites in the New South developed their own distinct traditions of sacred music born in part of a "fundamental struggle," in Robert Toll's formulation, "between aristocrats and 'middling' Americans" going on during this time.[57]

George Pullen Jackson was the first, and remains the most eloquent, scholar to anatomize the musical innovations that arose from this process of stratification and came to distinguish what he called "white spirituals" of the southern uplands from both antebellum music of the same region and other musical innovations going on in postbellum America.[58] Later scholars have identified northern influences on southern music, particularly the role of northern revivals whose music permeated virtually all segments of American life around the turn of the century.[59] What I wish to emphasize here is the value of the creative, economic, and intellectually synthetic act of music making itself within southern white gospel. Particularly during a period in history when poor and working-class whites were socioeconomically disadvantaged and culturally dispossessed, it is difficult to overstate the multifaceted compensations provided by an enterprise as aesthetically rich, technically innovative, and economically successful as shape-note white gospel rapidly proved to be in the two or three generations after the Civil War. Judging by the editors' prefaces from a cross-section of shape-note songbooks from the last quarter of the nineteenth century,[60] white gospel quickly became an indispensable idiom in which to shape postbellum identity both individually and collectively among those in the South or other culturally southern parts of America. The preface to an 1895 songbook attests to this dynamic: "The author of *Gospel Voices* has edited several song books, all of which have been well received. Much time and labor have been given to the preparation of this one, and it is confidently believed that it is the best of his life-work. . . . *Gospel Voices*, go thou, and do thy work! Strengthen the weak, comfort the sorrowing, bind up the broken-hearted, lift up the fallen, save the lost, and when thou returnest lay many precious sheaves at the Master's feet!" Passages like this are commonplace in songbooks from this era. "I say nothing in praise of *Harvest Bells*," another preface from 1892 reads, "because I hear so much of it from others who could not have any sinister or selfish motives. The very large sales and increasing demand are sufficient proofs of its popularity."[61] In the context of the economic depression that gripped most sectors of the southern economy during the 1890s,[62] white gospel music in the South distinguishes itself for standing on its own financially. Shape-note songbook publishers justifiably took pride in the fact that their books had "been well received" and that their "time and labor" created a self-sufficient enterprise. "No time, pains, or expense has been spared in the preparation of 'Happy Voices,' to make it the most popular of all," a preface from 1898 boasts. "The hymns have been carefully edited and are full of Gospel truth. The music is by the best authors, and is sweet and flowing. No piece has been put merely 'to fill up,' but each piece is a gem both as to poetry and music."[63]

By the capitalist logic of the day, shape-note gospel businessmen from Ruebush-Kieffer on (and sacred-music businessmen before them) viewed *profit taking* and *piety* as mutually reinforcing and synonymous terms, and they saw nothing contradictory in extolling a songbook's spiritual virtues in one sentence and, in the next, declaring that "I will prosecute any one to the full extent of the law who may use any of my Copyright Songs, either words or music, without my permission."[64] Publishers were understandably eager to protect their intellectual property. In many cases, doing so meant the difference between having a job in music and writing songs as a hobby. In the unstable economy of the late nineteenth century, unemployment consistently ran high and stayed in the double digits from 1894 to 1898.[65] What jobs were available to unskilled workers demanded hard labor in mines or lumber camps and often barely paid a subsistence wage. Certainly, these jobs could not provide the kind of self-actualizing enrichments that the *Gospel Voices* author gestures toward in describing gospel music as "his life-work."

Working in shape-note gospel brought with it the mastery of a craft for people who could claim to be master over very few aspects of their lives, and it provided command of a specialized skill at a time when the drive toward a workforce of industrial specialists was excluding many poor and working-class whites from middle-class prosperity. Singing schools and conventions were technically advanced and physically demanding ordeals—schools typically ran for ten-day stretches, twelve hours a day, and singing conventions would often go on into all hours of the night.[66] Both schools and conventions often included competitions at which amateur singers could distinguish themselves within the community. "For a rural youngster raised on a farm who had a talent for singing," Cusic writes, "this was a mark of

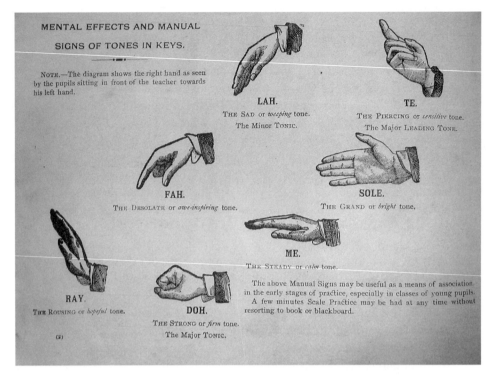

Conductor's guide for giving singers manual signs for tone keys, from *The Messenger of Song*, a shape-note songbook published by Ruebush-Kieffer in 1893. (From author's collection.)

prestige and honor. Watching the singing school teacher" (who was often referred to as "professor," though most lacked more than a singing-school diploma themselves), "many saw a way out of southern farm life, and a chance to make a living doing what they loved—singing." The songbook publishing industry was alive to this attraction and capitalized on it well into the twentieth century. One ad in a 1923 shape-note music magazine announced to readers with songwriting aspirations: "Your Song May Make You Famous." Dreams of fame were encouraged through published reports of shape-note students ascending "from janitor to professor of musical theory" by applying themselves in white gospel.[67]

Even when professorial renown was out of reach, very few jobs available to young white boys from the ranks of southern yeomanry could afford the kinds of satisfactions available in gospel music. Of his work in the Singers Glen print shop, Kieffer wrote, "I had the great satisfaction of seeing a score of music grow into shape in my 'stick.' The clefs, the sharps and flats, the notes, and the bars appeared as if arrayed in glory [before me]."[68] By contributing to the education and formation of the newest generation of southerners *and* turning a profit, southern white gospel neatly resolved in its own way an often insoluble political debate that raged on during (and well beyond) Reconstruction about whether to emphasize investment in education and cultural enrichment or economic redevelopment.[69] In the South, white gospel achieved both goals.

For Kieffer, as it was for the author of the *Gospel Voices*, white gospel music was more than a craft or a skill. It was a glorious *calling,* in the sense that Max Weber used the word to describe labor in the secular world that speaks to the status of the soul.[70] One employee at Ruebush-Kieffer who worked for the company in the 1870s described his experience on the job in nearly rhapsodic terms: "Those were the days when life was a dream of pleasure—when we literally lived on melody, and sang it, talked it, shouted it, dreamed it."[71]

From its modern inception in Reconstruction and continuing into our own time, a long line of self-taught lyricists, amateur poets, and (para)profes-sional musicians have found in gospel music a similar "dream of pleasure," or at least a means of escape from the economic and aesthetic impoverish-ment of subsistence wage labor that was (and remains) the fate of so many uneducated white men in rural America. The famous southern gospel bass singer George Younce wrote about coming of age as a young professional singer in the 1940s: "I literally came alive onstage. . . . [W]hen I was per-forming I felt like I had jumped up to Glory." His eventual business partner and co-owner of the legendary Cathedral quartet, Glen Payne, had a similar experience: "This music," he recalled of his first professional singing gigs, "had allowed me to *feel* heaven." More recently, Michael English, who came to fame singing southern gospel and inspirational music with the Singing Americans, the Happy Goodman Family, and the Gaither Vocal Band in the 1980s and 1990s, wrote about hearing the Blackwood quartet in 1976 and experiencing a "flash of calling" on his teenage life. Once he started singing southern gospel professionally a few years later, it gave him a "feeling of rightness" like nothing else. Compared to factory labor at the Barcalounger Plant in Turkey, North Carolina, where English worked for a while after graduating high school in 1980, a career in gospel music seemed to make possible a life "beyond anything someone like me, an ignorant fool from Wallace, North Carolina, ever could have dreamed."[72]

These types of stories are commonplace throughout the history of south-ern white gospel music: poor and working-class southerners finding through gospel music the affordances to "stretch our wings," as Payne put it, "and fly into middle-class life"—a life they experienced to be otherwise unattainable for them.[73] Several popular singers in southern gospel today testify to Payne's point: Glenn Dustin, the bass singer for the quartet Legacy Five, was a welder from backwoods Louisiana in 1998. After being hired to sing professionally in 1999, he was performing before twenty-five thousand fans at the National Quartet Convention. Rodney Griffin, a prominent songwriter and lead singer for the trio Greater Vision, often speaks from the stage about being plucked from the obscurity of office work in the Virginia shipyards to live his dream of singing gospel music professionally. For these people and others like them, white gospel music is more than a means of socioeconomic self-improvement. What Payne believed to be true of southern gospel's place in his life captures a feeling widespread among gospel singers from Kieffer's time on: "Without music, I had no dreams."[74]

Evangelical Equipment for Living

In his own time, Kieffer, who died in 1904, never realized the dream of musically literate legions raising their voices in sentimental songs of piety and reform. The author of a 1908 retrospective essay on Kieffer's life and work makes the unsubstantiated claim that more than three million people had come into contact with his songbooks at the time of his death. Perhaps. Certainly, Ruebush-Kieffer products were in widespread circulation at the turn of the century. But then again, subscriptions to the *Musical Million* peaked around ten thousand.[75] Whatever the precise number of people whose Kieffer's music impacted, Kieffer stands at the front of a line of defining contributions to white gospel from the South, and without them it is scarcely possible to imagine today's southern gospel music existing.

Of course, Ruebush and Kieffer were not the first to do what they did. Their business model in many ways reflects a form of sacred-music publishing perhaps most powerfully defined by Lowell Mason in the first half of the nineteenth century.[76] More contemporarily, there was the foundational influence of northern white gospel composer and singer Ira Sankey, the longtime musical associate of the evangelist Dwight Moody. Sankey's style of fervently pietistic revival music made gospel songs an international phenomenon in the 1870s, and his wildly popular collection of gospel music, *Gospel Hymns and Sacred Songs*, became a staple of the American evangelical music experience. First published in 1875 in collaboration with Philip P. Bliss and just as Ruebush and Kieffer were beginning to restart the family music business, Sankey's songbook and his spiritually exuberant style of gospel music making could not but have made an impression on Kieffer's creative impulses and the ambitions he and Ruebush had for their company.[77] Still, it would be a mistake to treat Ruebush-Kieffer as a derivative southern shadow of more successful figures and firms in the North. Though the popularity of Sankey's music indelibly linked gospel with the populist tastes of the working classes,[78] white gospel of the Moody-Sankey era emerged from the industrialized urban centers of the North and so remained a somewhat culturally alien form of expression for rural southern evangelicals in the generations after the Civil War. In this regard, southern shape-note music distinguished itself from other gospel as an indigenous cultural product of the Reconstruction South.

Ruebush-Kieffer convincingly proved the commercial viability of this culturally distinct form of white gospel when presented as a means of social enrichment, moral improvement, and spiritual sustenance for culturally southern Christians across the denominational spectrum of evangelical Protestantism "in every state in the Union."[79] Copies of financial records show that Ruebush-Kieffer posted a year-over-year increase in net worth annually from 1888 ($12,862.56) through 1911 ($41,654.62).[80] The company's market dominance in the South began to wane in the last decade of the nineteenth century as competition increased; around the same time, Kieffer appears to have retired, perhaps not fully by choice.[81] Yet even Kieffer's and the company's decline testifies to Ruebush-Kieffer's historical significance: the rival firms that started taking business away from Ruebush-Kieffer were in most cases founded by and reliant on the skills of students trained at the Virginia Normal School. These companies replicated the Ruebush-Kieffer approach that focused on establishing a catalog of original, copyrighted tunes; on building an interconnected network of self-reinforcing revenue streams around those songs (songbook publishing, monthly periodicals, singing schools, and ultimately groups of singing salesmen); and on using the connections that itinerant singing-school teachers made with student-consumers as initial points of sale in a primitive but effective retail-distribution system.

Beyond Kieffer's era, the technological advances of the twentieth century demonstrated that the Ruebush-Kieffer paradigm was fundamentally modern in its vision and scalability: as broadcast radio and long-distance travel by automobile—and later television and custom motor coaches and airplanes—made it possible to reach mass audiences in the South and beyond, white gospel music companies descended from Ruebush-Kieffer organically incorporated the use of "performance harmony to publicize the gospel music business."[82] These performers, usually quartets, fitted seamlessly into the hub-and-spoke network of supply and distribution built around singing-school teachers and established by Ruebush-Kieffer more than a quarter century earlier, before anyone heard of interstate highway systems or wireless radio transmission.

A big part of what makes Kieffer such an important figure in the history of the music is his apparently intuitive grasp of how modernity was changing southern evangelical popular culture, well before he himself had articulated a theory or philosophy of his work in that world. With time and age, Kieffer would come to develop a sophisticated concept of gospel music as a vehicle for the expression of modern evangelical life, anchored in traditional values. The outlines of this view are captured in Kieffer's 1881 book of mournful poems, nostalgic songs, and melancholy idylls, *Hours of Fancy; or, Vision and Vigil*. The book's value is not necessarily its poetic merit—Mary Kern not unfairly notes that "sentiment often sinks to sentimentality" in Kieffer's versifying.[83] However, in pairing imaginative vision with filiopietistic vigil, Kieffer's subtitle suggests the way the culture and language of rural white gospel music that emerged during Reconstruction and expanded into the twentieth century were partly about retaining a connection to southern pastoralism (vigil) and just as much about social and moral progress (vision)—of progressing, but in a traditional way.

The essence of this insight was latent in Kieffer's work from the first. The 1870 decision to drop *Southern* from the title of his grandfather's singing magazine and relaunch it as simply the *Musical Million* had early on signaled a shift away from antebellum pastoralism toward a more modern sense of gospel music as an example of—and exportable to—what might best be called a pan-southern culture. It is not that southernness ceases to be valuable in this new view. Rather, it ceases to be viewed as a purely parochial identity and emerges as a habit of being whose values and lifeways could—and ultimately did—take root widely among lower- and working-class Christians of southern extraction, wherever they may be found. In this Kieffer's worldview and work exemplify a southern form of socioeconomic development after the Civil War that James Peacock has called "grounded globalism," a term that describes the southern struggle in the late nineteenth and early twentieth centuries "to transcend regional oppositionality and dualism while retaining a regional identity and also defining its own global identity."[84]

Through both the music he wrote and the style of songs he and Ruebush published, Kieffer presided over the transformation of antebellum sacred music in the southern tradition—from his grandfather's generation of derivative vernacular singing deeply dependent on musical developments in

New England psalmody and its frontier successors to an independent musical idiom through which evangelical southern whites could effectively sublimate the anxieties of psychosocial crisis. If, as Kenneth Burke has argued, cultural texts are "proverbs writ large," then white gospel songs in the tradition popularized by Kieffer began in this era to function as southern evangelical "equipment for living"—structures of affect and expression that grounded the fluctuant experience of modern life in the nostalgic piety of the past.[85]

3. The Rise of "Southern" Gospel Music and the Compensations of History

Within current scholarship about southern gospel music, popular writing about the tradition, and the industry's own representations of itself and its past, no single figure enjoys the prominence and veneration accorded to James D. Vaughan. A songwriter and publisher, Vaughan studied at Ruebush-Kieffer's Virginia Normal School in the early 1880s. By the 1920s, Vaughan had built his own company, Vaughan Music, into shape-note gospel's dominant publishing house. In the 1940s, Vaughan was "claiming over 7,000,000 copies of its various books in use throughout the South."[1] In *Close Harmony*, the authoritative scholarly history of southern gospel, James Goff christens Vaughan the leading "pioneer" in the "birth of an industry." Similarly, Bob Terrell's account of gospel music's beginnings singles out Vaughan's efforts to "develop and popularize a new folk form of American music." In her 1978 history of the genre, Lois Blackwell describes Vaughan as a "progenitor." Novelist Fanny Flagg takes this founder's status as a given in her 2002 book, *Standing in the Rainbow*, which features a southern gospel subplot introduced with a synopsis of the music's history that begins with Vaughan.[2]

These accounts are restrained compared to the rhetoric surrounding Vaughan within the world of southern gospel itself. There, he is known as the father of southern gospel music.[3] The Southern Gospel Music Hall of Fame's highest honor for contributions to the advancement of the industry is conferred upon honorees in the form of the James D. Vaughan Impact Award. The James D. Vaughan Museum in Lawrenceburg, Tennessee, which claims to be the birthplace of southern gospel music, credits Vaughan with having "taught the South how to sing."[4] Today this view of Vaughan is considered settled history in most sectors of the southern gospel industry. While conducting archival research in Tennessee in the summer of 2009, I attended a social gathering in Nashville that included a number of people who work on the creative and administrative sides of the industry; one of them inquired after the subject of my research. At one point when I was talking about Aldine Kieffer and his pivotal post–Civil War contributions to the professionalization of southern gospel, a prominent record label executive turned to me and said, quite seriously, "Really? You mean James Vaughan wasn't the founder of southern gospel?"

It is easy to mistake a transitional figure for a foundational one, to confer the title of "founder" upon those historical players whose chief achievement is not original insight so much as a genius for building upon antecedent models. Still, the rise of Vaughanism in today's southern gospel is remarkable both for how recently and for how rapidly the view took hold in the popular imagination. In 1971 a book of biographical sketches of shape-note gospel songwriters gave no indication that Vaughan stood out in the history of the music any more than dozens of other prominent writers and publishers. As late as 1990, Don Cusic's history of gospel and Christian music emphasizes the contributions of Homer Rodeheaver (and to a lesser degree V. O. Stamps) in white gospel's transition from songbook publishing to performance harmony, over Vaughan's efforts.[5] It was not until 1993 that Vaughanism really took off. In that year, the magazine *Singing News*, the self-proclaimed "voice of southern gospel music" and perhaps the single biggest force behind Vaughan's resurgence in the past two decades, placed Vaughan's picture on the magazine's table of contents and proclaimed him the "Founder of Southern Gospel Music" on "May, 1910," in "Lawrenceburg TN."

The date and location are key to understanding Vaughan's appearance in the magazine, as Jerry Kirksey, the magazine's longtime editor, explained to me in a 2009 interview, because they pinpoint the time and place of Vaughan's decision to sponsor a quartet that began singing across trans-Appalachia promoting songbooks published by the Vaughan Music Company. Since modern-day commercialized southern gospel emerged from the popularity of professional all-male quartets in the mid–twentieth century, the formation of the first known gospel foursome made historical sense, according to Kirksey. "Everything has to have a starting point," he told me. Aided by the research that Goff was conducting in the early 1990s for what would become *Close Harmony*—which *Singing News* supported with a sabbatical grant of thirty-five thousand dollars—Kirksey became increasingly confident of where it all began.[6]

Goff's book is more circumspect about Vaughan than *Singing News*, but *Close Harmony* clearly reinforces the Vaughanist thesis: "Had James David Vaughan not happened upon the gospel music scene in the late nineteenth century, the expansion of the gospel music industry in the South might well have peaked with the contributions of Aldine Kieffer and Ephraim Ruebush." Without Vaughan's introduction of quartets into the shape-note publishing world, "the southern gospel music industry might never have been born. Something unique was needed to merge shaped notes, popular religious singing, and convention-style songbooks into a thriving industry. That something was the development of professional quartets." Goff's scholarly corroboration was pivotal for Kirksey. "Before Goff," Kirskey told me, "we knew a little about who we were as an industry, but not a lot." In Vaughan southern gospel had found "an anchor," as Kirskey put it, "a foundation."[7] Thus, every month for more than a decade, when the more than two hundred thousand southern gospel fans who subscribe to the *Singing News* scanned the magazine's contents for articles and information about their favorite singers, there was Vaughan, at the top of the page, presiding benignantly over the goings-on in an industry that he was purported to have founded in "May, 1910" in "Lawrenceburg, TN."[8] In 2010 the magazine began a yearlong celebration of what *Singing News* takes to be southern gospel's centennial—beginning, of course, with James D. Vaughan.

This view asserts an indisputably direct line of descent that leads inevitably from Vaughan to the present via the professional quartet. But this sort of sudden revision to a historical narrative, as Van Wyck Brooks first noted, often signals deeper disturbances in the warp and woof of culture.[9] With sufficient disruptive pressure, history can, in Robert Milder's words, even "work backwards," as "vestigial or outmoded" ways of thinking and acting "come to reassert themselves figuratively as interpretive categories that responded to personal or communal crises."[10] Guided by the notion of backward-working histories, this chapter itself moves backward from the emergence of Vaughanism in the late part of twentieth century, reading the sharp swerve to Vaughan as an indicator of a more deeply submerged "status inconsistency," to borrow Michael McKeon's term from another context, within contemporary southern gospel music.[11] Intervening in the Vaughanist view of professional southern gospel's historical development, I then move outward from Vaughan to an encompassing analysis of white gospel's mid-twentieth-century rise into industrial professionalism. Vaughan reappeared when and how he did in the music's more recent postmodern historical consciousness as part of a broader process of cultural redefinition going on within conservative evangelicalism in the last half of the twentieth

James D. Vaughan, included in an image that appeared in *Singing News* magazine in 2010 to mark
what the magazine declared as the centennial of
southern gospel music's founding. This founding date
coincides with James D. Vaughan's 1910 decision
to form the first all-male quartet dedicated to singing gospel music in a professional, commercialized
context. (From *Singing News* magazine. Courtesy of
the Southern Gospel Music Association, Dollywood,
Pigeon Forge, Tenn.)

century and continuing into our own time. As I show, this process played
itself out through the emergence of the phrase *southern gospel music* and the
religious identity it designates.

A Contested Legacy

There is no doubt that Vaughan was indeed a major force in the modernization of white gospel, most especially in the South. In addition to forming
the first professional quartet, he most likely underwrote the first recordings
of white gospel music in 1921 and launched the first radio station devoted
to shape-note gospel music in 1923.[12] Though the 1910 quartet was not
the first group of southern men who gathered to sing gospel songs in four-

part harmony,[13] it was the first paraprofessional ensemble to perform gospel music from the South in a commercial context. And it was a big hit, powerfully demonstrating to audiences "what knowledge of shaped notes could mean in a rural community."[14] Up until this time, shape-note music was typically sung by mass audiences in singing schools, which dated from the mid–eighteenth century, and later at singing conventions, which functioned for most of the nineteenth century as valuable opportunities for socializing within rural farming communities. As singing schools proliferated after the Civil War, shape-note singing conventions flourished into annual or biannual events, at which an area's best singers would come together and sing the latest so-called convention songs released by shape-note publishers.[15] At a time when "more music was bought for the home than was heard on the stage," these recreational, participatory gatherings existed somewhere between the domestic and public spheres in postbellum life. By the early twentieth century, "singing conventions flourished in almost every southern state and boasted organizations on the county, district, and state levels."[16]

In their initial conception, the first quartets—Vaughan put several on the road after the original group showed signs of success—existed as adjuncts to convention culture (a quartet would often be a bonus feature at singing conventions). This complementary role was what Vaughan clearly seems to have had in mind in May 1910. But as these singing performers started reaching mass audiences—first as traveling salesmen, then via radio broadcasts, and finally through mass-market audio recordings in the 1920s and 1930s—the quartet ultimately supplanted the singing convention as the defining phenomenon of shape-note white gospel. By the 1940s and 1950s, groups such as the Speer Family, which had come to fame working for Vaughan as singing-songbook promoters, had launched off on their own and were joined by a host of other groups such as the Blackwood Brothers, the Statesmen, Blue Ridge, the Weatherfords, and the LeFevres. These groups and others like them were succeeding as professional performers, especially in demand at all-night singings that, at one point, according to a promoter at the time, attracted upwards of two million paying fans a year.[17] By the 1960s and 1970s, television broadcasts such as the *Gospel Singing Caravan* and the *Gospel Jubilee* were turning the most prominent performers into national celebrities, and Elvis Presley was touring with a southern gospel quartet—first the Jordanaires, then the Imperials, and finally the Stamps.[18]

Where are Vaughan and his legacy in all this? Vaughan died in 1941. As early as 1939, he was being touted as the "Musical Father of Gospel Singers in the South," but this was in his company's own magazine, *Vaughan's Family Visitor*. Almost certainly, christening Vaughan the patriarch of southern singers reflects an increasing concern in the Vaughan circle about the precariousness of his place in the history of southern religious music as the balance of power shifted away from songbook publishers and songwriters and toward professional performers. Indeed, there was reason to worry. In 1924 V. O. Stamps, a longtime employee of Vaughan's, broke away from the Lawrenceburg empire and started his own firm in Texas. The formation of what would become the Stamps-Baxter Music Co. was "the biggest event in the world of shape-note publishing."[19] By the late 1930s, Stamps-Baxter was turning out more than two million songbooks a year.[20] This was still far fewer than Vaughan, but Stamps was strategically forming business relationships with the rising-star quartets and family groups of the new performance culture, performers who would sing Stamps-Baxter's new songs onstage, in turn driving sales of songbooks. Stamps's model reworked the Vaughan approach, in which performers demonstrated songbooks that were ultimately meant for use by ordinary singers. Stamps-Baxter instead sold books as mementos of professional singers' popularity and fame. The emergence of songbooks as not just instruments for participatory singing cultures but also an early apparatus of celebrity in evangelical culture tacitly signaled the coming era of professional performance.[21]

By emphasizing instruction in performance harmony, the Stamps-Baxter School of Music became the premier white-gospel singing school for aspiring singers. These singers' idols were no longer normal-school "professors" in the Vaughan mold, but celebrity performers such as James Blackwood, the lead singer and emcee for the Blackwood Brothers, and James "Big Chief" Wetherington, the legendary bass singer for the Statesmen quartet. The company's official connections with many of the most prominent groups in the white gospel business meant that the school's best students had a chance both to learn the craft and to land a spot touring with a top-tier group. Consequently, many of the quartet men and other prominent figures who have dominated southern gospel's more recent generations do not primarily associate the formation of their musical identity and career with Vaughan or the singing-convention tradition. Rather, they identify with Stamps-Baxter and live-performance harmony—among them George Younce, Glen Payne, Bill Gaither, and Gerald Williams.[22]

Meanwhile, the Vaughan Co., once the first to experiment with new technologies and strategies for spreading white gospel, began to stagnate, intensifying its affiliation with the older, more amateur world of participatory singing conventions that were being displaced and rendered increasingly obsolete by the emerging performance-concert culture.[23] Celebrity quartets were the sharp end of the wedge splitting southern white gospel apart.

Discomfort with changing musical mores on the shape-note side surfaced in *Vaughan's Family Visitor*, the voice of traditional amateur singing conventions. An editorial from a few months before Vaughan's death insists, "The singing convention should be a place where everyone meets on an equal footing and where all should enjoy the blending of voices in one grand pean [*sic*] of praise to a glorious Redeemer. Not a place where politics is played to get one of 'my crowd' on the program, but where brotherly love should prevail and the destinies of the convention left in the hands of a capable unbiased individual who has the good of the Song Cause at heart." Getting "one of 'my crowd' on the program" here figures as a failure of Christian charity that unsettles a benevolent patriarchy's commitment to egalitarianism in traditional singing-convention culture and compromises the raison d'être of "the Song Cause"—its ministerial and evangelistic function. But the intrusion of "politics" is also a symptom of how professional performance destabilized the experiential dynamics of southern white gospel. By the late 1930s, "the leading publishers of shape-note gospel music [were] James D. Vaughan, Stamps-Baxter and Stamps Quartet," and the former had very different ideas than the latter two about the extent to which performance harmony should define southern gospel.[24] Consequently, jockeying for position at singing conventions among these firms' representatives—whether an individual representative of a particular firm who would lead the singing or a quartet with close ties to one publisher or another—was one important way that competing visions of the music played out in public.

In this light, Vaughan's positioning himself as the patriarch of southern *singing*—not performing—makes most sense as a revanchist critique of spectatorial, commercialized white gospel that shape-note singing conventioneers often disdained for what they saw as its embrace of politicking, worldliness, and impiety. The Vaughan circle of singing conventions and publishing held on for a few more decades, but by the 1960s it was visibly contracting. The Statesmen and Blackwood Brothers formed a business partnership, Stateswood, that bought out the Vaughan catalog and *Visitor* in 1964, a move that gave Stateswood control of Vaughan's vast catalog of classic—copyrighted—songs. Once in possession of the publishing rights, Stateswood promptly discontinued the magazine and sold the singing-convention book line to the Church of God publishing house.[25] To speak of Vaughan throughout most of the twentieth century, then, was to speak in shorthand of fervent fealty to the "Song Cause," as distinct from—and often in direct conflict with—the growing southern gospel commercial music industry.

A southern gospel songbook published by the Blackwood
Brothers quartet in the early 1950s. Members are, *clockwise
from top right:* R. W. Blackwood, James Blackwood, Bill Shaw,
Jackie Marshall, Bill Lyles. The songbook explicitly invites
fans to link the Blackwood Brothers' music with its high-flying
celebrity status as the first gospel group to travel in an airplane.
A plane crash in 1954 killed members R. W. Blackwood and
Bill Lyles. (From the collections of the Center for Popular
Music, Middle Tennessee State University. Used by permission
of Blackwood Brothers quartet.)

If Vaughan began where Ruebush-Kieffer—and the firm's most direct heir, A. J. Showalter—left off and developed much of the basic industrial infrastructure essential to modern mass-market southern gospel, it is equally true that Vaughan was either uneasy with or incapable of fully exploiting the commercial potential of his own system at the end of his career. This idea is reinforced in the same *Vaughan's Family Visitor* editorial that complained about the defilements of pseudocelebrity politicking: "It was said some years ago that the radio would do away with singing conventions and all day singings and other religious services of this nature. It was a mistake, because radio has added to it, and more people are hearing the Gospel in song now than ever before. . . . Let the song wave roll and more people learn to sing and more new songs be written until the whole world is made to know of Christ through the songs telling of him."[26] Whether the evangelistic optimism here reflects a genuine, if false, belief that singing conventions were really on the way up, or whether it is so much whistling in the dark, the defiant undertone presages how the Vaughan wing of the shape-note subculture ultimately turned obliquely but decidedly resistant to the changes afoot. To a large extent, singing-convention culture remains so to this day. Even though the shift toward celebrity-driven performance culture was a natural extension of Vaughan's innovative insights, shape-note singers in the Vaughan tradition have commonly treated these developments as a corruption of the music's purity. This response intensified especially after Vaughan's death, when memorializing his life's work became closely linked to preserving the old-time way. In keeping an ambivalent distance from celebrity performance, the Vaughan circle effectively ceded the mantle of innovation to rivals such as Stamps-Baxter and Stateswood.

I experienced this resistance firsthand at a 2008 conference devoted to convention singing, where I presented a paper arguing for subtle but definitive continuities between the Gaither Homecoming phenomenon and the shape-note singing-convention movement, a connection I discuss in chapter 4.[27] One of the first comments I received during the audience discussion that followed was from a leading figure in what remains of the shape-note publishing community descended from Vaughan. Visibly emotional, he strongly challenged the existence of any link of the sort I proposed and insisted that singing conventions were about worship and spirituality, while modern southern gospel was about money, fame, and entertainment. This was not a compliment.

A Loss of Dominance

Given Vaughan's ambivalent relationship to modern spectatorial modes of commercial gospel in his own time, and the fierce claims placed upon his legacy by a remnant of singing-convention enthusiasts in ours, how did Vaughan become the icon of today's mainstream commercialized southern gospel music industry? Up to this point, I have been careful to use the term *southern gospel* only in reference to the mass-market commercialized white gospel music industry of roughly the past three or four decades. The use of the term *southern* to describe white gospel with a southern accent did not really begin until the late 1970s and did not gain widespread acceptance until the 1980s. Before then what is now known as southern gospel—the national network of performers, record labels, fans, and products participating in commercialized performance harmony descended from the white gospel shape-note tradition—had simply been "gospel" music to its practitioners and fans, and it was part of the mainstream of Christian entertainment on television, radio, and the concert stage.

What came to be called southern gospel, then, as we have seen, originated in the rural South. But it was always heavily influenced by popular religious music outside the culture of rural southern white evangelicalism,[28] and by the third quarter of the twentieth century, it had become far more than a purely southern phenomenon. The rapid development of northern industries and the pressure that urban industrialization put on hill-country farming in the years between 1930 and 1950 combined with the increasing ease of cross-country travel by car to fuel a great migration of southerners across America in the years after the Second World War. The migration, particularly after 1945, coincided with the decline of singing conventions and an explosion in popularity of live-performance gospel concerts. These concerts were sustained by the discretionary wealth of a growing middle class of mobile white evangelicals eager to signal their social ascendancy by choosing spectatorial modes of musical entertainment over more traditional forms of entertaining themselves, as earlier generations had done, in participatory convention singings and singing schools.[29]

At the same time, the music's deep historical and stylistic connection with southern culture meant it functioned for uprooted southern whites much the way shape-note music had in the years after the Civil War: stabilizing fluctuant experience in a moment of socioeconomic upheaval. Writing in *Harper's* in 1972 about the growing diaspora of southern whites, William Martin described "folk all over America who share a background of economic strain, hard work, church twice on Sunday, prayer meeting on

Wednesday night, and a close-knit family circle" that was the hallmark of rural southern evangelicalism in the late nineteenth and early twentieth centuries.[30] Because these people took their musical tastes with them, gospel music formed the basis for a pan-southern community among newly relocated white evangelicals of southern extraction even as attending concerts allowed them to align themselves with the modern, spectatorial American middle class. Church culture was still important, of course, but joining a local church did not necessarily address cultural differences born of geography or class. In this context, southern gospel became a kind a secret handshake, and the reliability of finding cultural kinship within the world of southern gospel held on well into the 1970s after its midcentury emergence as "the popular music of American Christianity" in the evangelical tradition.[31]

One key feature of southern gospel's mass-market success was its ability to function as what amounts to a nearly borderless constellation of popular musical possibilities, centered on the culture of the evangelical South. For example, the 1969 hit song "Jesus Is Coming Soon" borrows freely from country rhythms. The song was popularized by the Oak Ridge Boys, a country-gospel quartet that gained widespread crossover appeal among secular audiences in the 1970s before focusing exclusively on country music. Yet the song also uses harmonies throughout the chorus that echo traditional quartet music: most notably, the three voices around the lead answer his voice after each major musical phrase. This type of hybridity blended traditional approaches and ideas with modern trends and motifs, persistent features of southern white gospel. Going back to the influence of New England psalmody and its musical descendants on early white gospel in the South and its later incorporation of musical styles from northern revival songs, the music has always been defined to an important degree by its tendency to borrow sounds from other genres. The earliest Vaughan recordings from 1921, for instance, are striking for how similar they sound to black gospel styles of the era. By the 1940s, white gospel in the southern style begins to sound more like the "classic quartet" sound that most people associate with the genre today. This sound was epitomized by the Statesmen, the Blackwood Brothers, Blue Ridge, Couriers, and Florida Boys, among others: four well-blended male voices, a highly arpeggiated piano accompaniment, homophonic verses, contrapuntal choruses, and long suspended resolutions over which the tenor soars and beneath which the bass plummets. This polymorphic sound synthesized a host of American musical genres—secular pop music, country, blues, black gospel, and jazz among them[32]—in a way that sheds any pretense of being a definable style in terms of the music's formal features. Instead, southern gospel resembles nothing so much as a highly adaptable musical grammar that allows for a wide range of expressive possibilities, as the structure and style of "Jesus Is Coming Soon" suggest.

As long as the music remained a largely regional phenomenon of the (comparatively) homogenous South, such musical borrowing posed few problems and positively helped the music stay relevant and retain a wide appeal. Whatever influences it might absorb, shape-note white gospel through most of the first half of the twentieth century remained dedicated to "the Song Cause" and, more deeply, the cultural values of evangelical fundamentalism. But as the music was exported beyond the South, to a growing diaspora of culturally southern evangelicals dispersed throughout North America, it intermixed with more secularized cultures and absorbed their styles and even some of their songs. The result was a sound of the sort evident as early as the Weatherfords' 1959 album, *In the Garden*. Here, songs such as the title cut and an exquisitely urbane arrangement of the old hymn "Let the Lower Lights Be Burning" are full of standard pietistic lyrics joined to a musical sound of strikingly modern synthesis: vocal arrangements bring the instrumental harmonies of the midcentury vocal-jazz and American pop style to life by revoicing them in four-part gospel ensemble singing in the shape-note tradition, all of which is backed by lush big-band orchestral instrumentations.

This sort of synthetic musical mixing helped propel southern gospel's midcentury rise, but it also seeded a more fundamental crisis of status and identity among the fundamentalist evangelicals who composed the world of white gospel. The midcentury megahit "Gospel Boogie" encapsulated these crosscurrents. Most noticeably, the song relied on the popular boogie-woogie style of American pop music at the time. As Charles Wolfe has shown, the wildly popular tune's musical borrowing became a cipher for a "debate within the gospel community itself, as the ideas and values of the older musicians ran head-on into the ideas and values of the new professionals" such as Lee Roy Abernathy, who wrote "Gospel Boogie." Massive all-night singings and other stadium-size concerts thrived on this crossover style, which was rapidly overtaking the singing-convention movement. Many traditionalists were profoundly unsettled. One went so far as to compare this new form of gospel to communism. Clearly, "values were shifting," as Wolfe notes, "and a music that was once an expression of religious belief was now a business."[33] Commercial influences have been at work in the music going back well into the nineteenth century. What Wolfe seems to be driving at here is the degree to which the industry's old guard began during the mid–twentieth century to wield the perceived evils of a new hybrid style of commercialized gospel as a cudgel against the more modern ways of singing and making money.

Southern gospel's midcentury heyday is often treated as a "golden age," but the music's mainstream commercial success between the late 1940s and the mid-1970s belied the increasing fractiousness and discord rumbling just beneath the surface of the booming industry. In 1964 a group of gospel quartet men, led by James Blackwood, chartered the Gospel Music Association (GMA), "initially envisioned as an umbrella organization" for the rapidly commercializing world of white gospel.[34] What happened over the next few decades is a hotly debated topic inside southern gospel to this day, but the ultimate result was a split between white gospel and what came to be known as contemporary Christian music, with CCM displacing gospel as the dominant form of Christian entertainment within American evangelicalism.

Two incidents are emblematic of this struggle, and both date from the fall of 1971. The first was a vote-rigging scandal involving no less a personage than James Blackwood and his famous Blackwood Brothers quartet. After winning nine out of fourteen possible honors at the Dove Awards—the Grammys of gospel music—the group was not unjustly accused of buying votes and manipulating the balloting process. Eventually, Blackwood was forced to give back the awards and apologized for "unethical solicitation of votes by members of our organization."[35] People within southern gospel still debate whether Blackwood and his partisans actually went so far as to buy votes and mark ballots en masse. But the story's real value has less to do with the Blackwoods' reputation and more to do with the underlying struggle to chart the direction for Christian entertainment and to define American Protestant popular culture: less than ten years after founding the GMA, Blackwood—and, implicitly, the style of music he represented—had been rebuked in a public and symbolically powerful fashion.

At the same time that the GMA seemed to be leaving behind the very tradition of gospel music from which the organization emerged, much of white gospel was willfully withdrawing from the increasingly popular forms of progressive Christian music. In the September 1971 edition of *Singing News*, the Happy Goodman Family, led by Howard "Happy" Goodman, took out a large text-only ad complaining about the direction of Christian music: "It seems that you [the GMA] have decided to promote and condone the more hippie oriented crowd, and night club acts, other than the gospel music. To me, and the rest of the Goodmans, and many other groups that are not as bold to take the stand that we dare to take[,] promoting and condoning this type of entertainment is not 'Good News.' . . . In view of all these things, we are asking for the return of [our $]600.00 for Life Time Memberships."[36] The histrionic quality of the rhetoric here is typical. The Happy Goodmans were famous for pulling publicity stunts. They were known, for instance, to park their bus some distance away from a concert venue and rent a limousine to sweep them grandly up to the stage door. During their shows, Vestal Goodman would often enter the auditorium "unexpectedly" from the back or the side of the hall and start singing—bellowing, really—an a cappella chorus, creating the effect of a sudden, heavenly pronouncement, albeit in the vernacular. And then there was the group's ensemble singing style. In a marked departure from the smoother blended sounds of the all-male quartet and the mixed-gender groups typified by the LeFevres, the Goodmans popularized a "hard singing style,"[37] which subverts blend in favor of accentuating the downbeat of lyrical phrases and holding a fairly sustained—and loud—dynamic level across most musical thoughts. The group's endings were equally unsubtle: live recordings of the conclusion to the upbeat song "When Morning Sweeps the Eastern Sky" sound like nothing so much as a harmonized pig call. Each voice lands on the final word *sky* at different times and tonal positions on the scale, and the vocalists inflect their enunciation of the word itself with a heavy diphthong, discordantly sliding up a series of thirds before resolving into a bombastic consonance.[38] The ending brought crowds roaring to their feet in delight at the way the sound managed to teeter precariously between chaos and control, buffoonery and beauty, this world and the next. Late in life, Vestal and Howard Goodman—and after their death, their son—became notorious for selling almost anything the elder Goodmans were said to have touched, including autographed wing-backed chairs they sat in onstage, floral-print dresses Vestal made famous, and a seemingly unlimited supply of hankies that she had used in concert.

But even allowing that the GMA ad was in keeping with the group's penchant for melodrama, Howard Goodman was probably right in asserting that many other white gospel groups felt the way he and his family did about the drift toward CCM in the GMA. Though the Goodmans' sound was only one among many of the diverse styles contained within white gospel, their departure from the quartet norm was not atypical, as testified to by groups such as the Singing Rambos, who served as a performance vehicle for the songs of the famous composer and lyricist Dottie Rambo and in the process helped popularize a countrified form of gospel built around string instruments rather than the piano, or the Kingsmen quartet, which sang in their own simple, hard-driving manner they referred to as "three chords and a cloud of dust." Meanwhile, the Nelons were revolutionizing mixed-gender groups. Their 1977 album, *The Sun's Coming Up,* arguably their finest, aptly captures the way they departed from received models of quartet music by shifting the musical center away from a male lead singer

The Happy Goodman family in the early 1970s. Member are, *front row, left to right,* Jack Smith, Eddie Crook, Aaron Wilburn, Sam Goodman; *back row, left to right,* Rick Goodman, Larry Strzlecki, Howard Goodman, Vestal Goodman, Jim "Duke" Dumas, Rusty Goodman. (From the collection of Dean Adkins.)

toward a female soprano (most famously, Janet Paschal, who went on to become Jimmy Swaggart's lead soloist before launching her own solo career in southern gospel, and later Karen Peck Gooch). Their endings used this revoiced harmonic structure to create songs that ended in high, clear tones of surpassing brightness that could almost seem to herald a new heaven onstage, if not earth itself, and contrasted markedly with the typical staggered endings of the sort the Goodmans and more traditional male quartets used. These stylistic trends, combined with fundamentalist evangelical distrust of worldliness, put the traditional white-gospel world at cross-purposes with the increasingly professionalized, strategically ecumenical approach preferred by a younger generation of Christian musicians. The benchmarks of professionalization and success for these new performers were no longer pious songbook publishers or vernacular singing conventions but American pop music and the mass-produced culture of television—the very source of worldliness that traditional gospel leaders were decrying.

The Rex Nelon Singers in the early 1970s. Members are, *left to right, front row,* Janet Paschal, Kelly Nelson, Lamar Newton; *middle,* Rex Nelon; *back row, left to right,* Greg Cauthran, Rodney Swain, Robbie Willis. (From the collection of Dean Adkins. Courtesy of the Nelon Family.)

The tenor of the Goodmans' GMA resignation—"You can't fire me. I quit!"—reveals one side of the mutual distrust and wariness emerging between white gospel traditionalists and the more progressive musicians coming of age in the 1970s and 1980s. This dynamic is borne out in conversations I have had with industry leaders. One record-label executive I interviewed told me a story about attending the Dove Awards in the 1980s with several prominent industry leaders from white gospel, including figures who had helped found the GMA and its awards show. Upon entering the Tennessee Performing Arts Center, where the awards were being held, two of the most prominent CCM artists of the day conspicuously refused to interact with the gospel businessmen. For their part, the white gospel executives did not stay long, walking out halfway through the show, disgusted by performances of notionally Christian music that were to them indistinguishable from the most profane pop and rock acts of the day. The point of this story is that the white gospel executives, the Goodmans, and others like them saw CCM as one big conglomeration of "hippie-oriented" music. In turn, the performers in those "night club acts" saw the Goodmans' performance style as indicative of an outmoded folksiness and hopeless amateurism inhibiting the expansion of Christian music to more sophisticated consumers. While the world of white gospel recoiled at the shock of the new, a raft of record labels and producers filled the gap with a variety of new talent such as Petra, Steve Green, and the Winans, whose success only further disillusioned and alienated gospel traditionalists. But even if they had wanted to engage in this new mega-industry, many of them simply did not know how. "A lot of these guys," the record label executive told me, "were used to selling maybe a hundred thousand units of product a year. And here's someone like Sandi Patty selling millions of records!"[39]

By the 1980s, the forces that had coalesced to drive the midcentury explosion of white gospel music—mass-market technology, celebrity-driven entertainment, a burgeoning Protestant middle class, population relocation, and stylistic hybridity—were thoroughly scrambled amid two decades of counterculture backlash against middle-class norms in the 1960s and 1970s.[40] This backlash spawned a host of alternative sounds in Christian music, beginning with the Jesus People and early Christian rock such as the Crusaders and later Christian pop and rap.[41] Whatever else it achieved, the success of this new music eroded the (illusion of) homogeneity of tastes and values integral to the survival of traditional, filiopietistic white gospel in the southern tradition.

On the traditionalists' side, this loss of cohesion is registered most noticeably by the growing popularity of the term *southern gospel*. As more contemporary forms of Christian music—among them, inspirational, Jesus rock, Praise and Worship, and commercialized black gospel—began rivaling, then overtaking, gospel's traditional white male quartets and southern family acts for popularity among Christian-music audiences, both the GMA and those within the world of conventional white gospel themselves began promoting the term *southern* as a way to distinguish older forms of music from new styles.[42] From the point of view of those using the term, *southern* really means *traditional*.

Us and Them

More deeply, "southern" gospel initially emerged as a shorthand way to draw a line culturally between "us" and "them." Who "they" are has always been more fluid than the binary suggests: southern gospel versus contemporary Christian, obviously. But also evangelical versus secular, traditional versus modern, and, inevitably perhaps, white versus black. Following Goff's

claim that use of the "southern" designation helped "restore some separation between white and black gospel music" in "the wake of integration,"[43]
Suzanne Lee has described adoption of the term as a "deliberate 'whitening'
of the name" with potentially "racist" implications. "Although not explicitly anti-black," Lee concludes, "the choice [of] 'Southern' to mark off the
genre from African American music and simultaneously to refer to a sound
made popular during the height of legal and social segregation in the region
named, culturally references and celebrates a segregated society."[44]

Lee somewhat overstates things. I have found no evidence that "southern"
gospel gained popularity primarily or even implicitly as a racialized term.
But certainly race inflected southern white gospel music throughout most
of the twentieth century. In the years before Prohibition, prominent gospel
songwriters A. B. Sebren and James Rowe, whose pious poems were regularly
featured in *Vaughan's Family Visitor*, cowrote the 1914 temperance tune "I
Knows Bettah Now," which appeared in the 1917 Vaughan songbook *The
Modern Singer*. The lyrics, cast in a black dialect, tell the first-person story of
a rum-loving father and husband who "used to starve mah children for jags"
but who "knows bettah know": "Tho' black my face mah spirit is white. . . .
Ise jined de ranks, Ise ready to fight."[45] A 1924 song written by singing-school
mainstays Adger Pace and Walter Seale and published by Vaughan music
under the title "Wake Up, America and Kluck, Kluck, Kluck," extends the
temperance-era racial logic of "I Knows Bettah" to Jim Crow concerns with
race and (in)equality:

> "Not for self, but for others," the creed on which we stand.
> So brother, why not line up with this klucking band;
> Though each face is covered up beneath a crown of white,
> The heart beateth ever for all that meaneth right.[46]

The explicit equivalence here between "white" and "right" is not new or
unique to this song. The white-right rhyme has long been a favorite supremacist trope, used to suggest that white superiority is an essential fact of
existence embedded in the very fiber of language. But setting this notion to a
tune in the popular, upbeat gospel style and employing the linguistic formal-
ity of the King James Bible ("beateth" and "meaneth") intentionally blur
the lines between religious commitment and racist ideology. One becomes
a version of the other, as natural as humming your favorite gospel song.

It is this the casual, hop-along quality of the song that is so striking to
the modern listener, the way a musical celebration of unabashed white
supremacy literally falls just across the page from a "bonus" song—"Sweet
Little Girl of Mine," another Pace and Rowe tune—printed on the inside

The front cover to the sheet music for "Wake Up, America and Kluck, Kluck, Kluck," published in 1924 by James D. Vaughan Music Publishers. (From author's collection.)

cover of the first-edition sheet music for "Wake Up, America." The cover illustration for the printed score reinforces the offhand perniciousness of the ideology the song serves. To one side of the foreground, a patrician gentleman slumbers happily, a broad smile on his face, a cigar smoldering in hand, comforter over his legs, and "U.S." emblazoned on his smoking jacket. To the right, a cavalcade of Klansmen gallops toward the slumbering United States, a burning cross at the head of the hooded line. In the background, a deceptively bucolic scene unfolds: a setting sun, a white-clapboard country church, a rolling meadow, but in the sky, storm clouds gather. Five to be exact, each with a name—immigration, graft, lawlessness, bootlegger, and, the fifth, "isms." No regular cloud, this "isms," but a stormy, horned devil lurking menacingly over the scene with a grisly, blood-dripping claw outstretched and descending toward the hoary head of our stately gentleman in his blissfully ignorant repose. Like the song itself, this image stops just sort of explicitly articulating the barely submerged racial subtext. The giveaway in the cover illustration is in the far background on the left side, behind the church, where a dark grove of bushy-topped trees swallows up the backside of the white church in their malevolent darkness. James D. Vaughan's name is prominently embossed in ornate script at the bottom foreground of this disturbing image.

Racism in southern gospel was not just the province of the early twentieth century. In 1956 bass singer J. D. Sumner recorded the song "Sad Sam Jones" in flamboyant black dialect. In 1971 the Statesmen quartet recorded an album with the segregationist politician Lester Maddox while he was governor of Georgia. The album was titled *God, Family, & Country* and evoked many of the same ethnocentric themes of another Statesmen album from around the same time, *God Loves American People*. The Statesmen were not the only group to affiliate themselves with segregationist politicians. A group called the Sunshine Sisters sang at George Wallace rallies in 1960s, as did the southern gospel impresario Wally Fowler and an early gospel iteration of the Oak Ridge Boys. Overtly racist behavior persisted in southern gospel long after mainstream America considered public racism unacceptable. As late as 1982, the bass singer and owner of the Gold City quartet, Tim Riley, can be heard on a live album asking the emcee if he "got a piece of watermelon I could eat before I sing" the black spiritual "Ezekiel Saw the Wheel."[47] Riley was no aging throwback bubba shuffling with his racist connotations off the stage into retirement at the time. He stills owns and sings with the group today.

But by far, the mighty Statesmen are responsible for the nastiest expressions of southern gospel racism I have encountered in my research. In an unreleased 1959 recording on Mother's Day, Hovie Lister, the famously flashy piano player and gabby front man for the Statesmen, can be heard telling a story about the group's traveling to a gig in the nation's capital, where "brother, I found out firsthand that they already doing in Washington, D.C., what they been trying to do in Little Rock all these days." Once he and the group arrive at the church, Lister says, "It was 75 percent black . . . and the rest of it was niggers." Listening to the crowd's roaring laughter at this type of "joke," one is reminded of Wallace's explanation of his midcareer decision to espouse a hard-line segregationist position when he first ran for governor: "I tried to talk about good roads and good schools and all these things that have been part of my career, and nobody listened. And then I began talking about niggers, and they stomped the floor."[48]

Lister had a series of racist set pieces he regularly drew on from the stage for more than two decades. These stories typically involved various caricatures of audience members at black churches from which the Statesmen would have just returned. In the 1959 recording, Lister tells a story about a "great big ole fat nigger woman who weighed 350 pound if she weighed an ounce." Lister describes the woman as being conspicuously smitten with the quartet's lead singer, Jake Hess. The story ends with Hess running in delirious fear from the building after the woman makes amorous advances upon her beloved singing "sugar boy." Twenty years later, Lister was still at it, introducing the group's famous tenor singer, Rosie Rozell, in 1979 with a story about the group's having sung to a black audience in North Carolina "not long ago." Though Lister avoids using the racial epithets generously sprinkled throughout his emcee work in the Mother's Day concert twenty years earlier, his stories still pivot on cartoonish renderings of racial stereotypes: here, it is the emotionally uncontrolled black church experience with people shouting and crazily "running the aisles." "One woman lost her hat . . . twice, and the second time it come rolling down the aisle like a hubcap off a car." The climax of this story concerns another "large lady" in the fifth row whom Lister pegs as susceptible to the musical blandishments of the portly Rozell, because "fat folks love fat folks," the svelte Lister says. Lister claims that he decided to have Rozell sing directly to her because she seemed to be able to sway the rest of the audience's response to the group's performance. The ploy works, in Lister's telling, and the woman jumps up early on in Rozell's first verse, shouting, "Sang it, dahlun! Sang it!" This sort of paternalistic evocation of the mammy figure infatuated with sweet-singing white boys inverts the long-standing southern stereotype of the black male as sexual predator, a cartoonish inversion that smuggles in its supremacist message under the cover of a hyperbolic raconteur good-naturedly regaling southern whites with sidesplitting stories about the exotic fervency of African American worship experiences. Lister colorfully describes the outsized habits of expression to be found in the black church notionally in order to praise a worthy competitor: "Ain't nobody can outsing a good black quartet," he says in the 1979 recording. But David Vest is not far off in describing this routine as so much "clownish minstrelsy."[49]

Casual racism is, of course, still second nature both in the geographic South and other culturally southern parts of America (I grew up in southern Missouri in the 1980s, a place where the kinds of white paternalistic stories Lister told captured the conventional view of racial difference). But without diminishing the repugnance and danger inherent in the dialect skits and derisive stories not uncommon to southern gospel's recent past, I want to suggest that the overt racism is not the only story here.[50] What is at least as important is this rhetoric's mobilization of race within the context of white Christian entertainment. Be it reformist lyrics of the 1920s, minstrelsy dialects of the 1950s, or watermelon jokes in the 1980s, the effect of these racist rhetorical set pieces onstage is to reinforce a supremacist moral calculus that makes whiteness coterminous with social progress, moral superiority, and spiritual security of the (white) saints. Race is not nor has it ever been a predominant concern of most southern gospel songs or groups. But when lyrics and performers have explicitly engaged racial themes, the engagements often revealingly foreground the music's participation in much broader cultural processes. Initially, the music helped naturalize the ethnocentrism barely latent in the southern temperance movement. Then, during the civil rights era, the process effectively recast Jim Crow attitudes and actions as an extension of the evangelical struggle for moral improvement in America. And as this process was carried forward into the latter part of the twentieth century—a time when southern gospel's unreconstructed views of race began to occasion rebukes from mainstream America—these "politically correct" repudiations of evangelical culture could be worn like a badge of honor. A southern gospel singer being called a bigot by a *New York Times* columnist, for instance, confirms to gospel insiders their belief in secular humanism's overweening inability to accept God's sovereign administration of his kingdom, or to know the difference between racism and a joke about fat black people and watermelon.[51]

Nevertheless and at the same time, there is a much less polemical tradition of stylistic exchange between white and black gospel going at least as far back as the nineteenth century. Formally, the four-shape notation tradition borrowed songs and motifs from African American spirituals. More informally, "blacks and whites would often worship in the same congregation, albeit segregated within the building," before the Civil War. These sorts of formal and informal linkages persisted into the twentieth century. Rosetta Tharpe recorded Abernathy's "Gospel Boogie" (under the title "Everybody's Gonna Have a Wonderful Time Up There") in 1947 in the early years of the civil rights turmoil, and the songs of Thomas Dorsey had strong appeal among white audiences and performers.[52] W. E. B. DuBois thought white gospel hymns of the early twentieth century "well-nigh ruined our sense of song consist[ing] largely of debased imitations of Negro melodies made by ears that caught the jingle but not the music, the body but not the soul, of Jubilee songs." Nevertheless, as Kip Lornell observes, "it is difficult to underestimate the impact of black gospel music" on many influential white gospel performers, and I would add, vice versa. Whether consciously or not, white gospel groups borrowed heavily from the black gospel repertoire. From the 1950s to the early 1970s, the Oak Ridge Boys used a version of the black gospel song "Go Out to the Programs" in their act and recorded it more than once. The song is an up-tempo novelty number that urges listeners to go listen to concerts ("programs") by their favorite groups, of whom the singers then do short musical imitations. In their autobiography, the Oak Ridge Boys note that the song is "black music" (first popularized by the Dixie Hummingbirds) and cite it as an example of the "cornball stuff" in the group's repertoire that would help connect with "real Pentecostal, fundamentalist, traditional-style crowd[s]." In one recorded version, the song goes on some eleven minutes.[53] Southern gospel audiences have long responded powerfully to white versions of black gospel standards. For instance, most southern gospel fans associate "Get Away Jordan" with the Statesmen (and, more recently, the Dove Brothers quartet or Ernie Haase and Signature Sound) and "I Bowed on My Knees and Cried Holy" with Michael English. But although it is less well known in the southern gospel world, both songs were originally black gospel favorites: Dorothy Love Coates and the Original Gospel Harmonettes recorded "Get Away" long before the Statesmen latched onto it. Perhaps most famously, Mahalia Jackson mesmerized the world with her renditions of "I Bowed on My Knees" before English was even born.

In turn, black singers and groups have not infrequently succeeded in southern gospel at least since the 1970s: among them Teddy Huffam and the Gems, who worked many of the same concert dates in the 1970s and 1980s as the Nelons and the Kingsmen, two of the most popular white groups in the industry; Jessy Dixon, a soloist, songwriter, and accomplished keyboard player in both sacred and secular music who collaborated with, among others, Paul Simon and the rock group Earth, Wind, and Fire, was a fixture on the Gaither Homecoming tour from nearly its beginning until Dixon's death in 2011; and Charles Johnson and the Revivers and Reggie Sadler and the Sadler Family work many of their dates within southern gospel. As Stephen Shearon has written, both white and black gospel have "liked aspects of what the other was doing" from the inception of modern gospel music, and both have freely "borrowed those aspects, reinterpreting them for their own cultures."[54] If there is an inevitable air of tokenism surrounding nonwhite performers in an overwhelmingly southern, white musical culture,[55] the commercial success and genuine following these black performers have achieved among white audiences suggest that overmuch emphasis on black-white polarities diminishes our understanding of cultural dynamics submerged beneath the surface of the music, dynamics powerfully illustrated in the emergence of the term *southern gospel*.

From Dominant to Residual

Studying *Singing News* archives between 1970 and 1990 reveals that regular usage of the term *southern gospel* is a distinct phenomenon of the 1980s and its sociohistorical dynamics. In the 1970s, when the centers of power and influence within the GMA were still fluctuating between traditionalists and iconoclasts, references to *southern gospel* are mainly in relation to Dove Award subcategories. Only in the 1980s, when the balance of power in Christian entertainment was irreversibly solidifying around CCM stars such as Amy Grant, Michael W. Smith, and Sandi Patty, does *southern gospel* become a much more common way for the magazine to refer to the industry in articles, editorials, ads, and other acts of self-representation such as the *Singing News* Fan Awards, which became the southern gospel alternative to the Dove Awards. After a generation of turmoil among competing factions of Christian entertainment, *southern gospel* appears somewhat belatedly in the 1980s as a lexical feature formed in the decades-long torque of massive psychosocial and sociopolitical realignments within evangelical popular culture. Jerry Kirksey, longtime *Singing News* editor, acknowledged to me that the decision among a small group of leaders in the industry to adopt *southern gospel* for self-descriptive purposes was in no small part an acknowledgment that "we're stuck with this label" within the larger world of Christian music.[56] Thus, a geographical modifier was conscripted in service of a stylistic—and sociocultural—distinction.

In terms that Raymond Williams first developed to talk about the process of cultural change, a "dominant culture" in the midcentury mainstream, mass-market Christian entertainment industry was giving way during the

1970s and 1980s to the "emergent culture" of contemporary Christian music.[57] Williams's layered approach, which emphasizes the conflicting vectors of power, taste, and value within cultural traditions, is particularly helpful in the study of absolutist forms of culture such as southern white gospel music, whose monochromatic modes of thought and action tend to obscure the underlying strategies fundamentalists use to negotiate change. The catalyzing forces behind the changes were not primarily external conflicts between purity and corruption, white and black, or piety and worldliness, though the debate was and still is at times cast in these terms. Rather, this process of redefinition emerged from the self-embattling experience of being systematically relegated to what Williams refers to as the "residual" cultural position, distilled in this case into the term *southern gospel* and the increasingly marginalized identity it has come to represent.

It is no coincidence that the appropriation of the Vaughan legacy during the early 1990s comes amid fairly rapid reconfigurations within evangelical pop culture. Not least among these changes was the rise of the nondenominational evangelical megachurch, which supplanted denominations, where southern gospel has its strongest fan base, as the dominant force in conservative Christianity. In light of these and other fluctuations, repurposing Vaughan in service of modern southern gospel identity formation attests to an underlying anxiety about the sustainability of a fundamentalist, white evangelical monoculture in contemporary American society. This anxiety descends from the postbellum crisis of southern identity that Kieffer's story exemplifies and has been intensified by the exigencies of postmodernity: among them the great migrational shifts in rural populations after World War II, the fractionalization of American Protestantism, and the political radicalization of fundamentalist evangelicals who began to use politics as an avenue to redress a loss of cultural clout in mainstream America. These sorts of disruptions and realignments often manifest themselves culturally in a renewed concern with history and urgent efforts to create what Brooks first called a new, "useable past," whose retelling will ground communities in flux and orient individual identities in moments of upheaval and transition.[58]

Jerry Kirksey did not talk in these terms when he and I spoke about Vaughan and the origins of southern gospel. Nevertheless, he seemed to have something like a usable past in mind when speaking of Vaughan's value. Of particular importance to Kirksey is Vaughan's symbolic significance as a model of patriarchal piety. From his visit to Lawrenceburg, Tennessee, with James Goff, Kirksey was especially impacted by hearing a local story that after Vaughan died in 1941, the undertaker found "huge calluses" on his knees from praying so much. It was a galvanizing image, Kirksey said, for himself and Maurice Templeton, who owned *Singing News* at the time, ran a popular gospel music vacation business under the name Singing at Sea, and held stock in the National Quartet Convention. In Vaughan these southern gospel leaders had found "a good foundation," as Kirksey put it: "a brilliant businessman" nevertheless guided by prayer, not profit.[59]

This narrative is all the more striking given how much emphasis has been placed on making money in gospel music from at least Ruebush-Kieffer's time forward. Vaughan was no exception, which even his contemporary fans acknowledge. "Everything we do today [in commercialized southern gospel] had been done [by Vaughan]," Kirksey told me, "except for television." This sort of continuity seems to have value in contemporary southern gospel as historical evidence that this tradition alone remains unswervingly aligned with an originary vision of musical ministry in ways that no other form of Christian music can claim. So Vaughan's decision to launch a traveling quartet in 1910 is treated today in southern gospel as something close to divine inspiration that founded a genre and continues to define it. Vaughanism is not a style of music to be imitated. On the contrary, contemporary southern gospel is astonishingly diverse, even though the "classic quartet" sound continues to be highly prized. But Vaughan functions as a socioreligious landmark with which subsequent generations can identify under the term *southern gospel*. Today's southern gospel is held together mainly by self-selection among people who choose to associate themselves—as fans, performers, or other industry professionals—with the music and its culture, which has come to be metonymized in the pietistic, fatherly figure of Vaughan.

It is tempting to see latter-day Vaughanism as so much revisionist history, and there is doubtless some truth to this, especially insofar as historical revisionism in this case registers a delayed reaction to the loss of status and esteem for southern gospel in Christian entertainment. But the resurgent interest in Vaughan bears many of the distinguishing features of a more complex process of cultural transformation that plays out through revivals of declining musical traditions, as described by Bruce Feintuch. For Feintuch, when antecedent traditions and tropes are revived in the name of "continuity," often these revivals actually "recast the music—and the culture—they refer to." Taking a "selective" view of the past allows revivalists to "create their own canons and repertoire, of style, of authenticity."[60]

Within southern gospel, disproportionate emphasis on the Vaughan legacy had the effect of recalibrating the music's cultural equilibrium. Displacement from a once dominant position in Christian music is revalued as a kind of fortunate fall into a new appreciation for the roots of the music.

Seen as a godly cultural heritage bequeathed by Vaughan to today's industry leaders, southern gospel no longer measures its success by the standards of mainstream Christian entertainment. Were one to do so, the result would be grim: one record-label executive I spoke to estimated that sales of southern gospel fell from around 3.5 million units of music in 2000 to between 400,000 and 800,000 in 2008, or anywhere from 75 percent to nearly 90 percent in less than a decade.[61] Instead, the "rediscovery" of contemporary southern gospel's "true" origins in Vaughan's prayerful piety recasts marginalization as evidence of filiopiety even if that has meant loss of stature or status, both culturally and economically.

In this embrace of exile from the mainstream, there is an echo of the long-standing willingness in pietistic evangelicalism to be damned for the greater glory of God. To the extent mainstream Christian music has moved away from nostalgic sentimentalism and explicit expressions of piety and, over the past quarter of the twentieth century, adopted a sound that is often indistinguishable from secular adult contemporary music (what the music's detractors often call "Jesus is my boyfriend" songs), southern gospel has intensified its embrace of nostalgia, sentimentality, and piety. Musically, the result has been a precipitous decline in the value placed on creative originality and the related emergence of a conspicuously imitative, intensely nostalgic style of songwriting, musical arranging, and performance. In 2008 the *Singing News* Fan Awards Song of the Year was awarded to the Booth Brothers for their rendition of "Look for Me at Jesus' Feet," written more than thirty years ago and first made popular by the Kingsmen quartet in the 1970s and 1980s. In 2003 the album of the year went to the trio Greater Vision for *Quartets*, a novelty project on which the group's three vocalists were joined by a variety of southern gospel basses, including three famous but dead singers—J. D. Sumner, Brock Speer, and Rex Nelon—whose recorded voices were digitally combined with the living singers'. The resulting album gives the impression of Greater Vision singing with three of the most beloved members of southern gospel's greatest generation.

This is not to say that this nostalgic music is all bad. Artistically, *Quartets* remains one of the strongest southern gospel albums of the past decade. Nor is contemporary southern gospel devoid of new music. Rodney Griffin of Greater Vision, for instance, is among the most prolific and popular songwriters of his generation, and the Perrys—a mixed-gender family foursome—have demonstrated a long-standing preference for the flamboyantly emotionalistic music of songwriter Kyla Rowland. But this new music, like the more explicit reappropriation of the past, succeeds almost entirely on the basis of how intensely it incites religious affections through evocations of pietistic sentimentality and evangelical filiopiety beyond all other controlling ideas or aims. Of course, imitating or self-consciously gesturing back to antecedent values and approaches is more than just mimicry. In echoing the sounds and styles of earlier generations and evoking their memories, contemporary southern gospel's "representation of identity and meaning," to borrow Homi Bhabha's phrase from another context, "is rearticulated."[62]

This dynamic is perhaps nowhere more evident than in the popularity of Ernie Haase and Signature Sound, an all-male ensemble that styles itself as a devotee and descendant of the midcentury classic quartet. Like those earlier groups, Signature Sound sports flamboyant outfits and trendy hairstyles and conspicuously choreographed dance routines to many songs, especially upbeat numbers. Yet the group looks and sounds less like the Statesmen (the most obvious antecedent) and more like a southern gospel boy band—that is, conservative Christian sex symbols breathily crooning about a love beyond all measure. Of course, the Statesmen occupied a similar status in their day, but their fame came from using a repertoire of new songs that defined the leading edge of the musical moment in Christian entertainment. In contrast, Signature Sound endears itself to audiences by singing nostalgic music and engaging in sentimental showmanship in a way that transforms mimicry into homage.

Ernie Haase, the group's owner and emcee, is the son-in-law of the late, great George Younce, co-owner of the Cathedral quartet, and Haase has increasingly positioned his group as not just a quartet in the classic style generally (singing songs from that era or in the same way) but more particularly as the heir to the Cathedral's legacy. Under the cover of homage and filiopiety, the group has safely smuggled in a raft of sounds and styles from across the spectrum of American popular music and entertainment—most notably pop, Broadway, and Vegas shows—unconstrained by old debates about ministry versus entertainment. Signature Sound gives its audiences what they want: close harmony, fervent piety, a little cheesy humor, and a big finish, safe in their status as the good sons of southern gospel. This approach emerges most visibly in the group's 2008 live album, *Dream On*, recorded at Navy Pier in Chicago. Though the recording is thoroughly urbane in its aesthetic and technically sophisticated in its conception and execution, the show's innovations and adaptations are filtered through a heavily nostalgic lens: at least half the recording is devoted to covers of well-established songs from white and black gospel. Audiences are given permission by this type of stylistically innovative homage to embrace the new—the group's trendy look, their inventive takes on the old southern gospel sound—in the name of preserving gospel's most beloved history. In the process, nostalgia licenses transformations in the southern gospel repertoire.

It is no coincidence that contemporary southern gospel is dominated by musical homage. In the first place, the current generation of industry leaders and performers came of age in the 1970s and 1980s when the mainstream decline of southern gospel was already under way. On top of this, the past decade or so has seen the passing away of southern gospel's golden generation—the figures who were there for the music's midcentury boom. Many of these personalities found a second career in the Bill and Gloria Gaither Homecoming Friends series, which dominated the 1990s with concerts and videos of aging southern gospel greats singing old songs and reminiscing about old times together. The enormous commercial success of the Homecoming Friends has paradoxically cemented the popular notion that southern gospel's best days are behind it, that "good" southern gospel is synonymous with nostalgia, that the future has value mainly for what can be remembered. The result is that very few people are left for whom the cultural mood and commercial focus have not always already been primarily nostalgic—nostalgia for a time when tens of thousands of gospel music fans packed out stadiums for all-night singings and thousands more listened on the radio; when singing schools were reliably turning out backwoods virtuosi; when some of the most famous rock-and-roll and country stars got their start in, or only really ever wanted to sing, this music; when—in short—gospel music *mattered*.

Understood as an ongoing musical revival of a midcentury commercial repertoire, latter-day southern gospel both testifies to the half-life of nostalgic modernity in rural evangelicalism going back at least as far as the postbellum period, while also registering one important response to modern life within American fundamentalist Protestantism. Yes, southern gospel is beholden to nostalgic modes of thought and action in the late nineteenth and early twentieth centuries. It has, however, also shared with the larger world of Protestant evangelicalism an emphasis on progress and reform. This tendency is manifested generally in the shape-note movement's emphasis on music education as a path to right living and particularly by gospel temperance songs such as "I Knows Bettah." Daniel Walker Howe has argued that the enactment of Prohibition represents the apex of evangelical influence as a force for progressive reform, even as the Eighteenth Amendment turned American popular opinion against evangelicalism.[63] To a suddenly dry nation, the dedicated moral reformers who brought the country Prohibition started to look a lot more like moralistic scolds. In culturally southern parts of America, this displacement of evangelicalism from the mainstream was cemented by the solidification of Jim Crow laws and customs, largely supported by evangelical religious leaders, even as the rest of America slowly but inexorably moved toward integrationist attitudes and legislation. At the same time, the South failed on the whole to modernize in the New Deal era and the decades of economic transformation that followed, a failure that began to show itself most fully during the 1970s.[64]

The enthusiastic response to shape-note white gospel in the first half of the twentieth century drove the midcentury expansion of the music across America, music that ran headlong into a perceived process of secularization within mass culture. The rise of "southern gospel" measures one dimension of a resacralizing response from within evangelicalism to the increasingly liberal bent of American public life.[65] As we shall see, contemporary southern gospel has remained very much alive and responsive to these dynamics, relying on nostalgic modes of musical sentimentality to negotiate the increasingly conflictual, contradictory, and shifting relationship between fundamentalist evangelicalism and secular America culture.

4. The Gaitherization of Contemporary Southern Gospel

Within the overlapping worlds of gospel music, contemporary Christian entertainment, and multimedia televangelism in America, the long-standing success of the Bill and Gloria Gaither Homecoming Friends franchise has been a fact of professional life for almost a generation—a ubiquitous presence to compete with, admire, envy, or (when invited) join. What started as a happenstance gathering of "old-timers" from the heyday of midcentury southern gospel music at the Master's Touch studio in Nashville, Tennessee, in February 1991, has since become an institution in American evangelical life.[1]

Today, Homecoming exists as both an annual concert tour and a video series. Exact production and retail sales figures are difficult to secure, but as early as 1996, just five years after the launch of the first Homecoming video recording, Bill Gaither said that Homecoming sales had exceeded three million units.[2] Today the Gaither Music Web site offers more than two hundred different Homecoming-themed videos or video bundles for sale. These include installments in the regular Homecoming Friends series, children's videos, "best-of" recombinations of video recordings by particularly popular Homecoming personalities throughout their time on the concert tour, dozens of companion songbooks and other memorabilia, a magazine, and a subscriber-based online community. At its peak, the Gaither Homecoming was regularly drawing crowds upwards of twenty thousand and beyond, rivaling the largest single-night draw at the National Quartet Convention, the southern gospel industry's weeklong flagship event. In 2004 the tour's eleventh year and arguably its zenith, Homecoming ticket sales worldwide outranked Elton John, Fleetwood Mac, and Rod Stewart each.[3] In 2009 almost three-quarters of southern gospel fans and professionals reported having attended a Gaither Homecoming event in the past decade, nearly two times the number of people who report having attended the National Quartet Convention during that same period.[4] For decades now, Gaither's endorsement has launched the careers of numerous performers who have gone on to dominate gospel and Christian music. Meanwhile, the Gaithers have taken their popular brand of southern gospel and inspirational Christian music worldwide, recording events in the Holy Land, South Africa, Ireland, Canada, and Australia. Its enduring popularity and pervasive presence easily make the Gaither Homecoming franchise the Christian entertainment equivalent of the Grand Ole Opry in country music, if the Opry were constantly touring all over the world.

This is all the more remarkable given that Bill Gaither rose to fame not in southern gospel, but in contemporary Christian music as a songwriter and performer in the 1970s and sustained his place in the industry as a mentor to other CCM writers and performers.[5] Gaither often talks from the stage and has written about growing up enthralled with gospel music and attending the Stamps-Baxter singing school as a teenager. Though he is fond of telling audiences that he always wanted to be a singer, his songwriting made him famous, especially after his wife, Gloria, started collaborating with him on songwriting and performing concerts with him on the weekends. In the 1960s and 1970s, the Gaither Trio—most famously Bill and Gloria Gaither and Bill's brother, Danny—became a vehicle for original Gaither songs. By the mid-1970s, Gaither quit his regular job teaching high school and hit the road full-time. There he developed the style of aw-shucks showmanship that years later reinforced Homecoming's down-home bonhomie.

The Homecoming concept is deceptively simple. Gaither invites friends, peers, rising stars, and, most important, those gospel music idols from his childhood who are still alive to join him on a stage. Everyone sits around a piano and sings: old songs, new songs, gospel songs, hymns. Despite the connections between Homecoming and southern gospel music, no single song style predominates. Casual observers may come away from the Homecoming series thinking it more generically homogenous than it actually is because the songs on Gaither's shows demonstrate remarkable consistency in the arrangements, a consistency that mutes the variety of the music. Songs need not always be religious; for more than a year in the early 2000s, for example, the Homecoming tour opened with the chorus of the pop song "Lean on Me." More recently, the emotional centerpiece of the Homecoming concert tour involved a song that used the tune from Jean Sibelius's *Finlandia*, joined to Christian-humanist lyrics that were written by Gloria Gaither and emphasize the long-suffering charity necessary to make dif-

Bill Gaither (*far right*) and Gloria Gaither (*second from right*) and their Homecoming Friends. (Courtesy of Gaither Management Group.)

ficult relationships work.[6] Stories, jokes, testimonies, and the pageant of
Homecoming friends enjoying each other's company and talents hold the
shows together.

Gaither himself generally stands in the foreground of the frame, where he
cracks jokes between songs or reminisces about a lifetime spent in Christian
music. At other times, he will single out Homecoming friends to sing solos
or in groups. Near the end of most shows, he will join the group that bears
his name, the Gaither Vocal Band, to perform a series of gospel warhorses,
big ballads, and power anthems. Though he likes to describe himself and
his wife as a team—in addition to being his longtime cowriter, she usually
offers an ornate prayer, sentimental poem, or meditative reading at some
point during most Homecoming events—Gaither is obviously the impresario of his own show: the ultimate Homecoming friend . . . known and
liked by everyone, peer to all, rival to none.[7] Gaither's brand is built on
heavily nostalgic remembrances of legendary figures and a sharing of stories
and sentiment that both honor the dead and informally place the living
within an unbroken arc of cultural greatness that the videos and concerts

commemorate. In this Gaither has perfected displays of Christian friendship and gospel nostalgia as performance art.

The centrality of nostalgic enthusiasm in Gaither's music undoubtedly helps account for the dearth of scholarship about the Gaither oeuvre. For a long time, cultural critics considered the sort of unrestrained nostalgia typified by Gaither music to be a form of bad memory that relies on romanticized constructs of the past to elide the messier reality of history.[8] Certainly, there is something of a romanticized quality to the conspicuously sentimental remembrances of southern gospel greats coming from the Gaither brand. For instance, in *The Journey: The Happy Goodman Family*, a Gaither-series video tribute to the Goodmans, the singing family is depicted as a group of up-from-nothing, reluctant megastars whose struggles with fame and the strains of the road—being separated from children, experiencing vocal problems that threatened to derail the group's career—were kept in balance by their rustic faith, focus on God, and the gift of song. No mention is made of Vestal Goodman's struggle with an addiction to painkillers in the 1970s. Nor is anything made of the internal acrimony in the group over whether to pursue a less traditional path—a disagreement that ultimately split up the group in the 1980s.[9] These conflicts are glossed over in favor of more inspiring aspects of the Goodmans' "journey" and jolly saintliness—"people who live focused on the wonder of life," Bill Gaither says in a voice-over near the end of the video, "the goodness of God, and the destination beyond now." Historically, scholars have understood such sentimentalized evasions of history "along two compatible, nearly parallel lines: nostalgia abused individual and collective memory and nostalgia [obscured] the relations between producers and consumers. Either way, nostalgia was simply bad, bad, bad."[10] Viewed this way, Gaither and his Homecoming Friends matter mainly as a cautionary tale about the dangerous distortions of derivative history in the postmodern memory market.

It certainly is true that Homecoming has succeeded by commodifying the southern gospel past as a sepia-toned wonderland of harmony and wholesomeness—many of the covers to Homecoming videos include images reproduced in actual sepia tones or other antique colorizations.[11] But recent scholarly reconsiderations of nostalgia and its cultural function suggest that there is more going on here than merely merrily airbrushing the past. In more current criticism, old notions of nostalgia as bad memory have "given way to nostalgia as a more ambivalent, more engaged, critical frame. . . . Rather than an end reaction to yearning," nostalgia is being increasingly "understood as a technique for provoking a secondary reaction."[12]

Emphasizing nostalgia as cultural process encourages us to look at what nostalgic forms of culture are trying to achieve, often beneath or against the stated purposes of the subjects involved. This line of thinking suggests a richer and more helpfully textured approach to Gaither Homecomings. If, as Benedict Anderson has famously asserted, cultures share a tendency to construct imaginary communities for themselves based on clusters of common affinities, then one way to understand the operation of nostalgia in Homecoming is as the cultural adhesive holding together an increasingly diverse and fractious coalition of evangelicals by binding them to an idealized vision of the past.[13] Descended from and encoded in the nostalgic idiom of southern gospel music, Homecoming functions as a model of commemorative bonding and sentimental friendship within pan-southern evangelical culture.[14] In the process, the past and present converge in a nostalgic fusion that effaces the disjunctions between the sacred and the secular in contemporary American life. This has been a long-standing cultural function of southern gospel, as we have seen. Like all successful white gospel with a southern accent since the Civil War, Homecoming is ecumenical enough to attract a wide cross-section of contemporary Protestants, yet pious enough to distinguish itself from secular entertainment. What sets Homecoming apart is its adaptation of southern gospel's sentimental reengagements with the past—both religious and secular—to speak to the sociohistorical experience of those evangelicals who, like Gaither himself, came of age in cold war America. Indeed, Gaither's career and the concerns embedded in his music emerge from within a network of psychosocial tensions unique to late-twentieth-century American evangelical culture. As it engages these tensions, the Homecoming series comes to serve as an exportable method for evangelicals to negotiate the sweeping transformations taking place in American life near the turn of the twenty-first century.

That Homecoming Feeling

As Bill Gaither has often described it, the idea for the Homecoming series came from godly serendipity, caught on videotape. What started as a one-day session in Nashville to record some long-forgotten gospel music elders singing the old standard "Where Could I Go?" morphed into an unexpected, hours-long exchange of favorite memories, old stories, and beloved songs. The emotional poignancy of the experience is palpable, even viewed as a recording after the fact. The emotionalism is flamboyant, but not forced. In writing and talking about all this, Gaither is quick to credit the divine, but the surge of feeling so central to the video's success clearly seems also to have been intensified by the visceral sense of mortality and nostalgia that pervaded the atmosphere in which the singers assembled. Many of them were far past their prime, several of them mostly forgotten, if they were ever known at all, by the fans and leading figures in mainstream Christian music. A few were chronically sick. At least one singer—Jake Hess—was visibly unwell.[15] In this context of personal decline and professional obsolescence, the opening lines of the song to which most of the tape is devoted seem particularly apt: "Where could I go?" the chorus begins.

> Seeking a friend
> To save me in the end
> Where could I go but to the Lord?[16]

Or in the meantime, to Bill Gaither. According to Gaither, the process of editing and releasing the recording of the event suggested the possibility of other similar recordings, and thus was Homecoming born. Consequently, nearly every singer in the room that day in 1991 became a household name throughout suburban, white evangelical America by the end of the decade.

With time the Homecoming stage expanded its influence and visibility, extending its rehabilitative reach beyond the struggling stars of the past. In his rhetorical study of Homecoming videos, Michael Graves has identified a ceremonial function at work in the series that is tied to ritual reinstatements of celebrities from southern gospel and Christian entertainment who "have not lived up to their professed Christian behavioral expectations and ideals."[17] Michael English, Calvin Newton, and Mylon LeFevre are among the most prominent of southern gospel's favorite sons who openly transgressed conservative Christian cultural norms and were shut out of the mainstream of Christian music for their transgressions, only to be welcomed home much later by the Homecoming Friends in ceremonial rites of repentance, forgiveness, and reacceptance.[18] Though Graves is interested in a fairly narrow subset of prodigal-son moments in the Homecoming series, his argument suggests a broader psychosocial function for the Gaither Homecoming series as a tool that helps evangelical Christians understand their place in the world by reconciling competing ways of life and worldviews in musical dramas of love, acceptance, and graciousness. These need not be formal or highly visible ceremonies of reinstatement in order for a wayward performer's image to be rehabilitated by association with the Homecoming brand. For instance, Guy Penrod abruptly left his position as lead singer for the Gaither Vocal Band in 2008 amid rumors of some unspecified personal crisis or scandal. His status in gospel music remained in question until 2009, when he signed a record deal for a solo album with the Gaither Music label.

To many gospel music insiders, this was a signal that Penrod was once again welcome within the fold and, implicitly, absolved of any taint that may have attached to him given the circumstances surrounding his abrupt departure from the Vocal Band. Resolving these sorts of conflicts between orthodox believers and their prodigal sons within the Homecoming community constructs for its audiences a beatified image of Protestant Christianity in the Calvinist tradition triumphing over worldliness and sin in an effulgence of pious tears, humble repentance, and sanctifying harmonies.

To students and fans of the Homecoming series, effusions of fellow feeling—especially from "legendary" males in powerful or prominent positions—are nothing new. One main implication of Graves's analysis is that the Homecoming phenomenon creates an emotionally safe context in which men can express deep feelings about matters of the spiritual self and the soul without imperiling their masculinity or slipping into discrediting "feminine" roles often associated with displays of religious affect and effervescences of spirit in patriarchal cultures. The sentimental and histrionic manner of expression common to the most profound experiences of evangelical heart religion has always existed in uneasy tension with the element of machismo inherent in any patriarchy. Stretching back to the first Great Awakening, the revivals of Charles Grandison Finney in the Second Great Awakening, the big-tent evangelism of Billy Sunday and Dwight Moody, and running through the Billy Graham crusades in the mid–twentieth century to the megachurch televangelism of Joel Osteen and Rick Warren, male expressions of emotionalism and melodrama have always been prevalent in the more evangelical strains of American Protestantism. In one way or another, all these men exemplify versions of the same evangelical truth: real men love Jesus. But it can be easy to stray across the fine line between loving the Lord and aggrandizing the self, or serially misplacing religious affections on more sublunary objects of devotion. Witness Oral Roberts or Jim Bakker or Jimmy Swaggart or Ted Haggard. Not every weepy, flamboyant, evangelistically aggressive preacher on television is a womanizer or a swindler or a closeted homosexual. But enough have been to make the performance of pietistic masculinity a tricky business for evangelicalism's leading men of ministry and music.

In his impresario role, Gaither largely neutralizes the threat of feminized corruption in several related ways. First, Gaither is a megastar in Christian music, so his actions tend to weaken the gravitational pull of masculinist cultural norms to which he conspicuously does not conform. As a songwriter, publisher, and entertainment entrepreneur, Gaither has amassed four decades' worth of paradigm-shifting innovations in Christian musical styles and in business models for delivering content to Christian audiences. The American Society for Composers, Authors, and Publishers named the Gaithers "Songwriters of the Century" in 2000,[19] and though the title feels overwrought, it suggests the extent to which Gaither music has influenced American music, especially commercially viable expressions of religious nostalgia in our postmodern era of irony. His stylistic influence is vast. In the 1970s, he pioneered praise and worship music with "There's Just Something about That Name," "Family of God," and other now canonical choruses. His inspirational songs—most famously "The King Is Coming"—have become anthems of contemporary evangelicalism. And he has penned modern hymns—"He Touched Me" and "Because He Lives"—that achieved something approaching instant-classic status upon their first appearing in Protestant hymnals. At the same time, the Gaither Trio was releasing landmark albums, including the early-1970s recording *At Home in Indiana*. It is a seminal artifact in the evolution of Christian music. Stylistically, the album demonstrates that the Gaithers' original tunes would hold up against and could coexist alongside everything from the southern gospel standard "I'll Fly Away" to the Jesus-people campfire favorite "Kum Ba Yah." Conceptually, the album adroitly anticipates the loss of generic boundaries that would transform Christian music in the 1980s and 1990s—a transformation that arguably receives its most expansive fulfillment in Gaither's own Homecoming series.

Second, Gaither has created economic platforms for his music that have become templates for mass-market Christian music theater, making him a socioeconomic and cultural pacesetter. Before the Homecoming tour, there were the Gaither Trio national tours in the 1970s and 1980s that innovatively used a traveling troupe of friends and a variety-show format. The Gaither Trio both shaped and was shaped by another innovation, Gaither's Praise Gatherings. These latter events succeeded in the 1970s by merging music, religious motivational speakers, and evangelists as a means of creating an extended religious encounter built around music but going well beyond it.[20] In the 1990s, Gaither opened the short-lived Celebration Theater in Branson, Missouri—a venture leveraged in part against the successes of the Gaither Trio and the annual Praise Gatherings. The theater failed, but it contributed to a set of interrelated enterprises that each prefigured in one way or another the Vegas-Broadway-Praise hybrid that the Homecoming videos and tour ultimately perfected.[21] Collectively, Gaither's portfolio of business ventures and innovations has made the Gaither name and style omnipresent in American Christian music, and this omnipresence lends to Gaither a certain aura of untouchability in the Homecoming series.

Taken together these dynamics—Gaither's stylistic influence and his nonpareil status—mean that when Gaither presides over highly emotional forms of expression from men that in other settings might be emasculating or discrediting, he effectively indemnifies his friends from any loss of esteem. Respected for his artistic achievements as a songwriter, admired for his support of younger artists, and revered for his business acumen and enormous wealth,[22] Gaither is nevertheless viewed as the perpetually wide-eyed fanboy, awestruck by the beauty and power of his beloved gospel music—rather like the way Garrison Keillor creates (by becoming) the object of his own awe onstage.[23] As a result, the Homecoming stage appears professionally nonthreatening, a space in which the leading men of gospel music can show vulnerabilities to religious emotionalism and spiritual feelings without seeming to have been domineered or unmanned.

Gaither reinforces the notion of his stage as a safe zone by including self-deprecating displays of his own ordinariness: playing up his halting way of speaking and regularly relying on comedy skits and jokes that revolve around making fun of Bill Gaither—his highly coiffed hair and big nose, his affectations onstage, his mediocre singing voice, even his fame itself.[24] Oddly enough, Gaither himself rarely loses his composure or emotes as demonstratively as most of his friends. To a certain extent, this bespeaks his role as the reassuring, self-possessed father figure. Insofar as the Homecoming moniker evokes the story of the prodigal son in the New Testament, Gaither occupies the role of the forgiving father waiting patiently at the gate. The transcendent power of gospel music's nostalgic sentimentality in which his shows specialize becomes embodied in Gaither himself. His preternatural self-possession onstage imparts to Gaither the air of an emotional regulator, unflappably inviting the very demonstrative expressions of religious affections that he himself almost always avoids.

Gaither's achievement has been to popularize a commercialized form of patriarchal religious emotionalism that portrays it as the inevitable consequence of the gospel message in song, rather than any individual personality. If, as the old song says, "I sing because I'm happy / I sing because I'm free," Gaither's Homecoming friends might be said to cry, repent, lament, rejoice, and testify because they sing gospel songs.[25] These effusions of emotion are not only the province of men in the Homecoming videos, of course. But the patriarchal tendencies of conservative Protestant Christianity in America make displays of emotion from men rarer and riskier if they want to retain broad appeal. In creating a platform where expressions of emotion by evangelical males are safe and encouraged, Gaither has implicitly redefined ordinary evangelical masculinity in ways that cut against old gendered polarities of conservative Christianity.

This is not to say that Gaither is a gender iconoclast. In 1992 Gaither wrote an autobiographical book, *I Almost Missed the Sunset*, about the need to reclaim godly manhood from the corruptions of modernity. Gaither illustrates this concept with scenes from his music career and life experience, much like a religious motivational speaker. (Indeed, the book gives reason to believe that Gaither was positioning himself for a second career in motivational speaking on the Christian conference circuit if Homecoming had not come along when it did.) In contrast to Gaither's explicitly gendered approach to spirituality in *Sunset*, Homecoming largely disaffiliates emotion from gender, reorganizing celebrities' religious identities around their attentiveness to the spirit's movement in song.

All this plays out on the Homecoming stage as a notionally gender-neutral experience that emphasizes equal access to the emotional realms of evangelical community. Instead of explicitly gendered performances or personae, the Homecoming series more often than not reveals a decidedly androgynous preoccupation with forms of discourse that call into being the significance of the cultural traditions being celebrated.[26] The cultural capital generated by these celebrations in turn can be deployed to revalue the past and to address a range of concerns and aspirations enmeshed within conservative evangelical popular culture: fears about the legitimacy of self and community and their traditions, desires for recognition of one's achievements beyond insular religious subcultures, and other diffuse but persistent needs to feel that one's work in the world matters and can be validated both internally by one's peers and externally by outsiders.

The Private Origins of Popular Culture

Retelling the history of Homecoming in his 2003 autobiography, *It's More than Music*, Gaither writes that the Homecoming idea took hold at a time when "it seemed as though the big days of my career were over. I was fifty-five years of age, and after enjoying a successful career writing and performing music for more than three decades, in 1991 the music world was about to pass me by."[27] This was not the first crisis of Gaither's career. Indeed, as he portrays himself in his 1992 autobiography, Gaither's public persona and personal identity have been forged in periodic passages of intense anxiety or upheaval about his ability to fulfill God's plan for his life. In his childhood, Gaither—born in 1936—describes himself as coming into awareness of the "big Russian bear" and the omnipresent threat of communism that pervaded the American imagination. He positions his early songwriting and singing career as a personal effort to turn back the encroaching godlessness of the red menace.[28] Remembering the end of the 1960s, when his career as a songwriter and publisher was beginning to take off, Gaither describes important evolutions in his writing and performance style that emerged directly in response to the "negativity" of cold war American life:

> Astronauts had walked on the moon, but leaders had been struck down too. John F. Kennedy, Robert F. Kennedy, and Martin Luther King, Jr. had been assassinated. There had been riots and looting, even death on college campuses. The "God is Dead" debate had raged during the 1960s too. The 1968 Democratic National Convention in Chicago had become an ugly spectacle. All that negativity gnawed in the back of my mind, having been raised under the threat of communism and with memories of the depression recounted nearly every day. Somehow, the decade we had come out of and the warnings I had grown up with didn't mesh with the all the good things that were happening in our ministry [i.e., the Gaither Trio and Gaither's publishing company].[29]

This vision of a world rife with hidden danger and unseen snares that disrupt peaceful life in bursts of psychosocial turbulence recurs often in Gaither's autobiographical writings—especially at pivotal moments in his professional development. Throughout the formative years of his early adulthood, Gaither writes about what he felt in terms that emphasize persistent "wondering" and a series of "private debates with myself" and "my psyche" about "unconfirmed reports that someone was questioning me," doubting his sincerity. The reports turned out to be true. In 1970 a close friend is said to have ultimately confronted Gaither and accused him of being a sellout and a fraud. The accusation was, in Gaither's retelling of it, "devastating," sending him into a "black hole"—a yearlong struggle with depression, mononucleosis, and creative drought from which he says he was unable to emerge until the arrival of his first son, whose birth in 1971 inspired Gaither and his wife to write one of their most famous compositions, "Because He Lives," which sets the fear of "uncertain days" against the promise of Christic redemption.[30]

It can be initially difficult to comprehend the intensity of the reaction to his friend's accusation that Gaither attributes to himself. No doubt the charge stung, but the response Gaither writes about is considerably disproportionate to the allegation itself, one clearly rooted in petty jealousies and fairly tame as personal attacks in the entertainment business go. How could someone rise to such prominence and success without a thicker skin?

Understood, however, as symptomatic of a cold war predisposition to worry over invisible enemies and hidden forces waiting in the shadows to destroy faithful Christians in moments of vulnerability, Gaither's response makes more sense. Gaither's autobiographical writings are suffused with an abiding anxiety about ominous, lurking threats to personal or professional identity. These concerns seem to participate in a more deep-set and encompassing network of fears not just about his own motives but about the stability of the Christian basis for mainstream American society in the generations after World War II. Perhaps not coincidentally, this anxiety was particularly intense in the early 1990s, when the collapse of Eastern European communism precipitated the realignment of geopolitical superpowers and spurred a pervasive sense of mass cultural change at all levels of life.

Gaither was not alone in worrying over masculinity in a postmodern moment. The same year he published *I Almost Missed the Sunset*, Robert Bly published his poetic meditation on emotionally enlightened masculinity, *Iron John*, which grapples with a secular-humanist version of Gaither's anxiety about the changes afoot in late-capitalist, postmodern, globalized America. But few people have spent as much of their adult lives on the very large stages that Bill Gaither has called home for more than fifty years. Working backward from Gaither's public persona and putting it in conversation with the other versions of his own life that he has variously constructed over the years, I read his persistent concern about the psychosocial effects of world-historical changes taking place at the end of the twentieth century to be the gestalt of Gaither's life and work, the dominant paradigm through which he makes music and understands his experience and career.

Though *It's More than Music* is less intimately autobiographical than *Sunset* and more explicitly aimed at capitalizing on the success of the Homecoming tour in the preceding decade, both books function at one important level as Gaither's literary efforts to cope with pervasive personal and professional anxiety by describing successes or turning points in his career as the initially unrealized gifts of a God-sent crisis. These crises humanize Gaither, whose fame might—as is so often the case with the famous—make him seem one-dimensionally impervious to ordinary feeling and failure. As Gaither had done in his 1992 autobiography, he begins his 2003 memoir with his middle-age crisis of relevance that beset him in the late 1980s and early 1990s just before Homecoming took off: "I was discouraged and slightly depressed as I considered my options, but I wasn't upset. . . . I was accustomed to seeing one aspect of my career wind down while another area of opportunity opened up. Granted, the line between the end and the beginning is sometimes hard to discern, like the line separating the sand from the sea. They seem to run together for a while, and what we think is an ending often becomes a new beginning."[31] Beyond the experience of low-grade depression at the contemplation of the bittersweet approach of the golden years, an experience with which many of his reading fans will personally identify, the passage strategically universalizes Gaither's experience. His own feelings are typical, in his telling, of the eternal ebb and flow of existence, conveyed here in the sand-and-sea imagery. The tide of life comes in and goes out for the famous and the ordinary alike, and God is on his throne in heaven through it all. Indeed, Gaither's two autobiographies collectively leave the impression that he sees himself as a kind of evangelical everyman whose experience has been writ large by God's uncommon blessings on an ordinary life of Christian service, song, sacrifice, and strife.

In his study of the late-nineteenth-century American response to "over-civilized" forms of modern existence, T. J. Jackson Lears has shown how moments of general cultural anxiety about historical change can give rise to widespread reactive transformations in American life that take particular historical shape in the dominant modes of an era's art and pop culture. Extended to the post–World War II generations, whose creative imaginations were forged by the realities of cold war America, Lears's approach suggests that Gaither's life, as described in his autobiographies, typifies a common reaction against a familiar set of anxieties and fears: offsetting private tensions and problems with public, professionally stylized responses. The Homecoming series is the most successful phase of Gaither's professional life. As such it stands as one highly visible example of how conservative American Protestantism responded to psychosocial instabilities common to aging evangelicals in the early 1990s. Not least among these are the encroachments of age and the possibility of professional irrelevance at a time of widespread upheaval in the last days of the cold war, which was ending just as Homecoming was coming to life. The emergence of these anxieties echo those earlier fears Gaither expresses about the doomsday scenarios associated with cold war apocalypse and other forms of modern nihilism. Just as Gaither describes his early songwriting as an act of resistance to modern godlessness, the Homecoming series emerges in *It's More than Music* as an archetypal commemoration of Christian entertainment's greatest generation and its increasingly unfashionable values. Indeed, Gaither describes the initial idea of Homecoming as a way of memorializing a tradition that Christian entertainment had largely forgotten by the end of the 1980s.[32] But as Lears suggests, what starts as resistance to change often becomes a change agent itself. So it is with the Homecoming series. For a large sector of evangelicals, Gaither Homecomings have come to function as a new idiom in which to engage and symbolically resolve contemporary feelings of irrelevancy and aspirations for renewed spiritual vigor in later life, offering a cold war moral clarity for postmodern experience.

While the Homecoming series' success involves its appeal to the nostalgic sentimentality of fundamentalist evangelicalism, the Homecoming Friends are popular and meaningful to a much wider range of conservative and moderate Christians. Devoted fans of southern gospel, which is overwhelmingly fundamentalist, tend to assume that because the cast of Homecoming Friends is drawn primarily from the pietistic world of southern gospel music, Homecoming matters mainly as a piece of popular culture from within conservative and fundamentalist Protestant Christianity. But the evidence points in another direction as well. Fairly soon after its inception, the Homecoming series began to attract much wider audiences than its original southern gospel fans. This wider appeal is evidenced in general by the series' widespread syndication on cable and premium-content channels (most prominently the now defunct cable station TNN). In particular, the popular prime-time television show *Touched by an Angel* built a two-part 2001 miniseries around a fictionalized version of the Homecoming series. Several of the Homecoming Friends, including Gaither and his Vocal Band, made cameos in the episodes devoted to that story line.[33] These data points demonstrate that the phenomenon crosses denominational, sociocultural, and geographic boundaries to include a wide range of middle-class, North American Protestants.

Perhaps most important, the Homecoming tour's theology has always been studiously ecumenical and nondenominational, full of denominationally generic celebrations of Christian charity and grace that conspicuously avoid the various theological thickets that separate different Protestant sects. Gaither elaborates on this philosophy of ecumenical performances in his second autobiography. There, he writes that from the earliest days of his career as a performer, he consciously chose "neutral, nonchurch environment[s]" for his concerts in order to attract "people from all church denominations" who could, in the process of experiencing his music, "realize that they had more in common than they had ever imagined."[34] This ecumenism helps explain why the tour and series enjoy such tremendous success far beyond the borders of southern gospel. Homecoming speaks to concerns generated by conflicts between orthodox Protestantism and globalized, late-capitalist postmodernity. These concerns are widely dispersed throughout the American middle class and not solely the province of fundamentalist Christians. As a result, Homecoming reunions of famous friends serve as a model for pan-Protestant religious affiliation across wide swaths of contemporary American life. If Homecoming initially emerged from Gaither's own sublimated crisis of socioreligious legitimacy, then it has succeeded and thrived by using religious musical entertainment to address a wider crisis of relevance afflicting contemporary evangelicalism.

Psychodynamically, the effect of this sublimation as it manifests itself in the Homecoming series is to create a musical screen onto which people from a wide range of Christian cultural traditions within the American middle class can project their own religious concerns and spiritual aspirations. On-screen and in person, in one video and concert after another, the Homecoming Friends come together in the name of Christian unity from a variety of genres, religious backgrounds, levels of achievement, and, as Graves has shown, often checkered pasts. This display serves as a testament to the power of gospel music to transcend conflicts between the sacred and the secular, as the stories told between musical numbers about the idiosyncrasies of an individual performer's career or troubled life experience are subsumed into the collective singing of songs in a southern gospel style. Whereas traditional southern gospel music stresses the ongoing struggle of the beset Christian, Homecoming focuses on the lessons of spiritual questing and the common bond of "experience"—a word Bill Gaither loves to use—in gospel music that unites the Homecoming Friends. This is not a difference of kind but of emphasis.

If it can be difficult for outsiders to take conventional southern gospel expressions of pious sentimentality entirely seriously, it can be equally difficult to understand why the Homecoming Friends are so very visibly happy, to the point of seeming artificially joyous. Indeed, they often sing most songs with an unrestrained enthusiasm betokened by broad, beaming smiles and exaggerated motions of the head and body. This happiness can be all the more perplexing given how regularly it contrasts with tearful remembrances of things past. But reflections on the past function as the predicate for present happiness: emotional memories serve to remind the Homecoming Friends—and their audiences and fans—that the past is worth remembering mainly because it is past, because it has been endured.

For instance, in the 2007 Homecoming recording *Joy in My Heart*, Bill Gaither asks Mylon LeFevre, one of the prodigal sons in Graves's study, to "say a few words" about his mother, the legendary pianist and vocalist Eva Mae LeFevre. Despite having been welcomed back into the Homecoming fold years before after a raucous career in rock and roll, LeFevre obviously is still considered a cultural outsider. He seems to recognize this and comments on it obliquely by making a self-deprecating reference to his long hair—a shorthand in the conservative world of southern gospel for a general moral degeneration and spiritual danger associated with the worldliness of newer forms of music.[35] After the joke about his hair, LeFevre begins a sentimental encomium to his mother, who stands at his side while he praises her spiritual resolve and commitment to a life in gospel music, much of it spent traveling backwoods dirt roads to perform in unamplified churches where Eva Mae had "to sing loud enough over the piano she was playing." LeFevre connects this perseverance to his mother's constant Christian witness before her family—"you lived [your faith] in front of me"—and concludes by saying how proud he is to be the son of a "wonderful godly mama." He and his mother then sing "Without Him." The now famous gospel song, written by LeFevre himself as a young adult before his fall from grace, testifies to the helplessness of the struggling Christian without the ever-ministering presence of the divine.[36]

This episode encapsulates Homecoming's manner of symbolically engaging the clash between traditional religious and modern secular society in order to subjugate modernity to the nostalgic ethos of gospel sentimentality. Having implicitly evoked the tension between southern gospel's Christian conservatism and the mainstream American culture of long hair and rock and roll, LeFevre's presence becomes the occasion for the triumph of evangelical values—voiced in a son's sentimental celebration of Christian motherhood—over the secular sinfulness embodied in the prodigal's wayward past. Gospel music becomes the catalyst for spiritual self-correction and moral reformation. Just as he has come home from his prodigality, his friends and their fans watching this homecoming can themselves symbolically reunite with the values and traditions being memorialized. This melodrama of social crisis and spiritual overcoming resonates with fans, who experience these Homecomings as powerful pageants of Christian faith translated into models for ordinary living. Of the arc of emotions evoked by a particularly poignant Homecoming finale, one fan commented to me, "The grief, the dismay and resentment; then half-fear half-wondering shock and amazement. It was totally amazing." This sort of statement suggests that the Homecoming series extends to its viewers an ongoing series of symbolic resolutions to the conflictual relationships modern evangelicals have with pluralistic, multicultural American society. What might initially appear as one-dimensional nostalgia in the Gaither series actually works as a cipher through which Homecoming Friends onstage and fans in the audience publicly manage both collective and individual crises of relevance and other obstacles to stable identity construction.

The underlying anxieties and tensions expressed in this process would appear to mirror and magnify those of a fifty-five-year-old Bill Gaither, anxious about how his legacy would be understood and remembered, if at all, in the early 1990s. Then, too, there are the many older, struggling gospel stars of decades past, arrayed onstage with Gaither, whom he resurrected from obscurity for the first Homecoming video in 1991 and whose careers were salvaged and made over in abundance by their involvement in the subsequent franchise. Finally, there are the many overlapping Homecoming audiences—public and private, in performance spaces and homes—who see in the story of Bill Gaither and the successive choirs of his Homecoming Friends a heartening parable of nearly forgotten saints whose lives have been redeemed from the dustbin of a rapidly secularizing American history. In this way, Homecoming's nostalgic revaluations of subcultural tradition speak to the common threat of obsolescence running just below the surface of the series—as well as American life in general—and reinforce the vital role that strategically deployed structures of feeling play in ameliorating such threats.

The Consolations of History

Thus far, I have argued for the emergence of the Homecoming phenomenon that began with the 1991 *Homecoming Video Album* as a psychosocial response to—and at some level a critique of—the historical contingencies of late-twentieth-century evangelical life in America. Though it would not go undisputed in the orthodox world of southern gospel, my reading has been reinforced by the consensus view in southern gospel that the Homecoming phenomenon began when a bunch of old southern gospel friends gathered in a Nashville studio one afternoon in 1991 and started singing. Indeed, from Bill Gaither on down, this story has been told and retold so many times that "consensus view" barely begins to capture the near-mythic proportions of its explanatory power among southern gospel insiders. This view is attractive not least of all because it neatly reconciles two strands of Gaither's image: one of Gaither the aw-shucks superfan of southern gospel, the other of Gaither the savvy, ever-evolving entrepreneur of Christian music able to seize on the unlooked-for or unexploited opportunity when it arises. But there are several reasons to justify questioning this narrative. In the first place, Gaither was casting about in his fifties much more actively for something to do with himself than his books let on: the first Homecoming taping dates from roughly the same time as the book in which he hints at positioning himself as a motivational speaker, as well as his failed attempt at the Branson theater and another gambit (also failed) to restart the once mighty Statesmen quartet.[37] More important is the sustained evidence that Gaither's musical mind and creative imagination had been tending in the direction that would become Homecoming for some time prior to its actual inception in 1991.

At different times and places, Gaither himself has hinted at parts of this less well-known history of Homecoming. Writing in *It's More than Music* about the years leading up to the emergence of Homecoming, Gaither describes a 1990 benefit concert he hosted for Rusty Goodman, the bass singer and leading songwriter for the Happy Goodman Family, who was dying of cancer at the time. Drawing on his vast connections in Christian music, Gaither assembled a stage full of Christian entertainment luminaries: among them Amy Grant, Larnelle Harris, Bebe and Cece Winans, Russ Taff, Steven Curtis Chapman, Sandi Patty, Gold City, the Imperials, J. D. Sumner and the Stamps, Ricky Skaggs, and Larry Gatlin. The concert featured performances honoring Goodman, as well as a highly sentimental "dramatic reading" written by Gloria Gaither and a nostalgic video montage of Goodman himself singing songs that became the signature tunes of his career: "Had It Not Been," "I've Got Leavin' on My Mind," and "Who Am I?" The inescapable fact of Goodman's rapidly failing health combined with the emotional charge of so many Christian entertainers from across generations and genres coming together—*coming home*—in one space created the kind of nostalgic, lachrymose, song-filled experience that southern gospel old-timers often refer to as a three-hankie special. Country music has the Grand Ole Opry to anchor its identity, but gospel music has no physical place to call home. Instead, home becomes, as it did at the Goodman benefit, a feeling constructed—"imagined" in Anderson's framework—from a shared outpouring of sentiment and nostalgia. According to Gaither, this free flow of deep emotion and the sense of homecoming it created profoundly influenced him. The benefit concert, he writes in *It's More than Music*, "increased my desire to get some of the old songs and singers on tape before it was too late."[38] Less than a year later, the *Homecoming Video Album* was recorded.

At the same time, there were other influences at work. Gaither sat for an interview with James Goff in 1996 that led the interviewer to describe Gaither and Homecoming as "inspired by Charles Waller's Grand Ole Gospel Reunion, begun in Greenville, South Carolina, in 1988."[39] If Gaither elaborated on the exact nature of the inspiration, Goff does not say, so we must infer the details of the connection. But GOGR, as it is affectionately known in southern gospel circles, clearly shares many of the basic features of the Homecoming franchise: evening concerts that reunite well-known groups of the past to sing southern gospel favorites, companion performances of new talent and established artists, the use of archival videos to augment the live performances, and an emphasis on comedy routines and other humorous material drawn from the specific history and personalities of southern gospel.[40] Video from the 1989 GOGR shows Gaither onstage leading a round of group singing in the same manner that would become so famously familiar in the later Homecoming videos: head titled back, mouth open wide in full-throated song, eyes tightly shut in pious concentration, fist thrust out and up, song-leader style, in a gesture of invitation to the crowd to join in. At one point, Gaither sits down at the piano and leads the GOGR choir, which includes many of the same people who would become Homecoming mainstays, in singing, among other songs, "Where Could I Go?" which was to be the tune at the heart of the inaugural *Homecoming Video Album* two years later.[41] So strikingly do some shots of the GOGR video resemble those from the *Video Album*, an unsuspecting viewer might be forgiven for mistaking one for the other. The similarities go further: the first mainstream Homecoming video produced after the 1991 experiment *Reunion: A Gospel Homecoming Celebration* even seems to echo the Grand Ole Gospel Reunion name. These connections are probably not coincidental. In another GOGR appearance a few months after the first Homecoming video was recorded in 1991, Gaither remarks from the stage that he "got the idea [for the first Homecoming video] from Charlie Waller."[42]

Nevertheless, Gaither omits mention of his GOGR experience in *It's More than Music,* billed as the unofficial autobiography of Homecoming. Perhaps because of this omission (or what it has been construed, rightly or wrongly, to imply about his attitude toward the Waller event), the debt that Homecoming does or does not owe to GOGR remains a hotly disputed subject in some quarters of southern gospel even today.[43] These debates, however, miss the point. The originality of Gaither's idea matters less than the forces that shaped it. GOGR was one source of inspiration, as was the Rusty Goodman concert. But more than either of these, Homecoming reflected and responded to Gaither's own low-grade but persistent crisis of relevance during a period of personal and sociopolitical upheaval. As an artifact of this struggle, the Homecoming phenomenon functioned from the first as a vehicle for the transmission of cultural history in a religious monoculture struggling to retain coherence under the multiple pressures of postmodernity.

For this reason, it is important to acknowledge that the 1991 *Homecoming Video Album* does have value as a point of origin for a musical style and brand that would redefine Bill Gaither's career and guarantee the success of southern gospel as a relevant form of Christian entertainment well into the new millennium. But the birth of Homecoming is best understood not as a starting point alone, but also as an ending point: as the culmination of southern gospel cultural history in the twentieth century. This history stretches back to the all-night quartet singings that first captivated Gaither's attention as a boy growing up in the 1940s and '50s. And it reaches back further still, to the singing-convention tradition from which the Homecoming phenomenon descends in spirit, style, and function, as I argue in the remainder of this chapter.

The Neoconventional Homecoming Aesthetic

One way to understand the Homecoming emergence within southern gospel is in the context of another video that Gaither recorded in 1991, the Bill Gaither Trio and the Gaither Vocal Band's *Live at the First Baptist Church of Hendersonville, Tennessee*. The Hendersonville taping is a classic example of Gaither's midcareer, pre-Homecoming performance style. Built around the Gaither Trio and the Gaither Vocal Band, Gaither's midcareer concerts involved a rotating cast of friends: in the Hendersonville video, these included Buddy Greene and Allison Durham, who were arrayed in chairs behind center stage. Periodically throughout the concert, these friends would perform both alone and with various ensembles assembled from whatever recombination of singers struck Gaither's fancy (at least the appearance of spontaneity was the desired effect). In his books, Gaither repeatedly talks about this approach as a way to keep the pace of the program from dragging and, more altruistically, as a means to promote the careers of young artists in the field.[44] Gaither seems to see himself as a bridge between artistic eras and styles in Christian entertainment, writing songs that were popularized by southern gospel groups like the Speers in the 1960s even as the Bill Gaither Trio supplanted those older groups and became the cutting edge of Christian music. Often when Gaither describes the Gaither Trio's most successful years selling out arenas and civic centers in the 1970s and 1980s and electrifying audiences around the country with evocative vocal performances, he does so with the same kind of exuberance and excitement he uses to recall the high-energy all-night gospel singings that captivated him as a child in packed concert arenas.

Those midcentury singings that heralded the golden age of commercialized southern gospel were, as we have already seen, direct descendants of the gospel singing convention. The convention-singing tradition emerged in the late nineteenth and early twentieth centuries when amateur singers would gather between harvest and planting seasons in the agrarian South and Midwest to sight-read the best new music and the most beloved gospel favorites. By the 1920s and 1930s, singing conventions were beginning to spawn popular groups of particularly talented singers who were featured as special guests before or during regular convention singing. But by the 1940s, those special guests were parlaying singing-convention popularity into self-sufficient careers as professional performers whose concerts were luring participants away from singing conventions and turning them into paying audience members at live-performance concerts (even if the price of admission was often only a freewill love offering). The emergence of fully professionalized southern gospel music in the 1950s drastically diminished the vitality of convention singing, and ever since the 1950s and 1960s, which saw the rise of nationally touring gospel artists, southern gospel convention singing has tended to have more of a symbolic than a musical influence on the gospel industry.

Though the singing-convention tradition persists in pockets throughout the South, it shows up in commercial southern gospel today mostly as a novelty. Shape-note singing—the singing-convention method of music education that dates back to the postbellum South and uses shapes associated with one of the seven separate pitches on the Western major scale to teach sight reading—and convention-style piano playing are often featured in southern gospel concerts. The trio Greater Vision, for instance, has for many years now often included a "gather round the ole red book" segment of the show. During these interludes, the group sings an old convention standard, such as "I'm Wingin' My Way Back Home" or "Well Done, My Child," including at least one verse vocalizing the do-re-mis in place of words.[45] But even in these instances, convention singing appears mainly as a quaint relic or residual influence from an older generation of mentors and teachers.

Appropriated this way, the midcentury heyday of convention singing would seem to survive as a treasure in the collective imagination of southern gospel artists and fans. In this form, the convention tradition reminds audiences of a simpler era of music and fellowship before careerist tendencies hardened the lines between amateurs and professional musicians—a golden age revered but outmoded, much like the performers Gaither plucked from obscurity to help create Homecoming. But cultural legacies have a way of being subtly reimagined over time, whether consciously or not. So it is with the legacy of convention singing and Gaither Homecomings in contemporary southern gospel. Far from being an obsolete artifact of southern gospel's precommercial adolescence, the convention-singing culture not only persists today among a small group of shape-note devotees, but has also been absorbed, transformed, and repurposed in professional southern gospel music by the Homecoming phenomenon, which resembles nothing so much as a convention singing with brighter lights, more famous singers, and a transatlantic touring schedule.

The kernel of what I call Gaither's neoconventional Homecoming aesthetic is present in the midcareer performance style as captured in the Hendersonville taping. There, in the revolving host of friends performing with the Gaither Trio and the Vocal Band, it is possible to see a faint—and as yet undeveloped, but nevertheless real—echo of the singing convention's emphasis on variety of talent and stylistic diversity that Gaither so studiously scrutinized as a child at Wally Fowler's all-night sings in Nashville and later studied as a teenage student at the Stamps-Baxter School of Music.[46] Moreover, it is not just the presence of a diverse roster of onstage "friends" that signals the neoconventional element of Gaither's style. The positioning of gospel singers in the performance space itself has been of "utmost importance" in the convention style going back to the early years of singing conventions. Indeed, William Lynwood Montell's description of how convention singings were arranged could easily be mistaken for the stage directions in large ensemble moments of the Hendersonville taping: singers "often stood in a circle in the open space between the front pew and the pulpit" in "vocal groupings" that allowed the group to showcase their "musical expertise."[47]

The formal features of convention singing that remain latent in the Hendersonville taping receive more explicit development in the *Homecoming Video Album*. This latency reinforces the underlying significance in Homecoming of structures of expression and aesthetic organization first forged in the convention-singing culture. Because the *Homecoming Video Album* is a more informal recording than the Hendersonville taping, it captures the unfolding in minimally edited live footage of the Gaither vision in action—by which I refer not just to the vision of Gaither himself, but also to the collective effect of the decisions and efforts of those with whom he surrounds himself. On-screen, the *Homecoming Video Album* experience alternates between jolly pandemonium and nostalgic sentimentality. Often while people are singing and playing, others chat and stand on chairs in the middle of songs, calling out for different singers to come forward to sing in a way not unlike the calling out of songbook page numbers so common in convention singing. Other singers are permitted to mill about in the studio without any awareness or concern for camera angles and video sight lines. At other times, the group weeps openly over the past. Perhaps the most intense moment comes when Howard Goodman recites, from unprompted memory, the monologue in the middle of "I Don't Regret a Mile," complete with Vestal standing behind him and offering interpretative hand motions with her fist full of the trademark hankie she always clutched onstage.

Through it all, old habits of singing and forms of entertainment first popularized by singing conventions reemerge apparently spontaneously. Artists, most of whom were trained at singing-convention normal schools, line up in the familiar convention semicircle grouped by parts—at Gaither's direction during the "Where Could I Go?" taping—apparently by force of habit and memory during a later and even less formal afternoon session. A variety of selected voices from the larger group are combined and recombined to form small ensembles throughout the video. And as in the singing-convention tradition, a sense of good-humored competitiveness suffuses performances. Most memorably, Rosa Nell Speer Powell and Howard Goodman mount a four-handed attack on the piano during an old convention song. Goodman does his best to goad some kind of reaction out of Powell, first by muscling onto the piano bench with her, later with a series of high-handed antics—literally: Goodman popularized a method of playing rhythm on the piano that involves alternately flipping each hand at the wrist high above the keyboard, creating a dizzying blur. But Powell resolutely plays it straight with him the whole time.

At some basic level, the continuities between the Homecoming style and convention singing are not that surprising. People do what they remember, and the music of performers who came of age artistically at a time when singing conventions were still popular naturally bears the marks of its moment. But as Michael Kammen has shown in his landmark study of the transformation of tradition in American culture, resurgent interest in, attention to, or reliance on historical forms of cultural expression often signals a more deeply set and complex relationship between past and present than surface connections suggest.[48] In this context, Homecoming's neoconventional style draws on earlier traditions as a rich imaginative resource. Homecoming videos never slavishly imitate singing-convention forms. Nor do videos or the concerts that came later ever adopt specific techniques of the convention-singing method, except in conscious moments of homage like "gathering round the ole red book." Rather, the Homecoming phenomenon has come to succeed in no small part by reidiomizing the fundamental aesthetic structure of convention singing.

The branded image of "Homecoming Friends" musically commemorating their friendship works by commodifying the convention-singing emphasis on bonds of Christian community forged among singing saints. At the same time, individually highlighted voices or small groups assembled from within the Homecoming choir create their celebrity by commercially harnessing the esteem first accorded the skilled artisan or on-command performer in the singing-convention tradition. The insistence on high performance standards is an especially important connective tissue linking the two phenomena. Though Homecoming relies on the image of old friends drawn together solely by their regard for one another, they are actually each carefully selected by the Homecoming operation from among the ranks of professional musicians in gospel and contemporary Christian music. Mainstream southern gospel values personality over musical ability on the whole, and Homecoming would struggle to maintain its reputation for outdoing its own arrangements and performances in successive videos if just anyone could be counted a Homecoming Friend. Simultaneously, the series reinforces its own reputational appeal by staging concerts in increasingly sensational locations (Jerusalem, Carnegie Hall, South Africa) or nostalgic venues (the Ryman Auditorium, predecessor to the Grand Ole Opry, or the Paramount theater in Gaither's hometown of Anderson, Indiana).

This emphasis on musical excellence and renown contrasts sharply with the rise of amateurs and other performers of varying abilities who have come to dominate much of the southern gospel industry over the past three decades, especially since digital recording and reproduction have lowered the economic barriers to entry into commercial music careers. In this contrast, the Homecoming franchise mirrors midcentury convention singing, which prized musical craftsmanship over good intentions: "You didn't go [to conventions in the 1950s and '60s] to hear bad groups," as one Kentucky conventioneer put it. "If you couldn't do it right, you didn't stand up and sing," another recalls.[49] In light of all these parallels, Gaither's approach to the Homecoming series might well be described as a sustained effort to modernize the aesthetic of midcentury convention singing and create a participatory model of musical excellence in postmodern Christianity.

Just how consciously has Gaither thought of the Homecoming experiment as an artistic—as opposed to a purely historical—descendant of midcentury gospel singing conventions? By most available evidence, not very. The informality and chaotic nature of that first Homecoming video suggest participants, including Gaither, were relying mostly on habit and instinct. Even when the series has explicitly referenced midcentury convention singing, it has seemed to matter to Gaither only because of its historical significance and not because he thought of the Homecoming phenomenon or himself as artistically neoconventional. Instead, Gaither seems to have viewed himself in this period as an impresario bestride—or seated at the piano between—two worlds in the popular music of American evangelicalism. In this position, he was able to use his prestige in the mainstream Christian entertainment industry to reassert the relevance of southern gospel not just as a historically important style of religious expression but also as an artistic tradition with continued relevance.

As the pivot point between past and present, Gaither can symbolically fuse the contributions of younger artists and older performers in a dialectical synthesis of nostalgia and modernity. Of course, to some extent, Gaither's music has always emerged from some version of this synthesis, echoing the ways in which nostalgia served modernity throughout the twentieth century in southern gospel. But it was not until the Homecoming movement that the self-conscious juxtaposition of past and present came so explicitly to the fore of Gaither's work or southern gospel generally. As figures from gospel music's long ago come into musical contact with the newer generations of gospel artists in the Homecoming experience, the videos create a sense of their own historicity through a nostalgic reengagement in the present with the pastness of the past as represented by its faded stars and their stories and songs. The Homecoming series allows the viewer to create an illusion of experiencing the future significance of the recorded event in the present. In essence, audiences become participants in history.

The Frisson of Participation

Montell has argued that midcentury singing conventions ultimately lost their dominance in southern gospel because an emerging middle class was increasingly disinclined to support participatory forms of entertainment. Audiences for convention singing "gradually moved away from entertaining themselves and sought instead to be entertained," mostly by professional quartets that did not require audiences to participate the way convention singing did.[50] Montell is right to see the demise of the singing convention as a historical symptom of a shift in consumer tastes tied to broader socio-economic realignments within southern and midwestern working classes. Upwardly mobile evangelicals associated singing conventions with a less sophisticated lifestyle: informal, sometimes raucous, always crowded, and, in the summer, hot and sweaty.[51] But Homecoming's neoconventional performance styles suggest that the decline of participatory musical events among conservative evangelicals was not a rejection of the idea of participating in their own entertainment, as Montell claims. Rather, audiences were rejecting only the way that participatory entertainment was being delivered. Abandoning singing conventions was a way of implicitly putting pressure on popular modes of southern gospel performance to acknowledge the changing circumstances of life and shifting cultural norms for white, conservative evangelicals of southern extraction.

From the 1960s through the 1980s, the tastes and purchasing power of these middle-class evangelicals helped propel the development of mass-market Christian entertainment popularized by (among others) groups such as the Bill Gaither Trio and, later, the Gaither Vocal Band. Gaither's hybrid style of inspirational gospel music spoke to a generation of white Christians with tastes and tendencies very much like Gaither's. These people were imaginatively curious but still conservative, eager to experiment with new forms of religious expression—at least to the extent that traditional southern gospel rapidly came to seem too conventional—but unwilling to wander off into the high weeds of Jesus-movement spiritualism or the "Jesus is my boyfriend" style of music popularized by contemporary Christian music and its preoccupation with religious songs that sound virtually indistinguishable from mainstream American pop and rock.

If the psychospiritual concerns of a generation were writ large in Gaither's early work, then his midlife anxiety in the early 1990s about growing old in a postmodern world might help explain more than just his own openness to more explicitly nostalgic modes of musical performance foregrounded in the Homecoming series. Understood as a successor to midcentury participatory singing conventions, the Homecoming series succeeds by redefining the role of the postmodern evangelical consumer. Once passive spectators of musical events who dominated Christian music in the 1970s and 1980s, these fans become active participants in the making of history that the Homecoming series allows. After all, there are few historic events that no one is around to witness. Witnessing Homecoming music whether live or on a video becomes a commodifiable form of participation in a self-selected community of cowitness-participants. As the future's witness to gospel history being made in the present tense of the video or concert, viewers can experience and really *feel* the frisson of participation—*I'm a witness to gospel music history in the making at this concert*—without having to undertake any of the actual behaviors and actions that the average southern gospel audience would have been obliged to participate in fifty or seventy-five years ago. No need for the audience to sing, except for maybe a few bars of "There's Something about That Name" after one of Gloria Gaither's recitations. No unseemly Battle of the Songs[52] to decide who performed better or sang the highest or hit the lowest note. The audience's job is to *not* to do any of this. Instead, audiences watch and listen. They witness a version of what Hayden White calls the "present *as* history."[53]

Through Homecoming participatory Christian entertainment is shorn of the homemade do-it-yourselfness associated with midcentury singing conventions. Homecoming audiences can retain the spectatorial distance so essential to middle-class consumers' identity, without surrendering their status as meaning-making participants in a religious community constructing its own cultural identity and historical narrative through sacred musical arts. At a moment of great individual and collective upheaval for a generation of Christian music consumers preparing, as Gaither was in the early 1990s, for their sunset years, the Homecoming series reassuringly evokes the singing convention's long-familiar methods of making meaning about the self and world collectively. Simultaneously, Gaither's style of music creates an enormous fund of optimism about an idealized future rooted in the strength of Christian friendship renewed through the heritage of southern gospel music. Indeed, following Anderson's emphasis on the role of imagination in the construction of collective identities, Homecoming might be said to function as a framework within which evangelicals can construct an imagined, idealized religious community. These communities are capable of achieving a degree of moral coherence, fervent piety, and cultural distinction unavailable in the world of lived experience.[54]

This aspect of Homecoming's appeal testifies to the durability of nostalgia as a structuring component of (post)modern imagination, especially in contemporary evangelicalism.[55] Homecoming is not the first appearance of this dynamic in white gospel in the southern tradition, as I show elsewhere in the book, but it is the most explicit version of an imaginative process at work throughout the music's history. Indeed, one of the origins of this study has been my persistent uneasiness with the historically dubious way Homecoming performers and fans luxuriate in enthusiastic sentimentality and self-indulgent nostalgia, as if the experiences created during Homecoming concerts are meaningful primarily as efforts to escape reality and return to the simpler spiritual times of the all-day sings, dinner on the ground, and do-re-mis—an era that has never existed in such idealized form, except in the imagination. Appreciating how the present and past continually interact to reshape contemporary images of individual and collective identity almost inevitably means complicating the stories we tell ourselves about our relation to history and its meanings. But with complication also comes, in this case, a more complete and more meaningful sense of the sustaining effects of southern gospel as an imaginative tradition, and its ability to engender new forms of expression from the artistic legacies bequeathed from one generation of southern gospel music to the next.

5. Southern Gospel
   in the Key of Queer

In most quarters of the southern gospel music industry, it is axiomatic that behind every gospel song, there is a gay man somewhere. But then again, I would say that. I am, after all, what I have come to think and write about as a southern gospel sissy: a gay man who loves gospel music not despite the fact that he is gay but, as I argue in this chapter, *because* he is a queer, a misfit, a fag, a homo, a sodomite, or, most often, a sinner. There are many of us out there. Enough, at any rate, that even among those orthodox gospel music insiders who would find the very term *southern gospel sissy* to be blasphemous, the fact that queer people—particularly gay males—are involved in almost every aspect of the music's creation, production, performance, and consumption constitutes a widely accepted open secret.

As D. A. Miller has shown, such open secrets about homosexuality operate by a cultural logic that tacitly acknowledges the existence of queer lives and experience and readily accepts their contributions, but suppresses the positive reality of their presence with a "loquacity of prohibition."[1] Miller's interest centers on midcentury Broadway show tunes, and the title of his autoethnographic study of Broadway and queerness, *Place for Us*, prefigures the book's interest in locating the sites—onstage, within the audience, and in the imagination—where gay men have found surreptitious but meaningful affirmations of their identities despite the pervasive homophobia of dominant culture.[2]

Miller's formula has powerful explanatory potential for opening up the sustained inquiry I wish to undertake here into the gay male's fraught place in the world of southern gospel. The secretive part of the open secret about the gay side of southern gospel leads to a negating proscription of nonheterosexual identities and experiences that strives to render them invisible. This strictly enforced silence helps sustain the public illusion of southern gospel as always already straight and narrow. But as an *open* secret, the long-standing presence of homosexuals throughout white gospel culture generates theological and cultural dissonances that inevitably surface in intensely negative prescriptions of gay male lives, whether in the form of direct denunciations of homosexuality in written or spoken sermonettes from industry leaders or less overt repudiations of male homosexuality implied by a joke popular among gospel emcees about how hard it is to find a tenor singer who looks like a man but sings like a woman. Predicating the public discussion of homosexuality on polemics and punch lines—a southern gospel version of Miller's "loquacity of prohibition"—is one way that evangelical popular culture enforces what Adrienne Rich dubs "compulsory heterosexuality." As one prominent record executive said shortly after his company severed its relationship with a recently outed singer, "In our business, we deal with the market and the ministry. And those two issues have to mesh."[3] What he means is that the business side of southern gospel effectively monetizes fundamentalist evangelical biblical literalism. The southern gospel industry places a symbolic and an economic premium on monogamous heterosexual marriage as the ideal expression of Christian identity among southern gospel professionals, while simultaneously and radically devaluing nonheterosexuality.

Such silences and effacements are, as Nadine Hubbs has shown in her study of twentieth-century American composers and the role sexuality played in their artistic visions, powerful expressions of heterocentrism: "The denial and erasure of queer lives and contributions in historical accounts of twentieth-century U.S. culture reflect that culture's suffusion in homophobia. Homophobic culture provides ample incentive for nonqueer-identified commentators to uphold queer-effacing views, including the dominant myths that assert heterosexuals' exclusive place in cultural and social production and reproduction." In southern gospel, this heterosexual exclusivity contributes to an environment in which no prominent southern gospel artists have ever openly identified themselves as gay or lesbian while maintaining a full-time career in the industry. There *have* been cases in which homosexuality has become a prominent issue within the industry. Perhaps most famously, gospel tenor Kirk Talley was outed in 2003 when the FBI arrested a man who tried to blackmail Talley with indiscreet photographs he had shared on a gay chat site. Around the same time, Bill Gaither, arguably the industry's most successful songwriter and performer, and the eponymous impresario of the Homecoming Friends concert tour and video series, was photographed embracing an openly lesbian songwriter. Gaither had featured her music at one of his concerts and spoken from the stage about a song she had written in terms that many fans construed to be a tacit endorsement of homosexuality. But even these are the kind of exceptional examples that prove the rule of carefully enforced silence and denial surrounding the discussion of homosexuality in southern gospel: Talley subsequently sought the counsel of a "Restoration Team" comprising conservative evangelical pastors and a few prominent male figures from southern gospel. This group supervised a purification rite and a version of "reparative" therapy that concluded with a public statement from the team certifying Talley's fitness to return to the stage, although he has nevertheless largely been shunned as a performer. In Gaither's case, the outcry over the photograph and his public comments ultimately led him to issue a statement emphatically denouncing the songwriter and lamenting her "sad" life as a lesbian.[4]

These stories—the primary source of public information about what it means to be gay in gospel music—never end well. Such unhappy endings, combined with the emcees' jokes about "sister tenor" or onstage polemics about the biblical basis for opposite-sex marriage, doubtless help account both for the negative perception of homosexuality in southern gospel and for the widespread aversion among queer individuals to speak openly about their experience or involvement in evangelical popular culture for fear of reprisals or alienation.[5] Moreover, very few textual or artifactual traces of queer life exist to document the extensive role that nonheterosexuals play in the industry.

At the same time, my own experience as a gay man closely involved with gospel music—as a lifelong fan, an erstwhile Southern Baptist gospel pianist, and a scholar—attests to the powerful persistence of queer lives in, and contributions to, southern gospel culture despite its antimodern attitudes toward nonheterosexual ways of being. Though I have met all manner of gay and gay-friendly fans, performers, and other industry professionals through my writing and research about southern gospel, I can think of no better example of the thriving queer culture in gospel music than an annual social gathering in Nashville mostly consisting of gay male southern gospel professionals, who rather campily refer to the event as the Pink Party. Part religious experience, part cabaret, part family reunion, the Pink Party revolves around renditions of gospel songs by queer—though not always gay—writers or singers in an environment where there is no open secret, just openness. Still, the event has its critics. A columnist for *Inside Out Nashville*, a weekly periodical focused on the queer community in Music City, blasted gay men who choose to work in Christian entertainment as hypocrites and, and on that basis, described the Pink Party as "one of the most cynical and creepy statements of our society."[6] But this characterization bears no resemblance to what I have experienced there, which might best be described as unconditional affirmation of both the redemptive promise of evangelical spirituality and the experiential vitality of gay male sexuality. Looking around the room at this event, I have often marveled at how many of those present have been responsible for new hit songs and canonical favorites beloved by countless fans, how many have been and are recipients of the industry's highest honors, how many were or continue to be integral parts of famous groups revered for their orthodox piety. Which is to say, the Pink Party vividly captures the gay-gospel paradox of southern gospel music: the most culturally fundamentalist sacred music in evangelicalism could hardly be said to exist without queers and their contributions as fans, songwriters, performers, producers, players, and industry executives.

This chapter stands as my effort to recover the long-overlooked and serially misunderstood queer dimension of southern gospel. To be sure, there are significant cultural resistances and structural obstacles to documenting the history of individual queer lives and experiences reticulated throughout southern gospel. But this reality should not prevent a robust inquiry into queer modes of southern gospel expression, long obscured by the punitive silence and punishing stigma of fundamentalist homophobia. Although my aim here is to pierce that silence and challenge the stigma, it will fall to others to write the definitive documentary history of queer contributions to southern gospel. My goal is to reimagine southern gospel music as abidingly indebted to a fundamentally queer aesthetic. Judith Peraino has defined "queer" as "an unsteady state of questioning one's sexual identity," implying "that there might not be a conclusion, but also that 'identity' might not be restricted to 'sexuality.'"[7] Adapting Peraino's definition for my purposes, I use the concept of a queer aesthetic in southern gospel as shorthand for a transformational indeterminacy of psychospiritual identity generated in the experience of southern gospel music. This indeterminacy is defined by the presence of conflictual energies within the self and clashing components of identity held by the music in paradoxical, expressive tension—affirmed and integrated yet retaining their individual integrity—like notes in southern gospel's close harmony, whose captivating force often builds up around the movement from dominant to tonic, or within the space between discordance and consonance. In this model, the felt experience of idiosyncratic subjectivity matters more than whatever orthodox categories of identity that experience may be said to indicate (saved, saint, reprobate, sinner, and the like), just as experiencing musical sound matters more than its formal description. The centrality of a queer aesthetic in southern gospel raises the possibility that the self may exceed orthodoxy's available labels—a dynamic that is vividly captured by, but not limited to, the experience of the southern gospel sissy. The gay-gospel paradox I am identifying gives rise to a contest over cultural authority that, whatever else it may signify, fundamentally exemplifies a much more far-reaching heuristic struggle over what the music can *mean,* to whom and how.

Southern gospel piano teachers are fond of reminding their students that it is often hearing the notes you do not play that matters most. So it is with this undertaking. My approach here necessarily entails a careful academic reading of what is *not* said about nonheterosexuality in a heteronormative culture—or what is sayable only given the expressive freedom provided by written works of the imagination, on which this chapter periodically draws. Following what Miller, Judith (now Jake) Halberstam, and Adale Sholock have variously shown in their work on the first person in queer studies, my inquiry here is also deeply informed by my own experience as a gay man who has never known a time when gospel music was not an integral part of his life. In some ways, I have served throughout this book thus far as a version of what John Champagne calls a "privileged marginal," attempting to leverage my position with a foot in two worlds to mediate between the secular and sacred audiences encompassed by my approach.[8] In this chapter, my inquiry comes as close as I have yet been to the first person evoked by the book's title and the open-ended possibilities it is meant to suggest for transformative acts of self-fashioning in the idiom of southern gospel music.

The (Queer) Music of Misfits

I grew up and came of age as in love with southern gospel music as I was in closeted denial about my own sexuality. Similar to Miller's younger self cloistered in the basement of his family home with a stack of cast recordings from Broadway shows, a record player, and a vivid imagination of himself onstage, I spent countless hours at my family's piano learning every gospel song I heard or could find in the old songbooks I would pilfer from the choir rooms at the rural Baptist churches where my father was the pastor and where I was often the church pianist or organist. I have never been more than an adequate pianist, but in my imagination, when I played gospel songs, I was a flawless cross between Liberace and Hovie Lister, the famous, flashy pianist and showy emcee for the legendary Statesmen quartet.

It did not take much imagining to conjure this hybridized image. Most gospel groups tend toward a flamboyant, outsized, sentimental style—both in manner and in music—that is not as consciously queer as Liberace, but is certainly as campy. As is so often true in southern gospel, the Goodman Family singers typify the larger trend. The first time I saw Vestal Goodman in concert, she came sweeping down the center aisle of the auditorium, singing an a cappella chorus of the old gospel hymn "Revive Us Again." This was her signature entrance late in her career: moving majestically toward the stage in a flowing floor-length gown of clashing pastels, trailing clouds of glory and too much perfume. Vestal, as she is universally known, preferred big hair—in the Goodmans' heyday, it was not uncommon for her beehives to rise well over a foot off her head—an amplitude of maquillage and large, gaudy costume jewelry. Onstage she could call forth her own copious tears seemingly at will, inflecting her singing voice with a weepy quaver that threatened to disintegrate into unspeakable grief at any moment. She was large and loud and did nothing subtly, least of all when singing her lines. Her voice was an expansive, often bombastic alto, which gave her the capacity to sing lead in the ensemble with her husband and brothers-in-law or to help create unique harmonies unmatched by the all-male quartets.

The most famous Goodman ending to a song involved a chordal struc-ture that placed Vestal's voice at the top of the harmonic configuration. Whereas the highest harmonic position in southern gospel quartet music is typically a third above the chord's home base and sung by the tenor, Vestal could sing harmony a full fourth or more above the melody line, creating an uncommonly expansive sound. Her dream as a child had been to sing opera, and despite the vast distance between opera and gospel, something of the operatic diva infused her gospel singing style, particularly the way she deployed what David Bruce Murray has called "curly-cue endings," in which her voice "hung above the final pitch before resolving with a flour-ish."[9] Such vocal arabesques were thrilling crowd pleasers—and as she aged, an increasingly risky vocal move. It doubly taxes a singer not only to hold a pitch in harmony against other singers but also to sing an idiosyncratic musical phrase while three other voices are resolving to their own indepen-dent pitches. Late in life her voice would sometimes crack or go flat as she deployed her curly-cue finales, but she sang on, head turned heavenward while steadfastly waving her lace-trimmed hankie at audiences.[10] They—we—were transfixed by her.

For some time now, the thinking both within and beyond the Christian music world has been that the flamboyance and theatricality in Christian entertainment that Vestal Goodman epitomized explain why gay guys like me are attracted to the music. Anthony Heilbut is among the most promi-nent voices to assert this theory in his landmark history of black gospel.

"Since gospel is theatrical," he writes, "and theater is the paradigm for much of gay life, gospel has a special allure for gays." There is a certain attractive simplicity to this formulation's clean causal lines. It indeed neutralizes what is to many fans and professionals the off-putting presence in religious music of "gospel homosexuals" (as Heilbut calls us) to understand the phenomenon in terms of one-dimensional stereotypes about the stagy outlandishness of theatrical queens.[11] But as an interpretive model, it creates more issues than it addresses. As Philip Brett and Elizabeth Wood have persuasively argued, "The fact that homosexual people represent different, sometimes opposing, stylistic and ideological positions, no matter what part of the music business they are involved in, argues against a unified 'homosexual sensibility' in music."[12] In this light, Heilbut's theory perpetuates a heterocentric perspective that reduces nonheterosexuality to an oversimple monolith defined by its most unorthodox gestures or queerest tropes.

Heilbut is not wrong to observe a link between homosexuality and theatricality, but he deduces from this dynamic a dispositive explanation for the gay-gospel paradox by isolating gay experience and then completely ignoring the broader context. First, gospel's flamboyant pageantry does not exist on some frequency only homosexuals can hear. It is in fact an elemental part of the music that, statistically speaking, appeals to far more heterosexuals than homosexuals. Second, and more important, no matter how much southern gospel's style of show business may intensify its basic appeal, that appeal is more about the experience of the music and lyrics than about the costumes and personalities. What this situation indicates is not that homosexuals cultivate a separate connection to the music reflecting their queerness. Rather, the queer dimension of southern gospel is a fundamental part of its overall appeal that can be best understood by examining the queerer sectors of the southern gospel expressive spectrum.

Let me illustrate this point with an excursion into the world of musical divas and gospel drag, particularly the popularity of Vestal Goodman—both as a performer to be imitated by other southern gospel artists and as a character for drag queens to inhabit in performances in gay bars in the South.[13] Viewed as a manifestation of "gay culture" in a southern context, there is much that drag queens' performance of gospel reveals about the way elements of evangelical entertainment are repurposed in queer culture. Indeed, Jeffrey Bennett and Isaac West read drag-queen covers of "Looking for a City," one of Vestal Goodman's signature songs about the sainted pilgrim's lonely search for heaven's haven of rest while toiling here on earth, as a "utopic invocation of a more accepting world" for homosexual men marginalized in a heterodominant culture. In the context of the gay bar, gospel drag "transmutates the gospel classic into a call for action on the part of the audience."[14]

It may seem that we are far afield from orthodox southern gospel, but in fact these drag performances emerge from, and so magnify constitutive features ordinarily submerged beneath the surface of, southern gospel's psychodynamics. The drag scene, after all, is not the only—or even the first—place where Vestal Goodman's inimitable style has been memorialized by impersonators. The Perrys, a Goodmanesque family foursome comprising three males and the strong alto of Libbi Perry Stuffle, have capitalized upon both the similarity of Stuffle's voice to Vestal's as well as the two women's friendship while Vestal was alive. Since Goodman's death in 2003, Stuffle has become southern gospel's strongest link to Vestal Goodman, largely on the basis of Stuffle's striking ability to sing "God Walks the Dark Hills" in a manner that sounds eerily like Vestal. More recent imitators have even more explicitly paralleled the drag bar's male impersonations of Vestal. In 2009 a then fourteen-year-old boy named Cody Logan Smith became an instant celebrity in southern gospel for his imitation of Vestal singing another of her signature songs, "What a Lovely Name," at the National Quartet Convention and later at a Bill and Gloria Gaither Homecoming Friends concert. What Smith was unable to achieve in terms of Stuffle's precise stylistic verisimilitude he made up for with the novelty of an adolescent boy singing like the grand dame of southern gospel. At the NQC, the crowd roared with delight for Smith. His gender-bending performance in turn echoes what is perhaps the most famous instance of a male coming to fame sounding like Vestal. First tenor Johnny Cook sang Goodman's part in the 1970s when she had to take a sabbatical from the road and remained with the group for a short time after Goodman returned. Cook was a short, slight man—the Goodmans, a famously girthy group, made much of Cook's stature, often announcing his weight (135 pounds) as one would a boxer's before he and Vestal would "compete" to sing the vocally demanding chorus of "Looking for a City" in successively higher keys. Cook—a man imitating a woman who competes with a male version of her own voice—invariably won these sing-offs in a way that indirectly queered the stability of what Judith Butler has called "coherent gender" roles prescribed by dominant culture.[15]

These increasingly queerer appropriations of Vestal Goodman from within the mainstream of the southern gospel imagination—from Stuffle and Smith through to Cook—clearly exist, it seems to me, on a continuum with gay-bar drag queens (who, it is worth noting, often stage their own "Looking for a City" sing-offs).[16] Though they do so at different levels of visibility and intentionality, each imitation has the effect of redefining Goodman's status as a gospel diva. The musical diva is a fixture of gay culture—Judy Garland is the classic case—brash and bold yet self-consciously affected and emotionally needy. Divas "encourage a shared emotionalism, vulnerability, and perseverance" that can be "captivating to gay audiences,"[17] intimately familiar as so many gay people are in the experience of being vulnerable and with the necessity of learning to be perseverant. In southern gospel, divas are more commonly referred to as gospel's leading ladies: among them Goodman, of course, but also Dottie Rambo, Karen Peck, Brenda Ruppe, Kim Hopper, Peg McKamey, Taranda Greene, and, not least of all, Libbi Stuffle. These women each have their own idiosyncratic appeal, but their performance personae share a basic preference for melodramatic and emotionally self-indulgent engagements with the tragic element of evangelical spirituality. Insofar as the gospel diva appeals to audiences in a manner very similar to the ones divas of mainstream American music have relied upon to amass enormous gay followings, it is possible to read the phenomenon of the gospel diva as implicitly deconstructing evangelical fundamentalist rhetoric, and in the process, creating sites for potential queer resistance. Yet the gospel diva and her performance style enjoy widespread appeal throughout southern gospel—not despite but *because* of the fundamentally queer nature of the diva's persona and the emotional paradigm she activates, in short because of the unique manner in which she marshals the power of southern gospel lyrics and music. Brought to life by the gospel diva, a song about how "God will make this trial a blessing though it sends me to my knees," the opening line to the chorus of a song that made Peg McKamey made famous (and generates a boisterous response at gospel drag), becomes an opportunity for the diva to shine, to rise, to epitomize the genre's fixation with spiritual self-embattlement.[18]

The rise of the strong but vulnerable celebrity female singer is a phenomenon of the last half of the twentieth century in southern gospel, and continuing into our own time it has coincided with the music's displacement from the mainstream of Christian entertainment. This seismic shift in evangelical popular culture was itself an effect of the much broader modernization of American social attitudes, a process that intensified feelings of dispossession and vulnerability among a subset of evangelicals. These feelings were not new,[19] but they largely remained latent in professional southern gospel's early years. This earlier era was defined by the classic quartet tradition, which attempted to overcome the historically marginal status of southern white evangelicalism by emphasizing professionalized craftsmanship and a strict dedication to systematic principles of shape-note music theory. What ultimately came to be seen as the emotional austerity of this earnest style constricted its capacity to voice deep feelings of loss, anxiety, and alienation generated by the erosion of evangelicalism's cultural authority in the age of postmodernity. Perhaps no other single response typifies the fallout from this process of realignment more than evangelicals' perception of themselves as a persecuted Christian majority, under attack from, and surely to be undone by, the secular world's godlessness, but for the unmerited interposition of God's saving mercies via Christ's Crucifixion.[20] A large part of the Goodmans' success in the 1960s and 1970s is attributable to the fact that they offered audiences a new, unguardedly emotive way to express what it felt like to be an evangelical from the South—or in other culturally southern areas—in postmodern America. Vestal Goodman, the archetypal gospel diva otherwise known as the queen of southern gospel, came to epitomize not just the Goodman Family itself but also the dominant style of highly emotional southern gospel expression popular since the 1960s. To "classic quartet" traditionalists, "the Goodmans ruined everything," as one performer once put it to me in conversation. Nevertheless, in her popularity and the southern gospel persona she typified, Vestal Goodman's career bears out celebrities' function as "models of selfhood" for mass audiences, particularly those feeling "dislocated and rootless."[21]

The more culturally dispossessed and rootlessly vulnerable evangelicals have felt in postmodernity, the more powerfully they have responded to more explicitly emotional models of self-fashioning. The diva persona—emotionally beset but spiritually undaunted—embodies evangelicals' perceived vulnerability to secularism, their preference for emotional displays of piety in crisis, and their desire to see themselves as ultimately perseverant in the sweep of divine history. Yet while she encapsulates this volatile, not entirely rational flow of fear, faith, and feeling, the diva's onstage charisma and force of personality transform the inchoate gestalt of contemporary evangelicalism into an emotionally legible drama of Christianity's unfashionable piety.

Though these images are most often constructed by song lyrics in southern gospel, the diva gives a literal, embodied presence to the lyrical emphasis on dramatic spiritual transformations. There is perhaps no better example of this than the gospel diva's preference for an outlandishly flamboyant style infamously associated with Tammy Faye Bakker. Though most people recall Tammy Faye from her role as a televangelist and (at least unofficially) a coconspirator with her husband in their Praise the Lord (PTL) enterprise, Tammy Faye got her start in Christian entertainment as a gospel singer. Indeed, the qualities that made her so popular and infamous as the cosmeticized queen of evangelistic celebrity exist throughout southern gospel music and are powerfully demonstrated by its fashion: the conspicuously prosthetic fingernails and eyelashes; the heavily embossed eyebrows (Tammy Faye's were permanently tattooed); the thickly applied eyeliner; the gold-lamé, bejeweled, or otherwise elaborate costuming; and the boldly conceived coiffures. It is tempting to dismiss these and other easily lampooned excesses that often seem to attend the rise of evangelical celebrities as so much Beverly Hillbilly camp couture at best, as distasteful phoniness at worst. But "phoniness" is just another way of describing a departure from certain normative expectations or assumptions.

As a highly visible deviation from secular American culture, this style of adornment participates in a semiotics of evangelical nonconformism. PTL-style cartoonish extravagance holds outs to the ordinary evangelical an example of what it looks like to obey the scriptural command that Christians live in the world, but be not of it (Rom. 12:2). The outsized proportions of evangelical celebrity signal ascendancy to wealth and success, satisfying audiences' desire to see "what we think and feel" writ large, "in a way that is profound, intense, and highly emotional."[22] In southern gospel, this need stretches at least as far back as Reconstruction, when rural white evangelicals longed to see themselves and their unique values and traditions represented in modern modes of mass cultural expression.[23] At the same time, the unmistakable gaudiness of the Tammy Faye aesthetic has the self-authenticating effect of binding the evangelical celebrity to her fans. Outsiders see in the celebrity evangelical appearance a tacky amateurism and transparent fraudulence; to cultural insiders, this appearance communicates a refusal to surrender or succumb to the blandishments of the secular celebrity's worldly elegance and all the human frailty it hides.[24] That this style may appear "cheap" or "overdone" is the point at some level. Faith Hill, Martina McBride, and other secular female stars with southern connections may look like—and be worth—a million dollars. The gospel diva as a model of Christian nonconformism revels in her appearance as a conspicuously pious Christian. As the mascara runs down her cheeks, she demonstrates her abiding concern with the gospel in song over the allure of the secular celebrity's stylistic equipoise, much the way many female impersonators succeed most fully when they accentuate the disconnect between themselves and the imitated original. Not for nothing has Tammy Faye been described as a drag queen herself.[25]

By exemplifying dominant structures of feeling and belief at work within postmodern evangelicalism, the gospel-diva phenomenon demonstrates the extent to which the southern gospel imagination has far more in common with queer habits of feeling than orthodox culture could ever officially allow. The diva's persona encourages evangelicals to imagine themselves occupying a psychosocially marginal position—oppressed, according to the narrative of the persecuted Christian majority, for who they are by dominant culture—that parallels nothing so much as the underclass status of the non-heterosexual in gospel music.[26] The appeal of the diva as an icon for gay men appears to be on the decline, now that being homosexual in general carries with it far less stigma than it did for the Stonewall and AIDS generations who turned *Judy* into a byword for the never-give-up spirit of embattled homosexuality.[27] True as this may be in mainstream American life, being gay and evangelical continues to be about as isolating and punishing as being a religious absolutist in a postmodern pluralistic society is believed to be in the collective imagination of contemporary evangelicals. Whether or not "gospel music *is* gay music," as Yvette Flunder has claimed, there is indeed something fundamentally queer about the paradigmatic modes of thinking and feeling in postmodern southern gospel.[28] If orthodox evangelical popular culture has a vested interest in portraying the gay-gospel connection as a sinful paradox, it is in no small part an attempt to efface the fact that sinner and saint alike come to the music as nonconformists—real or imagined, gay or straight, and everything in between—drawn to southern gospel's dramatic rendering of spiritual marginality and social misfittedness.

The Limits of "Sin"

The gay-gospel paradox is only truly paradoxical if one uncritically adopts the orthodox evangelical view that openly embraced homosexuality and meaningful Christianity are mutually exclusive. The prohibition against homosexuality in evangelical fundamentalism is theoretically absolute, but practically speaking nonheterosexuals have always found or created ways to retain meaningful connections to religion. Most southern gospel evangelicals treat homosexuality as a particularly destructive kind of sin that befalls the spiritually inconstant. This was especially apparent in southern gospel after Kirk Talley was outed. Jerry Kirksey, editor of *Singing News* at the time, spoke for this way of thinking within the industry in an editorial a few months after the FBI case involving Talley became public: "Sin is not news. Sin is between God and the sinner. . . . If *Singing News* gets into the sins printing business, where do we stop? Whose sin, and what sins deserves coverage? How about 'pride' or 'disobedience.' The Bible says, 'he who has broken the least of these has broken them all.' Does that put 'gluttony' and 'murder' on the same level?"[29] The notional aim of Kirksey's column is to explain why faithful Christians, including Christian journalists, are compelled by scripture to turn away from the spectacle of sin. But the column's main point is to justify *Singing News*'s response to the Kirk Talley ordeal, without ever actually mentioning Talley by name. Kirksey goes on to cite the scripture that declares "all have sinned and come short" to explain the magazine's silence surrounding Talley's outing, and true to Kirksey's word, *Singing News* not only steadfastly remained silent about the Talley case after it went public, but also seemed to have scrubbed its pages of paid advertisements that made reference to Talley. Kirksey never explains why, under his unified theory of equivalent sin, Talley alone is excluded for his sinfulness, given that "all have sinned." Most likely, Kirksey saw no logical inconsistency in his argument. Nor did most of his peers in the industry. Talley's label dropped him shortly after he was outed, his product was returned en masse by retailers, and his touring schedule evaporated.[30] Meanwhile, the patriarchal deference to authority that suffuses southern gospel culture guaranteed that *Singing News*'s official code of silence surrounding all things Talley was enforced in the music's less formal public spheres. Prominent Web sites hosting discussion forums devoted to southern gospel news, including the popular sogospelnews.com (now called absolutelygospel.com), banned all but the most anodyne references to the Talley ordeal on the grounds that artists' private lives were out of bounds—at least when private lives turned into very public gay scandals.

The response from Talley's fellow performers reflected, and magnified, the unsteady mixture of silence and stigma present in Kirksey's column. In September 2004, Jonathan Wilburn, one of southern gospel's most popular performers, used an acceptance speech at the *Singing News* Fan Awards ceremony at the NQC to declare that "God made Adam and Eve, not Adam and Steve." Just like Kirksey's editorial, Wilburn made no mention of Talley's name, but the Talley scandal was clearly understood to be the context for Wilburn's commentary. After I blogged about the incident, criticizing Wilburn's outburst as a "mix of hatefulness" and "red-meat political invective" that was generally offensive and particularly insensitive to Talley's sister-in-law,[31] who was standing a few feet away from Wilburn onstage, a prominent artist from a famous family of singers who own a top-tier southern gospel quartet emailed me to defend Wilburn, and to complain about the scourge of homosexuality: "I must agree that a fan awards acceptance speech may not be the best place to air this matter. However, many of us in this industry are sickened by the people among us who are blatantly homosexual. Sure, there are a lot of other problems, but this one just seems to be going crazy right now. It just happened to be on Jonathan's mind at the time."[32] Southern gospel is culturally patriarchal, so *homosexual* is almost exclusively synonymous with *male homosexuality*. As indicated here by the language of heterosexual privilege, sexual pathology, and the perceived cultural crisis surrounding "blatant" homosexuality, southern gospel's response to male queerness is overwhelmingly shaped by the siege logic of homosexual panic—a term that Eve Kosofsky Sedgwick usefully deploys to describe the complicated regulation of male relationships in patriarchies.[33] In southern gospel, evangelicalism's abiding antipathy toward homosexuality demands a strictly guarded, Kirkseyean silence about all but the most distorted and distorting depictions of queer life and experience. At the same time, Christian fundamentalism's stigmatization of homosexuality drives the evangelical imagination in the opposition direction: toward a fixative proliferation of chronically indirect talk about the sinfulness of homosexuality that, as Kirksey and Wilburn illustrate, stands in for the realer, much deeper anxiety that *homosexual* is not just an adjective but a fact of human existence—a fact that constitutes perhaps *the* most feared threat to fundamentalism's masculinist orthodoxy. Whether consciously or not, this type of evangelical homosexual panic—a punitive way of talking about homosexuality but not talking about homosexuals—aims to deny the legitimacy of queer claims on religion and religious culture by making nonheterosexual ways of being solely about the "sinful" act of gay sex.

Yet "sin" has limited utility as a framework for understanding the presence of gay men in gospel music. The persistence with which gay men claim affiliation with such an overtly homophobic form of fundamentalist evangelical pop culture bespeaks the power of the desire for self-transcending integration of the dissonant parts of queer evangelical identity. Michael Warner makes a version of this point autobiographically in his essay about growing up gay and Pentecostal: "Jesus was my first boyfriend. He loved me, personally, and he told me I was his own. This was very thrilling, especially when he was portrayed by Jeffrey Hunter."[34] What Warner seems to be getting at here is that habits of evangelical conversion and piety impress themselves deeply into the psychospiritual character of queer adolescents whose formative years are spent under the shaping pressure of fundamentalist idioms and imagery.

For gay men such as Warner, Talley, myself, and many others who come of age within southern evangelical culture, certain experiential symmetries may emerge between the struggle to come to terms with homosexuality and evangelical salvation experiences as a religious rite of passage. Each involves deep-set and even more deeply felt shifts in identity, accompanied by public statements of personal transformation (so-called professions of faith, in evangelicalism), suggesting that the phenomena might well serve similar psychosocial functions. And in both coming-out and salvation experiences, identity is (re)constructed simultaneously in the public renunciation of an earlier way of living and in the embrace of new narratives and norms that help disambiguate an individuality in flux and integrate it into a community of support and understanding. In the evangelical vernacular, this experience is understood as the conviction of the holy spirit and the work of redemptive grace being imparted to the soul that has come to be aware of the lapsarian state imputed to all humankind through original sin. Perhaps unsurprisingly, contemporary evangelicalism commonly locates this so-called age of accountability during the years of childhood leading up to and culminating in puberty. This emphasis on the conversion of adolescent and early-teenage children inevitably blends and blurs religious experience and sexuality. For those (post)pubescent religious strivers coming into comprehension of their incipient homosexuality, the crisis of religious awakening can easily also become a crisis of psychosexual identity.[35] Consequently, the orthodox salvation experience can become a lived metaphor for making sense of queer identity. In effect, evangelical religion can supply for some gay men what Warner terms "a language of ecstasy, a horizon of significance within which transgressions against the normal order of the world and the boundaries of the self *can be seen as good things.*"[36]

A Musical Theology of Queer Experience

There are some people for whom same-sex orientation is not necessarily an acknowledged obstacle to identifying with orthodox evangelicalism and its emphasis on the individual's denial of the "sinful" self before the sovereign, redemptive power of the divine. As a man wrote to me in response to my online writings about the Kirk Talley scandal: "I have same sex attraction also. Notice I did not say I was gay. I am struggling with it, as I am sure Kirk Talley is, daily. All the counseling, all the prayers, all the countless days of struggles, and yet it does not disappear. I am 49 yrs. old and have been in this struggle my [entire] lifetime."[37] Tying nonheterosexual identity to psychospiritual "struggles" descends from evangelicalism's "hate the sin, love the sinner" paradigm, which rhetorically links homosexuality with the same language of self-embattlement used to talk about other "sins" in conservative Christianity. In this view, one struggles with homosexual feelings much the way one would struggle with the temptation of adultery, alcoholism, gambling, covetousness, and so on. "Gay" or "homosexual" becomes an action, not an orientation. Same-sex desires are manifestations of sinfulness to be overcome, not structuring components of identity to be embraced.

But what about those nonheterosexuals from conservative Christian backgrounds who reject this orthodox paradigm of the self-embattled homosexual yet wish to retain a sense of their native spirituality in ways that positively affirm their sexuality? If, as Brett and Wood suggest, musical language operates on a "doctrine of autonomy" from social issues, then it makes sense that queer evangelicals would turn to sacred music as a strategic way to manage conflicts between private feelings and public expectations of orthodox culture. The specific drift of gay men toward southern gospel attests to its particular power to activate feelings and intuitions essential to psychospiritual transformation, without placing preconditions on access to these experiences. This quality is a key part of what enables the music to contain conflicting sets of privately individualized meanings and possibilities simultaneously, while also publicly functioning as a catalyst for culturally conservative consensus. This creates a situation in which the more intense and overt the resistance to homosexuality, the more deeply and surreptitiously do queer habits of experience and expression become embedded in the fabric of evangelical culture, even or especially, it seems to me, when it appears to be at its least queer.

Del Shores's 2001 play, *Southern Baptist Sissies*, dramatizes this dynamic in the unfolding story of four gay friends—Mark, Andrew, TJ, and Benny—growing up and coming out (or not) in a tiny Southern Baptist community in rural Texas during the final decades of the twentieth century. As children their lives revolve around a religious community suffused with hymns in the gospel tradition.[38] As they mature into young adults, music functions as a paralanguage with which to engage constructively with their fundamentalist pasts. Mark is the play's resident thinker: introspective, defiantly queer, and deeply vulnerable beneath his anger and polemical outbursts about evangelicalism's hateful treatment of homosexuals. In a soliloquy at the heart of act 2, he begins to come into half-sighted realizations about the relationship between his fundamentalist childhood and his angry defiance as a gay adult enraged by the evangelical rejection of homosexuality. At the conclusion of the soliloquy he says, "Sometimes . . . Sometimes I think Benny's right (*A look at Benny*) Just live your life and let them live theirs—and shut the fuck up. But I can't. (*Chokes up, BROTHER CHAFFEY enters and starts softly playing 'Pass Me Not, Oh Gentle Savior.'*)"[39] Here, Mark considers embracing a live-and-let-live detachment from the world in response to the way antigay evangelicalism not only rejects the homosexual but also dispossesses him of the intellectual and emotional resources needed to redirect the evangelistic impulse into a more humane reform agenda. The problem for Mark is that such a pose would mean abandoning the affective structures and emotional logic of Protestant evangelicalism as a primary framework for understanding the self. "I can't," he says, suggesting both that he can't "shut the fuck up" about evangelicalism's bigotry, but also that he can't live with the simple binaries that put "gay" in insoluble conflict with "evangelical Christian." This tension is as much a phenomenon of secular American culture as evangelicalism. Words dissolve into sentimentality and tears precisely when and where rational categories for identity break down.

His reluctance to surrender evangelicalism's familiar idiom (even if in service of an incipient gay activism) coincides with—indeed seems catalyzed by—Brother Chaffey's appearance onstage and the opening strains of the plaintive gospel hymn, "Pass Me Not, Oh Gentle Savior." For the first time, Mark begins to evince a gospel-induced awareness of the deeper significance of his angry defiance, not as a rejection of all that is familiar, but as a desire for self-transcending integration of the dissonant parts of his identity. As Mark's soliloquy ends and "Pass Me Not" continues to build, the scene concludes:

> BENNY: [singing]. "Savior, Savior . . ." (he rises and begins to exit.)
> BENNY/ANDREW: [both singing]. "Hear my humble cry . . ."
> (*ANDREW rises and follows* BENNY.)
> BENNY/ANDREW/TJ: "While on others thou art calling . . ."
> BENNY/ANDREW/TJ/MARK: [all singing]. "Do not pass me by."[40]

As the song unfolds, the scene evokes the traditional four-part male formation of the southern gospel sound, reinforcing the way that the gospel style specifically—in ways separate from contemporary Christian music or other derivative forms of religious pop music—has the power to catalyze meaningful experience of spiritual self-transcendence. Yet a foursome of *sissies* necessarily undercuts the normative values of the southern gospel tradition by voicing queer feelings of pain and isolation through the singing of a standard Baptist hymn in the gospel tradition. At one important level, this scene critiques evangelical fundamentalism by effectively queering a traditional form of Christian musical expression. For the orthodox evangelical, the scene's implication is clear: the singers up there onstage movingly harmonizing about the straight and narrow path may themselves be neither, and they may *mean* something quite different than you assume. But the deeper significance of the scene seems to be its evocation of what I would call a queer double consciousness of subjectivity derived from dissonant spheres of postmodern life: fundamentalist evangelicalism and transgressive sexuality. As each boy tentatively joins his voice with the others', they form a queer quartet that transcends false dichotomies and transforms the vicissitudes of individual suffering into a basis for belonging in community formed as much from identification with the part of the self expressed by gospel music as from the queer component of identity.

Both in my scholarly understanding of the gay-gospel paradox and in my personal experience of the music as a gay man, this scene resonates with me as a powerful representation of southern gospel's ability to convert otherwise insoluble cultural conflicts over sexuality and spirituality into moments of self-recognition and unconditional acceptance for nonheterosexuals. Other gay southern gospel fans confirm this to be true. As part of my research, I have asked hundreds of fans and professionals to tell me about a memorable experience associated with listening to gospel music. Dozens of nonheterosexuals responded to my query about the ways people experience southern gospel. One gay man responded that the song "'Always Enough,' ironically by Kirk Talley, ministered most to me when I was dealing with my orientation and coming out." It "assured me that God's Mercy was plentiful and always enough for me!" Another respondent, this time a gay gospel performer, also emphasized the music's palliative effect in the psychosocially claustrophobic environment of an antigay industry. Speaking of his connection to the song "Sheltered in the Arms of God," he wrote, "I was on the bus of the group I was singing with at the time and I heard it come on the radio. It was at a time in my life that I felt rejected by most of the world and most of the people important in my life. But I heard it that night while driving the bus and I literally had to pull the bus over because I began weeping so hard. It is an anthem of assurance to me—no matter what—no matter my orientation—no matter my circumstance—that I can be and I am Sheltered in His Arms." Gay fans and performers return again and again to this theme in their discussion of their bond with southern gospel: that the music and its meanings cannot be separated from the culture that produces them, yet they develop independent of cultural norms and orthodox belief. This distinction is vital to understanding how southern gospel functions as a contemporary idiomatic bridge between the modern humanist values that embrace a prismatic variety of identities and subjectivities, including homosexuality, and antimodern fundamentalist evangelicalism. One gay man made this notion explicit. In response to my query about the reasons people remain affiliated with southern gospel, he wrote: "Listening to and watching the McKameys are unique in the impact they have had on me. Peg has the ability to create an experience for the audience that isn't, for me, hampered by her musical limitations. This, to me, is memorable because I reject both emotive religion and fundamentalist beliefs. However, her talent for communicating piety and the derivation of joy from a lifestyle that appears sheltered is affecting. I mention these times where I have been 'moved' by her concerts because it is so contrary to my own experiences and feelings."[41] The psychospiritual response to the music—being "moved"—is revealingly set off by quotation marks here. This emphasis suggests both suspicion of the experience and—recalling Mark's teary breakdown—the inadequacy of rational language to convey the momentary experience of being "moved" by southern gospel out of the insoluble binaries customarily deployed to categorize identity.

Taken together these responses testify to the vital, if overlooked or ig-nored, work gospel music accomplishes as a bridging mechanism in post-modern American society. The common thread binding Shores's sissies, these respondents, and my own intuitions about the music is a kind of gay grace that emerges in the often unlooked-for mingling of sentiment and song that momentarily remakes one's entire perceptual apparatus. The incipi-ently queer protagonist of Dorothy Allison's novel *Bastard Out of Carolina* captures what I mean by this. Her friendship with the daughter of a southern gospel music promoter has exposed her to both the corruption of the south-ern gospel industry—the drinking and philandering and generally coarse living that have always gone on offstage—as well the music's incantatory power to transport her out of herself and the sexual violence and domestic abuse of midcentury southern, white poverty: "Aunt Alma swore all gos-pel singers were drunks, but right then [while listening to southern gospel music] it didn't matter to me. If it was whiskey backstage or tongue-kissing in the dressing room, whatever it took to make that juice was necessary, was fine. I wiped my eyes and swore out loud. Get that boy another bottle, I wanted to yell. Find that girl a hardheaded husband. But goddam, keep them singing that music. Lord, make me drunk on that music."[42] When I teach this novel to students unfamiliar with southern gospel, their initial impulse is to take Aunt Alma's side, to read the disconnect between gospel performers' publicly pious personae and their often personally compromised private lives as evidence that the music is self-discreditingly peopled with hypocrites. What this reaction masks is the way the always already claimant prerogatives of heterosexual privilege cloak themselves in the depoliticized language of authenticity and hypocrisy. A straight wife and mother like Aunt Alma, with the ensured social status and sense of belonging afforded by heteronormative matriarchy, sees hypocritical frauds on the gospel stage, perhaps because there are few correspondences in her own comparatively stable and well-adjusted life to the experience described in gospel songs about wayfaring strangers striving in solitary struggle after the home of the soul just beyond the ever-moving horizon of suffering. But the maladjusted queer kid hears the same song and immediately feels the truth of music commemorating the beset soul.

From the social outcast's position at the margins of community, southern gospel sounds like something very close to a musical theology of queer experience. The close harmony of southern gospel models a mutuality in which each voice is allowed to exist individually *and* as part of a family of singers simultaneously—without effacing genuine differences of identity or character. In insisting on the inextricable link between gospel songs and sinful selves, Allison—herself a lesbian from the same white-trash world her characters inhabit in *Bastard*—dramatizes how gospel music becomes an entrée to metaphysical experiences for the queer self cut off from the regular forms of spiritual transcendence. To "keep them singing that music," to "make me drunk" on it, is to consecrate queer-identity formation and life experience in the reassuringly familiar patterns of evangelical feeling and expression communicated through southern gospel.

Coming Out from Among Them

Allison and Shores are not alone in linking music and metaphysics. Indeed, there is a long-standing connection in the literature of religious experience between musicality and transformative upwellings of spiritual energy going back at least as far as Augustine. In book 8 of *Confessions,* he describes his religious conversion experience beginning at the sound of a child singing in the garden. The singing voice seems to be a sign from God to turn to scripture as a guide to salvation. For Augustine, music collects a set of disaggregated spiritual aspirations into a coherent feeling of epiphany or insight: "take and read," the child's voice sings, "take and read." And "in an instant," Augustine concludes, "it was as though the light of confidence flooded into my heart."[43]

In general the queer turn to religious music manifests little concern that experience align with the literal meaning of the doctrine as expressed in lyrics. Instead, the focus is on the feeling of salvation (which is to say, unconditional acceptance and belonging) that emerges in the close harmony of gospel music sung in the ensemble. One of Shores's characters recalls a version of this experience from childhood, describing it as "that moment" when "everybody would start to start to sing" some old gospel chorus and "I'd feel that tug . . . [that] I didn't quite understand" until "a feeling of peace, of joy, and happiness [would] flood through my entire being."[44] What matters about the song in these moments is the incorporating effect of southern gospel music's participatory harmony.[45] To join a community of singers is ipso facto to partake—palpably, viscerally through the voice's uplifted song—in a musical version of what scripture refers to as the eternal promise that "whosoever-will may come," independent of orthodox doctrine's attempt to regulate this experience. At a general level, this dynamic is not unique to southern gospel. Kiri Miller has shown, for instance, how Sacred Harp singing permits singers of diverse faiths—or no faith at all—to feel equally invested in a musical tradition whose centuries-old roots translate singers' conflicting ideologies, beliefs, or identities into a welcoming "community of uncertainty." Brett and Wood have described this sort of pluralizing effect as the "non-specificity of musical language." But for queers particularly, the malleability of musical meaning creates a "special situation in which music [plays] an important part as both safety valve and regulator in the mechanism of the 'closet.'" [46]

My own experience singing or surrendering myself to songs about the soul's plea for salvation has confirmed the slippery truth of this proposition as it relates to meaningful queer identification with music so often associated with antigay ideology. In addition to being popular within the world of southern gospel generally, many of the songs I have written about in this book were originally and indelibly seared in my memory during my own queer encounters with southern gospel: blasting the Cathedrals' live recording of "Oh, What a Savior" as a salve against homesickness—and a bulwark against my fear about the consequences of coming out—in the first lonely months after moving from Missouri to northern Minnesota right after college, or sitting in the nosebleed seats in 2005 at the NQC, listening with what I thought was the researcher's necessary degree of analytical detachment, only to be brought up short when Mike Bowling joined the Crabb Family for their electrifying cover of the old Hinsons song "That I Could Still Go Free."[47] During these and other countless moments like them, lyrics have occasionally been part of the explanation, as they often are in my scholarly analysis of the music. Part of what propelled my absorption in the Crabb Family performance at the NQC, for instance, was the realization that I was, at that very moment, personally experiencing the dynamics I had been studying for years: the way southern gospel lyrics establish a surface rhetoric of consensus beneath or behind which elaborately individualized complexes of feeling develop.

Just as often, lyrical content recedes into the interpretive background. "Oh, What a Savior" is, on the one hand, a cultural by-product of the world whose regressive view of sexuality made coming out from among that culture so painful and costly for me. Nevertheless, the song stands in my memory of those days as a kind of emotional Rosetta stone, uniquely able to translate feelings back and forth across the ever-widening space between who I had been and who I was becoming under the daily shaping pressure of all the tiny tragedies and personal triumphs that constitute the process of coming out.

This process of identity formation is, of course, a lifelong process to some extent. Often what the song may mean or how it functions psychosocially emerges only later, in glimpses of the remembered self filtered through time and experience. Shores's treatment of the self's interaction of past and present suggests as much in *Sissies*. Remembering his own baptism by full immersion—and the experience of seeing his friend TJ naked as they both changed clothes afterward in a small room off to the side of the church baptistery—Mark confesses that "that blend of religion and sexuality was just almost too much for my almost teenage body to deal with. I was supposed to feel different. And I did! But now, in hindsight, on that day, the day of my baptism, my twelve-year-old . . . body and soul . . . (*Stares at TJ*) . . . fell in love." This memory is part of a flashback scene in which young Mark and TJ are both welcomed into the communion of Christian fellowship following their baptism. Standing at the front of the church, Mark "walks over and joins TJ, throwing his arm around him," and they sing with the rest of the congregation:

> Hallelujah, thine the glory
> Hallelujah, amen
> Hallelujah, thine the glory
> Revive us again.[48]

As with so many of the psychosexually pivotal moments of the gay-gospel experience, this one relies on the presence of some classic gospel hymn or other song from the southern gospel tradition or in that style to catalyze an imaginative and emotional resolution of the dichotomies that beset the gay male evangelical caught between the vise of self and society. The transgressive attraction that Mark feels when looking at TJ's body in the baptismal dressing room is—he realizes looking back on it—ceremonially sanctified in the experience of gospel singing. A touch that is verboten in the erotically charged changing room is permitted and encouraged in the evangelical public sphere, which sanctions homosocial bonding as an expression of Christian brotherhood.[49] Mark throws his arm around TJ in a gesture that is not satirical or ironic or blasphemous, but suffused with vectors of identity originating in both religion and sexuality. Under the auspices of evangelical religious cultural practices like baptism and the ceremonial exchange of affection between Christian "brothers," ordinarily conflicting impulses of gay evangelical identity are momentarily and wonderfully harmonized through the experience of the gospel music that helps consecrate these rituals and feelings.

From this point of view, the link between gay men and gospel music begins to make sense as an experiential context in which to feel the queer, evangelical equivalent of what William James referred to in *The Varieties of Religious of Experience* as "the high-water mark of his spiritual capacity." That this experience should emerge within such an openly homophobic environment comports with the structure of feeling and desire found in strictly patriarchal societies. Indeed, Sedgwick's study of homosociality in "male-dominated kinship systems" has shown "the tendency toward important correspondences and similarities between the most sanctioned forms of male-homosocial bonding" (sports, politics) "and the most reprobated expressions of male homosexual sociality" (cabarets, drag shows, gay strip clubs).[50]

Yet for all this, as Mitchell Morris has written, "it so often seems that in the absence of impossibly detailed proof . . . historical figures are treated as straight by default—or as unreadable, and therefore straight by default again." To this I would add that it is not just people themselves, but often the ambient cultural atmosphere that is presumed always already to reflect the heteronormative bias of dominant culture. Take, for instance, the all-male southern gospel quartets that spend long stretches of time on the road in the necessary intimacy of a custom coach bus (the preferred mode of travel in southern gospel). Unaware of the pious explanations of southern gospel music as a high calling and an evangelistic ministry, one might observe this dynamic as an outsider and easily draw far different conclusions from the sight of four comely (or at least highly coifed) men spending most days and nights together in a confined living space they share for the purposes of eating, sleeping, bathing, and passing most of their waking hours between concerts. For their part, many gospel singers speak of the bonds they form with other singers as akin to brotherhood, strongly suggesting that a great deal of intimacy inevitably builds up between men who not only live this closely together for (often) years at time, but also join their voices night after night in close harmony to sing of the soul's striving after grace and salvation. "I count it an honor," the manager of one of the most prominent southern gospel all-male quartets said in a statement referring to the group's lead singer, "to stand beside this man night after night. He is not only the finest lead singer in Gospel Music, but he has a passion for this music and the message it delivers. I love him like a brother and thank God for his friendship."[51]

I am not suggesting that such dynamics are in the majority of cases manifestations of repressed homosexuality or explicitly genital attractions. But
these networks of religious camaraderie and spiritual intimacy can nevertheless combine with the rhetoric and experiential force of southern gospel to
function as a powerful idiom for understanding evangelical sexuality. Through
this idiom, those involved at any stage of the music's creation and consumption may sublimate a range of homosocial, homoerotic, and homosexual
feelings or desires that build up within evangelicalism's repressive culture.
In my own case as an adolescent and young adult, idolizing gospel music's
leading performers and imagining what life on the road must be like reflected
a genuine affection for the music that validated my identity as the queer,
closeted, musical son of an evangelical preacher. In the process, the "abnormal" psychosexual energies associated with my malformed queer identity
were recoded into a notionally asexual esteem for performers' musical ability.

This kind of thing goes on more often, and in more prominent ways,
than southern gospel culture is typically prepared to acknowledge. A few
years after being outed by the arrest of the man who tried to blackmail him,
Kirk Talley wrote and recorded a song titled "Intimacy with Jesus." In the
song, the singer describes his desire to touch Christ's face daily and be near
enough to feel the Savior's heartbeat and to "completely lay upon your
chest."[52] It is not uncommon for southern gospel songs to rely on images of
physical or romantic intimacy to dramatize what evangelicalism imagines to
be the believer's ideal relationship with the divine—around the same time
Talley recorded "Intimacy with Jesus," Karen Peck and New River released
"Hold Me While I Cry." But the New Testament's prominent descriptions
of Christians as the bride of Christ (Eph. 5:25) and Jesus as a bridegroom
(Matt. 25:10) provide a scriptural rationale for desexualized interpretations
of such imagery as purely metaphorical. Read in light of Talley's ordeal and
the very public way he subsequently discussed having "wrestled and dealt
with same-sex attraction" for many years, "Intimacy with Jesus" is notable
for collapsing the traditional distance between the tenor and the vehicle
of the metaphor.[53] The song's explicitly homoerotic imagery transparently
displaces homosexual desire onto evangelical religious experience.[54]

It is debatable whether Talley would have ever recorded a song quite
this explicit about the relationship between religion and sexuality before
he was outed, or whether even now he would concede the legitimacy of
the psychosexual reading I have provided here. What is incontestable is
that this song was part of a 2005 live album that Talley used to appeal to
orthodox fans, many of whom interpreted this and other postscandal songs

as evidence of Talley's rehabilitation.[55] Whatever else it may signify, the song's relationship to Talley's own psychosexual ordeal demonstrates what it means for southern gospel to function as a culturally authorized language in which to speak of deep feelings of the heart and intuitions of the soul. Talley himself has come very close to acknowledging as much. In the same interview in which he discussed his same-sex attractions, he also said that "people are just now finding out" about his sexuality because of the criminal case he was caught up in. But "all my life I put myself and my personal struggles in my songs." His music, he concludes, is and has been a "transparent look into my real life."[56] If we take Talley's words seriously, then one function of southern gospel music indeed seems to be to redirect culturally forbidden desires of the gay male—on either side of the footlights, whether out, repressed, closeted, or questioning—into pathways of expression that are both psychospiritually familiar and culturally acceptable.

In matters of the spirit, soul, and identities in transition, we deal in penumbras just beyond our focal distance; in evidences felt, not seen; in substances hoped for, but never fully grasped. Gospel music raises the alluring possibility that the outcast might find a single language through which both the desires of the heart and the habits of the soul can merge and find expression. The queer evangelical is drawn back by this prospect to the mysteries of Protestant grace and Christic redemption, even as the limits of contemporary evangelicalism's homophobia obstructs strivers' progress and attempts to turn them away.

When I have felt for myself the self-authenticating force of gospel music at its best, the experience has been as authoritative and affecting in the moment as it has proved difficult to explain or describe after the comedown. The explanation always seems to exist just beyond the limits of language, between orthodox evangelicalism and secular gay culture, in a space where certain types of religious songs take on the underlying character of one's psychospiritual desires for belonging in community and, by externalizing the feelings in song, legitimize them. In these moments, the narrow limits of absolutism's monochromatic categories for identity (rightness-wrongness, saved-lost, saint-sinner, white-black, straight-gay) dissolve in the frisson of suspended resolution. This thrilling, momentary fusion of typically opposing energies into a single feeling of redemptive, liberating totality constitutes the ne plus ultra of glory bumps. In these moments, the good news of southern gospel is that "whosoever-will" may feel this heavenly harmony of assurance, as the ever-striving soul is momentarily transfixed by gospel's glory-rolling joy.

Epilogue

The Soul's Best Song

Throughout this book, I have treated southern gospel music as a tool for implicitly but meaningfully expressing unorthodox experience within an orthodox culture. Encounters with this music create a safe space in which to try to reconcile the evangelical identity to those aspects of the self that orthodoxy stigmatizes as variant, subversive, or sinful. With this effort to queer southern gospel—in which "queer" encompasses not just explicitly sexualized expresses of identity but a range of aberrancy as judged by conservative evangelicalism—I have attempted to demonstrate how abnormal subjectivity exists within the context of, and is inextricably entangled with, evangelical Christianity. This entanglement, I have suggested, makes a particular kind of complex sociopolitical statement. The result is a form of expression that moves beyond the exclusivity of southern or northern, rural or urban, gay or straight, of believer or unbelieving, of sacred and secular identities. Southern gospel, it turns out, contains multitudes.

This state of affairs arises in no small part because of music's ability to evoke and harmonize a set of often contradictory feelings, responses, and insights within diverse audiences. What may be less obvious is that, in the case of southern gospel, its capacity to hold conflicting states of mind and feeling in productive tension stands out as much for existing largely outside traditional church culture as for being a musical mode of religious self-fashioning. Southern gospel music draws most of its fan base and talent from rank-and-file evangelical churches, and the survival of southern gospel depends on the willingness of local churches to book touring artists. But the habits of thinking and feeling associated with the music originate, as I have argued in the preceding pages, from intricate psychosocial dynamics and complex socioeconomic realities that outstrip the epistemological boundaries of orthodox evangelical church culture. Evangelical churches are comparatively good at carving out socially conservative and religiously cohesive communities from within the prevailing secular society; these churches have proved far less adept at providing personalized responses to the crises of identity and faith that often emerge for evangelicals when secular life and sacred life intersect in America.

Beginning in the 1970s and continuing for at least a generation, the scholarly understanding of these types of dynamics in evangelicalism was dominated by the so-called strict-church thesis. Proponents of this thesis argued that "strict churches proclaim an exclusive truth—a closed, comprehensive, and eternal doctrine. They demand adherence to a distinctive faith, morality, and lifestyle. They condemn deviants, shun dissenters, and repudiate the outside world." Consequently, the strict or "strong" church "increases commitment, raises levels of participation, and enables a group to offer more benefits to current and potential members" by providing a modern-day rhetoric of assurance and a community of absolute moral clarity. More recently, scholars of evangelical megachurches (such as those started by Joel Osteen, T. D. Jakes, and Rick Warren) have argued that, rather than quashing dissent and heavily policing the boundaries between the sacred and the secular, as the strict-church thesis would predict, these churches succeed by surreptitiously addressing controversial social and cultural questions. In this view, contemporary evangelicalism as a "movement is far more elastic, far more complex, and far more contradictory than what [most] popular accounts reveal."[1]

This reconsideration of the strict-church thesis provides a useful case study in the broader trends in the study of religion and American culture over the past two decades or so. In that time, scholarship on religion in American has shifted "away from the denominational focus and toward a study of how particular people, in particular places and times, live in, with, through, and against the religious idioms available to them in culture." In the study of American evangelicalism, this shift to the study of so-called lived religion has occasioned an invaluable recalibration of scholarly perspective and generated an impressively diverse body of literature on evangelical culture, practice, and experience. The result is that "the scholarly understanding of American evangelicalism is the most intricate for Christian cultures worldwide."[2]

Yet for the most part, contemporary evangelical culture as an object of scholarly study continues to be conceived of as a field of experience and practice defined by or in some way responding to the church—whether individually or collectively.[3] So, for instance, a (para)church-centric view of American religion sees the shift away from strident, Falwellian, strict-church orthodoxy in evangelical congregations as evidence of cultural innovation in a postdenominational era. In this view, churches must evolve into less dogmatic and antimodern religious communities, lest they waste away into irrelevance. And this is true, so far as it goes. But the study of southern gospel music goes further to inquire after those domains of religious experience that are not exclusively—or even always primarily—organized around church affiliation or (the threat of) its rejection.

The trend in current scholarship toward uncovering the way evangelical churches today are figuring out how to validate unorthodox experience shares with my own interest in southern gospel a commitment to upend one-dimensional assumptions about the evangelical worldview and experience. What I wish to emphasize here is the value of scholarly frames of reference in which the church exists within a larger world of overlapping but distinct spheres of evangelical cultural practice that are not always exclusively rooted in congregational affiliations. This approach recognizes the church both as the central repository for evangelical norms and ideals and at the same time as a powerful force for obscuring the ways evangelicals often really live.

Southern gospel as a field of religious thought, action, and feeling asks us to reimagine the concept of "organized religion" as a phenomenon—in this case, a popular music culture—that exists alongside, within, and beyond the church. What I am describing is not an oppositional relationship with an essentially fixed power differential defined by stable boundaries (southern gospel as set over against the church, or subservient to it, for instance). Rather, what I have in mind is a relational dynamic in which evangelical habits of mind and feeling and the expression of feelings shift along lines of individual and collective needs and desires. For a large segment of evangelicals in America, these needs and desires may appear in congregational contexts and find satisfaction there at times, but they are predominately organized and powerfully activated by the experience of southern gospel, an experience that is capable of affirming the idiosyncratic beliefs and feelings of the individual while also giving coreligionists a chance to imagine and forge new communities of social solidarity and spiritual affinity constructed from the raw materials of spiritual striving and gospel music. Those southern farming families in the years after the Civil War did not undertake daylong journeys to participate in weekend-long gospel singings because they were looking for more of what they were already getting at church, though neither were these journeys a repudiation of congregational membership or experience. And what of the tens of thousands of evangelicals who make a yearly pilgrimage to the National Quartet Convention in Louisville, Kentucky? Do they choose to sit in a cramped and smelly arena for hours at a time, for days on end, because they want the chance to see what church feels like—or escape from it—in a space normally used for livestock exhibitions and gun shows? The available evidence suggests not.

The data of experience from the world of southern gospel consistently indicate that southern gospel transforms typical assumptions about what is meant by "the body of believers"—unmetaphorizes it, if you will—as a concept for understanding how religion is lived and recenters scholarly attention on the embodied experience of evangelical belief and practice situated within particular historical circumstances and cultural contexts.[4] In its best moments, southern gospel quickens the sense of what it means to feel (and to study) the truth of belief, to inhabit—and embody it as a fan, performer, and scholar alike—yet simultaneously to slip the short chain of the ordinary self, set free the soul, and feel oneself to be, in effect, a body of belief. It is, in my experience, to become a kind of spiritual transistor tuned to the glorious gospel sound. As the old song puts it, "Everybody is a radio receiver, / all you gotta do is listen for the call."[5]

Southern gospel fans and performers refer to this kind of self-transcending embodied presence in a vocabulary of heart feeling. As one fan reported to me in discussing the difference between the experience of church and southern gospel, "Good southern gospel music has 'heart' to it. Not saying that church music does not, but church music can be presented 'well' but have no emotion tied to it, no depth of experience, no mind's eye of the lyrics." Another fan reinforced this view of southern gospel as distinct within evangelicalism: "Southern Gospel Music is what I call 'heart music.'" A third fan summed up the experiential quality gestured toward by the first two respondents by drawing on a vernacular metaphor: in effect church culture says, "sit quietly and mind your manners." Southern gospel, meanwhile, "invites you to join in," to feel a sense of individual and collective validation. It is the difference, this fan concludes, between the "fun grandma" and "the stern one."[6]

Beyond the pithiness is a substantive point. To take this kind of perspective seriously, the phenomena of evangelical popular culture must be treated as something other than either a series of paracongregational subcultures that orbit the sun of the church or sets of highly individualized practices that try to break free from its gravitational pull.[7] Accordingly, the study of southern gospel music and culture approaches evangelicalism as a constellation of overlapping but distinct expressive vocabularies that includes church membership, but in which it does not necessarily always predominate. Viewed from this angle, modern evangelicalism has been systematically smuggling heterodox feelings and ways of life into (and out of) the epistemologically closed systems of conservative Protestantism for well over a century now. That a version of this dynamic should so recently begin to predominate in evangelical congregational culture, as recent scholarship suggests, reminds us that there is more to evangelical life as lived through organized religion than what goes on in and immediately around the church. A corollary to this reminder is that innovations in church life and culture do not occur in a vacuum; the church not only exerts a shaping force upon but also is itself shaped by the surrounding world of evangelical popular culture. Plotted along the broader historical arc of evangelicalism, the spiritual smuggling operation now belatedly transforming twenty-first-century evangelical congregations serves as a cultural coda to psychodynamic trends afoot within evangelicalism since at least the late nineteenth century. As one powerful response to the exigencies of modern American life, southern gospel vividly embodies the long-standing, ineradicable desire within evangelicalism for felt validation of religious commitment, for a wonder-working song of glory to sing.

* * *

Finding effective language to describe ineffable moments of spiritual transcendence has long been a defining preoccupation of American Protestant heart religion. No less gifted an evangelical divine than Jonathan Edwards complained in his 1743 treatise, *Religious Affections*, about "spiritual things being invisible, and not things that can be pointed forth with the finger," so that "we are forced to use figurative expressions in speaking of them, and to borrow names from external and sensible objects to signify them by."[8] This problem is especially acute for those individuals seeking affirmation of their spiritual experience *and* the queerer aspects of identity within the culturally conservative world of evangelical Protestantism. What little language does exist in the antimodern environment of contemporary evangelicalism is very often aimed at forcing separations between spirituality and nonnormative experience of all kinds. As a result, attempts to integrate the disparate parts of the identity into a coherent religious self create complicated constellations of emotion shot through with contradiction and elisions. Efforts to achieve this integration through southern gospel leave one with a nagging feeling that to enjoy gospel music is to implicate oneself in Protestant fundamentalism's often retrograde worldview.

To those unfamiliar with, or unreceptive to, the many varieties of evangelical religious experience, the notion of gospel music as a meaningful language for postmodern transcendence may well defy credulity. But it would be a mistake to dismiss gospel's ability to engage postmodern individuality, lest we substitute one set of moral dogmas for another. The lyrical and stylistic tendencies of gospel music have historically emphasized the felt human struggle of trying and failing to live up to impossible goals of official doctrine. At the same time, American literature that explores the gospel music experience—a diverse corpus of texts that run the gamut from white to black, straight to gay, North to South, and, in at least one case, all the way to Paris and back—variously demonstrates the inextricable link between singing about Jesus and living like the devil in one form or another.[9] To ignore this persistent linkage is to deny the persistent role that misfits, outcasts, nonconformists, and strugglers of all sorts have played in the history of gospel music and evangelicalism more broadly.

However, even as I place emphasis on the experiential diversity that southern gospel music allows within fundamentalist evangelical culture, I am also mindful of the risks associated with any discourse of religious pluralism or diversity. As Mark Hulsether has insightfully shown in his study of religion, culture, and politics, emphasizing a plurality of religious experiences can inadvertently mask concentrations of hegemony and the operations of dominant cultural power that shape contemporary religious life, especially marginal and minority identities.[10] In the case of southern gospel, evangelicalism's reliance on effusions of sentiment and nostalgia about the saint's struggle in this vale of tears tends to mask the inescapable fact that most members of the "persecuted Christian majority" in America experience very little of the inequities, biases, and various forms of violence directed at genuinely persecuted people. Mainstream evangelicals enjoy the luxury of putting on and taking off the marginal status of the pious nonconformer whenever it is or is not convenient to experience the jouissance of spiritual transgression, without accruing to themselves any of the actual disenfranchisement of being socially or culturally outcast. Thus, in speaking of southern gospel's surreptitious heterodoxy or covertly queer aesthetic, one must emphasize the clandestine quality—its invisibility and the burden of self-regulation that falls to the nonconforming individual who wishes to forge a religious identity beyond what orthodoxy strictly permits or heaven will allow—as much as the heterodox nature of that experience.

Taken together, then, the evidence from beneath the pious surface of evangelical life—behind the gospel music stage, from the back of the bus, beyond the reach of the spotlight—tells an alternative story about southern gospel music and its cultural function, but also about evangelicalism. The queer sides of southern gospel do not yet—indeed, may never—definitively disrupt orthodox power structures or discredit orthodox accounts of the music's purpose. But they are considerably complicated even so. If there ever was a moment when it was possible for a southern gospel song about heaven as a place where "little children will play and our hearts will be gay" to come out innocently free from the burden of entendre or paradox, that time has surely passed.[11] The more emphatically the dominant culture of southern gospel tries to make the music mainly about rejecting the complexities of postmodern life, the more inextricably entangled the song becomes with the fallen world whose fallibility energizes so much of the southern gospel imagination. In effect, modern southern gospel deconstructs the very orthodox doctrines it depicts. The true value of southern gospel music is its marvelous, incantatory, ever-dawning power to transcend orthodoxy's efforts to control what it means or put limits on the transformational work it accomplishes for all who hear in it the soul's best song.

Appendix A

Songs Referenced

The following songs are referenced in some way in the preceding pages and are representative of the predominate styles and eras found in modern southern gospel (roughly since Reconstruction). Consult endnotes where applicable for information about sheet music and sound recordings of these songs.

"Always Enough," by Kirk Talley
"Amazing Grace," traditional, with lyrics by John Newton
"Because He Lives," by William J. Gaither and Gloria Gaither
"Brethren, We Have Met to Worship," by George Atkins and
    William C. Moore
"By the Gate They'll Meet Us," by Aldine S. Kieffer
"Can a Boy Forget His Mother?" by J. H. Weber
"Can't Nobody," by Andrae Crouch
"Cry for the Children," by Lois Gail Sypolt
"Down in the Licensed Saloon," by W. A. Williams
"Evergreen Shore," by Aldine S. Kieffer
"Expenses," by Harold Leake
"Ezekiel Saw the Wheel," traditional
"Family of God," by William J. Gaither and Gloria Gaither
"Famine in Their Land," by Niles Borop, Dick Tunney, and Melodie Tunney
"Get Away Jordan," traditional
"God on the Mountain," by Tracy Dartt
"God Walks the Dark Hills," by Andra Czarnikow
"God Will Make This Trial a Blessing," by Terry Lee Tidwell
"Go Out to the Programs," by Ira Tucker (with several variations)
"Gospel Boogie," by Lee Roy Abernathy
"Grave on the Green Hillside," by Aldine S. Kieffer

"Had It Not Been," by Rusty Goodman

"He Touched Me," by William J. Gaither

"His Eye Is on the Sparrow," by Civilla Martin and Charles Gabriel

"Hold Me While I Cry," by Gerald Crabb

"How Great Thou Art," traditional, with lyrics by Stuart K. Hine

"I Bowed on My Knees and Cried Holy," by E. M. Dudley Cantwell

"I Don't Regret a Mile," by Rusty Goodman

"I Knows Bettah Now," by A. B. Sebren and James Rowe

"I'll Fly Away," by Albert E. Brumley

"I'm Bound for That City," by Albert E. Brumley

"I'm Wingin' My Way Back Home," by J. B. Coates

"Intimacy with Jesus," by Kirk Talley

"I Still Glory in the Cross," by Belinda Smith and Marty Funderburk

"I Then Shall Live," by Jean Sibelius, with lyrics by Gloria Gaither

"I've Come Too Far to Turn Back," by Nancy Harmon

"I've Got Leavin' on My Mind," by Rusty Goodman

"I Will Glory in the Cross," by Dottie Rambo

"Jesus Is Coming Soon," by R. E. Winsett

"Jesus Will Let You In," by Aldine S. Kieffer

"The King Is Coming," by William J. Gaither and Gloria Gaither

"Kum Ba Yah," traditional

"Lean on Me," by Bill Withers

"Let the Lower Lights Be Burning," by Philip P. Bliss

"Life's Railway to Heaven," by Charlie D. Tillman

"Look for Me at Jesus' Feet," by Squire Parsons

"Looking for a City," by W. Oliver Cooper and Marvin P. Dalton

"Lord Build Me a Cabin in the Corner of Gloryland," by Curtis Stewart

"Love Lifted Me," by James Rowe and Howard Smith

"Oh, What a Savior," by Marvin P. Dalton

"Oh That Wonderful Promise," by Kyla Rowland

"Pass Me Not, Oh Gentle Savior," by Fanny Crosby and W. H. Doane

"Power in the Blood," by Lewis E. Jones

"Revive Us Again," by William P. MacKay and John J. Husband

"Sad Sam Jones," unknown

"The Savior Calls," by Aldine S. Kieffer

"Sheltered in the Arms of God," by Dottie Rambo

"Sweet Little Girl of Mine," by Walter B. Seale and Adger M. Pace

"That I Could Still Go Free," by Ronnie Hinson

"There's Just Something about That Name," by William J. Gaither
    and Gloria Gaither

"This World Is Not My Home," by Mary Reeves and Albert E. Brumley

"Through the Fire," by Gerald Crabb

"Till the Storm Passes By," by Mosie Lister

"Too Much to Gain to Lose," by Dottie Rambo

"Truth Is Marching On," by Jim Brady, Barry Weeks, and Tony Wood

"Turn Your Radio On," by Albert E. Brumley

"Twas Rum That Spoiled My Boy," by L. F. Cole and Martin Towne

"Twilight Whispers," by Aldine S. Kieffer

"Vote as You Pray," by J. Calvin Bushey

"Wake Up, America and Kluck, Kluck, Kluck," by Walter B. Seale
    and Adger M. Pace

"Well Done, My Child," by Byron Faust

"We'll Understand It Better By and By," by R. E. Winsett

"We've Got to Get America Back to God," by Jerry Thompson

"We Want America Back," by Jeff Steele

"What a Lovely Name," by Charles Wycuff

"When I Knelt the Blood Fell," by Tim Greene

"When Morning Sweeps the Eastern Sky," by Oren A. Parris

"Where Could I Go?" by J. B. Coates

"Who Am I?" by Rusty Goodman

"Without Him," by Mylon LeFevre

Appendix B

*Methods and Preliminary Findings
of a Survey of Attitudes and Beliefs
about Southern Gospel Music*

This appendix details the methodology and basic demographic findings of
a large-scale qualitative survey I conducted to understand better some of
the popular attitudes and beliefs held by southern gospel fans and performers about the music. Selected data from this survey appear throughout the
book. The following is a preliminary report. A comprehensive interpretive
treatment of the data is the focus of a larger, separate scholarly work. For
this reason, the following discussion is expository, rather than analytical,
in nature.

The survey was conducted online, using proprietary interactive survey
software. Participants were drawn from the substantial readership of a blog
about southern gospel music and culture (averyfineline.com) that I have
maintained for more than seven years. A total of 756 respondents interacted
in some way with the survey. Of those, 507 respondents completed the entire
survey; 681 provided answers to at least some questions.

Basic Demographic Findings

At the beginning of the survey, respondents were asked a series of questions
related to demographic information (nine common questions for all respondents and two unique questions for respondents who identified themselves
either as southern gospel fans or as professionals).

Respondents predominately identify themselves as fans (385/58%). The
next largest group is performers, part-time and professional (202/30%),
followed by nonperforming professionals, such as songwriters, bus drivers,
executives, and so on (81/12%).

A plurality of respondents (241/38%) report being between the ages of 35 and 49, followed by 25–34-year-olds (138/22%), 50–59-year-olds (125/20%), 60–69-year-olds (55/9%), 18–24-year-olds (54/8%), and 70 and older (26/4%).

Most respondents identify themselves as male (478/72%), compared to 187 women (28%).[1] Respondents overwhelmingly identify as Caucasian/white (655/98%) and straight (616/92%), 42 respondents (6%) identify as gay, and 14 respondents (2%) identify as bisexual.

Annual household income presents as fairly evenly distributed across a range of income brackets. A slim plurality of respondents (193/30%) identify themselves as part of a household earning $50,000–$74,000 annually, followed by those from households earning $25,000–$49,000 (157/24%), $75,000–$99,000 (122/19%), $100,000–$250,000 (128/20%), less than $25,000 (33/5%), and finally more than $250,000 (20/3%).

Church affiliation clusters heavily around the Southern Baptist denomination (167/25%). The next most represented congregational affiliation is nondenominational evangelicalism (83/12.4%). The remaining affiliations with which respondents identify in double digits are: Independent Baptist (74/11.1%), Assemblies of God (41/6.1%), Church of God (33/4.9%), Methodist (33/4.9%), General Baptist (26/3.9%), Nazarene (21/3.1%), Free Will Baptist (15/2.2%), and Church of Christ (10/1.5%). A total of 41 respondents (6.1%) identify themselves as Christians with no religious affiliation. The "other" category accounts for 72 respondents (10.8%).

Roughly equal numbers of respondents identify themselves as having a bachelor's degree (229/34%) and some college (225/34%). The next proportional tier of respondents indicates a high school diploma as their highest level of education (98/15%), followed by those holding master's degrees (80/13%); those with advanced terminal degrees such as the Ph.D., M.D., Ed.D., Th.D., etc. (24/4%); and those who report having completed some high school (10/2%).

Geographically, a majority of respondents identify their place of residence as being in the South (389/58%), followed by the Midwest (146/22%), the Northeast (37/6%), the West (25/4%), and the Southwest (24/4%). All other regional affiliations are negligibly represented.

Most respondents identify themselves as residing in an urban or suburban environment (419/63%); the remainder (250/37%) identify themselves as residing in a rural setting.

Those respondents who identify themselves as fans were asked to indicate about how much money they spend annually on southern gospel music. Responses vary widely: 94 respondents (24%) report spending $100–$249 annually, followed by $250–$500 (70/18%), less than $50 (67/17%), $75–$99 (53/14%), more than $500 (56/14%), and finally $50–$74 (48/12%).

Fans were also asked to report on their attendance over the past ten years to two major musical events in the world of southern gospel: the National Quartet Convention and the Gaither Homecoming Tour. By far the latter presents as the preferred event: 286 respondents (74%) report having attending a Gaither Homecoming event in the past ten years, compared to only 157 respondents (41%) who report attending the NQC in the same time period.

Those who identify themselves as professionals were asked to indicate about how long they have been involved in southern gospel music. Answers vary considerably: 5–9 years (53/19%), 10–14 years (48/17%), 15–19 years (41/15%), 40 years or more (40/14%), 20–24 years (38/14%), 25–29 years (26/9%), and 30–39 years (21/8%).

Southern gospel professionals by a considerable margin indicate that they earn less than $25,000 in annual income from southern gospel music (171/63%), followed by $25,000–$49,000 (60/22%), $50,000–$74,000 (22/8%), and $75,000–$99,000 (8/3%).

Qualitative Responses

The remainder of the survey consisted of various qualitative questions or other prompts designed to gauge dominant perceptions of the music and its culture, as well as discern finer-grained variations of thought and habits of response associated with the southern gospel experience.

The most involved portion of the survey centered on a series of open-ended prompts to which respondents were asked to provide prose-based responses. The prompts are as follows:

- What makes a gospel song "good" in your estimation? (644 responses)
- Describe a memorable experience you've had while listening to gospel music. (601 responses)
- Name your favorite gospel song and describe the most powerful or meaningful associations, memories, feelings, or other reactions you have when you recall that song. (573 responses)
- What do you think is the main difference between listening to/creating southern gospel music and church music? (551 responses)

These prompts were followed by a series of Likert-scale questions that tested a series of working hypotheses developed in the research phase of the book about participants' perceptions of what ministry and entertainment mean in the context of southern gospel music. For each of the statements below, respondents were asked to rate their response on a 1–5 scale, where 1 is "strongly disagree" and 5 is "strongly agree."

- Ministry is about converting non-Christians to Christianity. (513 responses)
- Ministry mainly involves convicting backslidden Christians of the need to repent. (511 responses)
- I know I've been ministered to when I get that feeling of chills that seems to come out of nowhere. (514 responses)
- Ministry means supporting and encouraging people who are struggling. (515 responses)
- Entertainment should give people a pleasant diversion from ordinary life. (508 responses)
- I know I'm being entertained when I get that goose-bumpy feeling from the music. (508 responses)
- Entertainment is about enjoying fellowship with other people who love this type of music. (509 responses)
- Entertainment helps people enjoy themselves in a wholesome way. (508 responses)

The final item in this series asked respondents to read a qualitative statement and select one of six possible responses that best captured their attitude or feeling.

Statement: No matter how you defined ministry and entertainment, please select the phrase below that most closely describes what you think about this issue (513 responses):

- Southern gospel is about ministry.
- Southern gospel is about entertainment.
- Southern gospel is somewhat entertaining but mostly about ministry.
- Southern gospel is somewhat about ministry but mostly entertaining.
- Southern gospel is equal parts ministry and entertainment.
- Southern gospel is about neither ministry nor entertainment.

Four concluding Likert-scale prompts asked respondents to interact with a series of statements about their engagement with and attitudes toward southern gospel. For each of the following statements, respondents rated their response on a 1–5 scale, where 1 is "strongly disagree" and 5 is "strongly agree."

- When my favorite group releases an album, I will always buy it. (305 responses)

- Most songs mean the same thing to most southern gospel fans. (509 responses)
- The main measure of gospel music's quality and value is whether or not the performers are making a joyful noise to the Lord. (510 responses)

Before exiting the survey, respondents were given the chance to share any additional thoughts or responses that they were unable to include in some earlier portion of the survey. There were 520 responses of this kind. Finally, 505 respondents voluntarily chose to provide an email address as an indication of their willingness to participate in further research along these lines.

Data Sorting

Except for the final open-ended response, all data generated in the qualitative portions of the survey were analyzed for identification of themes by a four-member team, including three graduate research assistants who had completed a graduate seminar on gospel music in American literature and culture, and myself, serving as both a participant-sorter and research supervisor.[2]

The theme-identification process used a latent coding method, beginning with "analyst-constructed typologies."[3] As the principal investigator and the team member most familiar with the habits of thought and feeling in southern gospel culture, I conducted a cursory review of the responses to each prompt prior to team sorting activities. From this orientational exercise, I developed a preliminary set of categories for data sorting. Each team member received a roughly equal number of responses to each open-ended question or prompt and a list of the preliminary categories.

Through a collaborative discussion about recurring images and ideas, word and concept patterns, and common points of emphases identified in each team member's data set, the team revised and modified my original analyst-constructed categories to reflect the most relevant or dominant "indigenous categories" of response emerging from this more rigorous review of the data.[4]

Once a stable set of themes was in place, each team member coded responses in his or her data set based on the established categorized themes. Team members assigned a common code to responses that seemed not to fit in any of the collaboratively constructed categories. Any response that seemed to stand out—perhaps for vividness of expression, a particular use of language, or evocative style of writing—was assigned a common code.

Because the final prompt by design invited a range of responses as varied as respondents themselves, the data generated by this prompt received separate attention. I conducted a review of the data, marking any particularly evocative, insightful, or otherwise notable responses. Then, in light of the theme identification process conducted among the team, those responses that fitted within existing categories were coded accordingly. All responses that fell beyond the team-generated categories were resubmitted to another review to sort further the remaining items.

Notes

Introduction

1. R. W. Apple, "On the Road: Polishing Nashville's Twang," *New York Times,* July 28, 2000, E27.

2. Susan Friend Harding, *The Book of Jerry Falwell: Fundamentalist Politics and Language* (Princeton: Princeton University Press, 2001).

3. *The World of White Gospel* (London: BBC Four, March 21, 2008). This documentary illustrates both the allure of southern gospel as a quasi-exotic folk object of fascination in the view of mainstream culture as well as the ways that southern gospel is serially misunderstood by outsider assumptions about the music's history and value. The documentary's conflation of southern gospel with the history of white gospel more generally as suggested by the title—*The World of White Gospel*—is forgivable. But the film's serial ignorance of even the most basic differences between Sacred Harp and convention singing, southern gospel and country music, and Elvis Presley's relatively marginal role in the history of quartet music makes for a risible and virtually unrecognizable distortion of the southern gospel tradition. In other words, the documentary mistakes southern gospel for a far a more culturally foreign phenomenon than it really is and, on that basis, proceeds to construct a historically bizarre account of the music's emergence that matches the imagined exoticism.

4. Anthony Heilbut, "Black Urban Hymnody: Gospel," on *Brighten the Corner Where You Are: Black and White Urban Hymnody* (New World, 1978, NW-224). It would be impossible to document all the instances in academic and popular culture of this phenomenon. Sticking with the former, neither Heilbut's nor Robert Darden's history of black gospel (*Gospel Sound* [New York: Simon and Schuster, 1985] and *People Get Ready! A New History of Black Gospel Music* [New York: Continuum, 2004], respectively) evinces any meaningful interest in the notion of *gospel* as a racially capacious term. Heilbut seems to accept the commonly held meaning of the term, though elsewhere he acknowledges its limitations ("Black Urban Hymnody"). Darden, writing in the

wake of the African American studies movement, is interested in definitively tracing the African roots of the music as a way of countering the ethnocentric view of black gospel as an outgrowth of white culture—a view that dominated scholarship for much of the twentieth century. Still, the terminological failure of gospel studies to grapple substantively with the fact of multiple gospels in American religious music is striking, no matter how inadvertent. The *Cambridge Companion to Blues and Gospel* (Cambridge: Cambridge University Press, 2002) is focused on blues and *black* gospel, and many authors take pains to distinguish between black and white traditions, but the title of the volume does not. *The Encyclopedia of American Gospel Music* (New York: Routledge, 2005) copiously documents a subtle range of voices in and influences on black gospel and white gospel. Yet the treatment of southern gospel includes persistent gaps and lacunae. For instance, there is no dedicated entry for Bill and Gloria Gaither or the Gaither Homecoming Friends franchise, even though the Gaither name is equivalent in white and southern gospel to James Cleveland's in black gospel. What to make of this phenomenon? The conflation of *black* and *gospel* stretches as far back as the nineteenth century (e.g., Mark Twain's promotion of the Fisk Jubilee Singers). In the postmodern popular imagination, this conflation was powerfully reinforced by the introduction of black gospel characteristics into the American pop mainstream via the performances of Ray Charles, Sam Cooke, Aretha Franklin, and others. Equating "gospel" with "black gospel" may well have been intensified when white chroniclers of popular music—usually nonsouthern or western urban white chroniclers—who had little or no knowledge of the rural white North American tradition of gospel music, adopted the same language as the black artists they were covering. Thus, black gospel became known as just "gospel" in American pop culture. In humanities scholarship, a commitment to recovering lost or underrepresented traditions may have added to the problem, focused as so much of humanist studies (justifiably) is on the multiplicity of lives masked by dominant culture and the range of experiences often excluded by normative histories.

   5. For the Sunday-school movement, see V. A. Cross, "The Development of Sunday School Hymnody in the United States, 1816–1869" (D.M.A. diss., New Orleans Baptist Theological Seminary, 1985). For a standard view of white gospel as descended from northern traditions, see Harry Eskew et al., "Gospel Music," *Grove Music Online* (*Oxford Music Online*), http://www.oxfordmusiconline.com/subscriber/article/grove/music/40056 (accessed July 7, 2010). I use the terms *northern* and *urban* here with no little circumspection, aware of how easily they can become little more than a dialogical alter identity for southern gospel music. Scholars (typically following Harry Eskew and James C. Downey, "Shape-Note Hymnody," in *Grove Music Online* [*Oxford Music Online*], http://www .oxfordmusiconline.com/subscriber/article/grove/music/25584 [accessed July 8, 2010]) usually refer to the "urban" gospel of the "North" as a way to describe popular religious music produced by people who were not from the South or culturally southern. But if the term hits the ear wrong all the same, it is in the first place because after the Civil War, *northern* has meaning only within the context of a culturally southern perspective. In any case, the rapid commercialization and mass-marketization of religious music in the first half of the twentieth century effectively nationalized regional, subculturally indigenous forms of sacred music by midcentury—North, South, and otherwise. One result: despite the geographically inflected names people may have used (and continue

to use) to describe "their" gospel music, it has become very difficult to say that gospel music comes "from" any particular area or region. Instead, it has for some time now been defined by cultural practice, social affiliation, and normative values associated with its various forms and phenomena. Certainly, as I argue here and elsewhere, this is the case with "southern" gospel, which paradoxically started appropriating a geographic modifier for the purposes of self-identification at almost the exact historical moment when the music was becoming a national phenomenon (see chapter 3). Moreover, the term *urban* denotes very different cultural identities and experiences (especially for Protestant Americans) when describing life before and after the rise of suburban America in post–World War II society. Just as *northern* serves as a shorthand for "neither from the South nor culturally southern," *urban* used as a descriptor of life before World War II in discussions of gospel music typically connotes "nonrural, averagely educated, and socioreligiously similar white evangelicals from within the industrial working and middle classes." After World War II, gospel music initially affiliated with "northern urban" life began moving to the suburbs along with middle-class whites, so that by the 1960s and 1970s in mainstream Christian entertainment, the music that might have at one time been accurately described as northern, urban gospel was becoming (and remains) largely a suburban phenomenon going by the name contemporary Christian music (CCM), with suburban white evangelicals driving into urban centers to see headliner concerts from CCM stars (or perhaps to attend a Billy Graham revival) at the stadiums and auditoriums that were missing in the suburbs, at least until the past few decades in major American metropolitan areas. By the last quarter of the twentieth century, southern gospel was the only professional form of white Christian music making use of the name "gospel" to describe itself. Although it is true that all white gospel has not historically been southern (and not all southern gospel is professionalized), *southern gospel* and *white gospel* are today effectively synonymous terms, given that there is no professional, commercialized white gospel tradition distinct from southern gospel that recognizably persists in the "urban" "North." To the extent that I make reference here and elsewhere to northern, urban gospel, I do so fully aware of its limited descriptive power. For my purposes, the term appears as an economical way to gesture toward broader and sometimes contrasting historical developments in the world of gospel music beyond its southern variety.

6. This is not to discount the long-standing tradition of academic and archival work focused on gospel's contributions to American music and culture broadly construed. The twentieth century produced numerous state-sponsored folklore collections in the South, which include artifacts and analyses of different gospel music traditions. Moreover, studies of blues, jazz, and country almost invariably must account for gospel (see, for example, chapter 1 of Bill Malone, *Southern Music, American Music* [Lexington: University Press of Kentucky, 2003]). Similarly, southern gospel has found a place in studies of American sacred music expression. Of scholarship in this latter vein, see Stephen Marini, *Sacred Song in America: Religion, Music, Popular Culture* (Urbana: University of Illinois Press, 2003), 296–320. Marini provides the most theoretically vigorous exploration of today's evangelical pop music culture since the rise of white gospel. Given that his aim is to trace the historical development of the music within the broader context of American sacred music traditions, Marini tends to focus on isolated phenomena to exemplify his larger claims, but this approach complicates his treatment of southern gospel (a family of

bluegrass singers popular among southern gospel audiences is presented as representative of the southern gospel tradition, and the cultural and structural relationship between professional southern gospel and contemporary Christian music remains unsorted). This inadvertently tangled treatment of southern gospel is but a small part of an impressively sweeping view of public expressions of religious music in contemporary America and, for my purposes, is particularly valuable in tracing gospel music forward as a psychosocial development of postmodern late capitalism growing out of the Sankey-Rodeheaver eras. In any case, my point here is to emphasize that there is a comparative dearth of academic work devoted to nonblack gospel music traditions and scholarly studies in which southern gospel music plays a central—rather than peripheral—role.

7. Heilbut, "Black Urban Hymnody."

8. Eskew and Downey, "Shape-Note Hymnody."

9. For exemplary treatments of southern gospel music within the context of country music, see Malone, *Southern Music, American Music*, which is a notable exception to this trend. For work that sees gospel's significance primarily as a context for understanding broader aspects of southern culture, see David Fillingim, "A Flight from Liminality: 'Home' in Country and Gospel Music," *Studies in Popular Culture* 20, no. 1 (1997): 75–82; Stephen Tucker, "Pentecostalism and Popular Culture in the South: A Study of Four Musicians," *Journal of Popular Culture* 16, no. 3 (1982): 68; Charles Wolfe, "Presley and the Gospel Tradition," *Southern Quarterly* 18 (1979): 135–50; and Cheryl Thurber, "Elvis and Gospel Music," *Rejoice* 1 (1988): 6. It is worth noting that the insights and research generated "on the way to somewhere" else can be enormously valuable (see, for instance, the work of a folklorist such as Mike Seeger on the music of southern Appalachians, which helps contextualize an understanding of the repertoire of musical possibilities available to early southerners). Indeed, the body of academic, archival, and documentary resources about the gospel music of the South that has emerged from the work of researchers, archivists, and scholars in related or adjacent fields of interest is enormous. Unfortunately, it is also widely dispersed and, so, often difficult to locate.

10. Peter Guralnick, *Last Train to Memphis: The Rise of Elvis Presley* (Boston: Back Bay Books, 1995), 77; "Celebrating America's Musical Heritage: A Salute to Gospel Music," Gaithernet.com, http://gaither.com/news/news.php?uid=340 (accessed October 28, 2006); "George Younce Biography," GeorgeYounce.com, http://www.georgeyounceonline.com/biography.htm (accessed October 28, 2006); "Schedule," Otghquartet.com, http://www.otghquartet.com/index.cfm?PID=10933 (accessed October 28, 2006); "Grammy Nominated Crabb Family 'Driven' to Share Faith," Cbn.com, http://www.cbn.com/700club/guests/bios/crabbfamily_020305.aspx (accessed October 28, 2006); "Mercy's Mark Scheduled to Appear on TBN," Singingnews.com, October 4, 2005, http://www.singingnews.com/news/sg_wire/story_detail.lasso?id=35023; "Greater Vision to Record Live Album," Singingnews.com, August 9, 2001, http://www.singingnews.com/news/sg_wire/story_detail.lasso?id=32775; "Legacy Five to Perform at Southern Baptist Convention," Singingnews.com, June 2, 2005, http://www.singingnews.com/southern-gospel-news/11591659/.

11. Mark Allen Powell, "There's Just Something about That Man," *Christianity Today*, April 2004, http://www.christianitytoday.com/ct/2004/april/1.32.html.

12. James Goff, "The Rise of Southern Gospel Music," *Church History* 67 (December 1998): 723.

13. Don Cusic has also written about the history of southern gospel, and despite its cursory nature, Cusic's is probably the best treatment of southern gospel's intersection with emerging forms of contemporary Christian music in the second half of the twentieth century. Cusic, *The Sound of Light: A History of Gospel and Christian Music* (Milwaukee: Hal Leonard, 2002). No volume of critical (as opposed to historical) scholarship devoted to southern gospel existed until the 2004 publication of *More than Precious Memories: The Rhetoric of Southern Gospel Music*, ed. Michael Graves and David Fillingim (Macon: Mercer University Press, 2004), a collection of ten essays from a constellation of authors who draw heavily on communication and rhetorical theory in their analyses (I have commented more fully about this volume in "Why Southern Gospel Music Matters," *Religion and American Culture* 18, no. 1 [2008]: 27–28). The most comprehensive existing scholarly treatment of southern gospel is James Goff's *Close Harmony: A History of Southern Gospel Music* (Chapel Hill: University of North Carolina Press, 2002). One of the most valuable contributions of this work to the scholarly understanding of southern gospel is Goff's emphasis on the music's infrastructural evolution over time. By placing southern gospel within a stream of historical influences and socioeconomic contexts that shaped its development into a mass-market music industry, Goff implicitly defines southern gospel as stylistically and historically coherent, yet also porous at all its borders so that it shapes and is shaped by musical styles and traditions adjacent to it. This approach treats southern gospel not as a single entity, but rather as an elastic network of musicians who work along a continuum of styles rooted in American hymnody and folk traditions and reliant on contemporary church music and secular musical genres for creative infusions. In this my work shares with Goff an emphasis on the open-ended quality of a musical tradition that cultivates close ties with other musical genres (praise and worship music, bluegrass, CCM, and country, especially) in order to remain responsive to the present needs of its practitioners and listeners. At the same time, the emphasis in Goff's book on changes over time in the way the music was created, sold, and consumed leaves very little room for any meaningful engagement with the sonic experience of southern gospel music in all its lived, immediate, soul-stirring power. Thus, one finds in *Close Harmony* a great deal about marketing innovations in southern gospel's economic development, important technological advances that were brought to bear on old ways of music making, and fortuitous marriages and other impactful personal alliances in the music's history. But the fundamentally inductive element to this approach—southern gospel as the sum of the material, historical, and social changes it absorbed over time—limits the scope of its insights into southern gospel's cultural function as a means of forming and expressing religious identity, which is the central concern of this book.

14. David Fillingim, "Oft Made to Wonder: Southern Gospel as Musical Theodicy," in *More than Precious Memories*, ed. Graves and Fillingim, 49. Janice Rushing suggests a similar approach to gospel music in "Gospel Music Rhetoric," *Religious Communication Today* 1, no. 1 (1978): 29–35.

15. In general, "modern" describes habits of thought and action rather than a specific period or moment. As Theodore Adorno describes it, "modern" is a "qualitative," as

opposed to chronological, distinction. Adorno's theory of modernity is particularly useful in emphasizing a purposeful self-consciousness about the products of the mind and imagination, especially skepticism about the value of mere "replication." Instead, modern modes of imagination and creation consciously reposition the self in relation to the past. Adorno, *Minima Moralia* (London: Verso, 2005), 218. Here and throughout, I use the term *modern* in this spirit, as a functional designation for the emergence of an actively cultivated self-conscious dimension to the conceptualization, creation, and dissemination of southern gospel in the years after the Civil War, when a specific set of psychosocial dimensions began to be realized in this music. At the same time, I use *modern* in the materialist sense to describe the emergence in the long twentieth century in America (Civil War onward) of popular music publishing, professional music performance artists, sound recording, electronic amplification, radio, television, and ultimately digital modes of content provision.

16. Goff, *Close Harmony*, 35.

17. Michael Kammen, *Mystic Chords of Memory: The Transformation of Tradition in American Culture* (New York: Vintage, 1993), 300; Stuart Patterson, "'The Dream Then and Now': Democratic Nostalgia and the Living Museum at Arthurdale, West Virginia," in *Defining Memory: Local Museums and the Construction of History in America's Changing Communities*, ed. Amy Levin (Walnut Creek, Calif.: AltaMira Press, 2007), 110–11.

18. Here and throughout, I will place emphasis on the structuring influence of shape-note music culture on today's professional southern gospel music, largely to the exclusion of other expressive traditions and influences, religious or secular. I do so with awareness that a whole universe of musical possibilities was available to southerners generally, and to evangelical southerners particularly, in the nineteenth and early twentieth centuries. My decision to focus here on the constellation of practices and approaches to southern sacred music making bound up in the seven-shape gospel notational tradition is a way of circumscribing a vast and sprawling hydra-headed topic that—if tracked long enough—can lead just about anywhere in American life. More important, this approach is a way of honoring and attempting to understand better the genealogy that today's professional southern gospel fans and practitioners themselves claim as a defining ancestry.

19. Blackwood Brothers, "Lord Build Me a Cabin in the Corner of Gloryland," on *Close Harmony: A History of Southern Gospel Music*, vol. 1, *1920–1955* (Dualtone, 2004, CDC-959240).

20. Though most of American evangelicalism has been theologically Arminian since roughly the Second Great Awakening in the early to mid–nineteenth century, I prefer to describe contemporary voluntarist evangelicalism as "in the Calvinist tradition" because it places its emphasis as much on the predestinarian aspect of salvation as on the choosing of it (one must choose to be saved, but what makes that choosing important is that God has personally known you would do so since the foundations of time). In its lived paradoxes, this theological outlook more closely resembles the self-embattlement most powerfully associated with the Calvinist tradition.

21. I am grateful to Mark McClellan for sharing a copy of his play with me.

22. Fillingim, "Flight from Liminality," 80. Here and throughout, and following Douglas Kellner and Steven Best, I use the term *postmodern* and its derivatives to designate the late-twentieth- and early-twenty-first century era of "contemporary high tech media

society," defined by "increased cultural fragmentation, changes in the experience of space and time, and new modes of experience, subjectivity and culture" that proliferate in globalized, late-capitalist formations of Anglo-European civilization(s). Kellner and Best, *Postmodern Theory: Critical Interrogations* (New York: Guilford Press, 1991), 3–5.

23. Benedict Anderson, *Imagined Communities: Reflections on the Origin and Spread of Nationalism* (London: Verso, 1991). Anderson's analysis implicitly takes up lines of inquiry set out by earlier theorists of the role of imaginative constructs in society. See particularly Cornelius Castoriadis, *The Imaginary Institution of Society*, trans. Kathleen Blamey (1975; reprint, Cambridge: MIT Press, 1998). More recently, scholarship on the social imaginary has moved beyond Anderson's framework to posit society as constituting a coexisting network of "multiple modernities," another promising framework for thinking through the subterranean complexities of evangelical popular culture. Charles Taylor, *Modern Social Imaginaries* (Durham: Duke University Press, 2004).

24. Raymond Williams, *Marxism and Literature* (New York: Oxford University Press, 1977), 132.

25. Marini, *Sacred Music*, 74–81.

26. Edward Ayers, *The Promise of the New South: Life after Reconstruction* (New York: Oxford University Press, 2007), 397–98.

27. Eskew and Downey, "Shape-Note Hymnody."

28. Malone, *Southern Music, American Music*, 67. On both the southern and the midwesterly spread of gospel music, see Eskew and Downey, "Shape-Note Hymnody"; and A. D. Horsley, "The Spatial Impact of White Gospel Quartets in the United States," *John Edwards Memorial Foundation Quarterly* 15 (1979): 91–98. On hymns and gospel music in the nineteenth century, see Sandra Sizer, *Gospel Hymns and Social Religion: The Rhetoric of Nineteenth-Century Revivalism* (Philadelphia: Temple University Press, 1978).

29. William Lynwood Montell, *Singing the Glory Down: Amateur Gospel Music in South Central Kentucky, 1900–1990* (Lexington: University Press of Kentucky, 1991), 4.

30. Demographic data obtained from a large-scale survey of southern gospel fans and performers regarding popular attitudes and beliefs about southern gospel music. For a more complete discussion of southern gospel's demographic profile, see appendix B, discussing the survey's method and its basic demographic findings.

31. Horsley, "Spatial Impact," 91.

32. David Crawford, "Gospel Songs in Court: From Rural Music to Urban Industry in the 1950s," *Journal of Popular Culture* 11 (Winter 1977): 555. On hymns, see *Sing Them over Again to Me: Hymns and Hymnbooks in America*, ed. Mark Noll and Edith Blumhofer (Tuscaloosa: University of Alabama Press, 2006).

33. Crawford, "Gospel Songs in Court," 555; "Brethren, We Have Met to Worship," in *The Baptist Hymnal* (Nashville: Baptist Press, 1975), 260; "Too Much to Gain to Lose," in *The Dottie Rambo Collection: Songs of a Lifetime* (Nashville: Daywind Music, n.d.), 30–31.

34. Montell, *Singing the Glory Down*, 4.

35. Qualitative comments drawn from this survey appear throughout the book and are cited as online responses to author's query. Appendix B at the back of the book describes the method of this survey in more detail.

36. Eskew et al., "Gospel Music."

37. Judy Spencer Nelon and Niles Borop, ed., *The World's Greatest Southern Gospel Songs* (Chester, N.Y.: Shawnee, n.d.).

38. Jane Tompkins, *Reader-Response Criticism: From Formalism to Post-Structuralism* (Baltimore: Johns Hopkins University Press, 1980), 53.

39. Barbara Rossing, *The Rapture Exposed: The Message of Hope in the Book of Revelation* (Boulder: Westview Press, 2004); Mark Noll, *The Scandal of the Evangelical Mind* (Grand Rapids: Eerdmans, 1995), 3; Franky Schaeffer, *Addicted to Mediocrity: Contemporary Christians and the Arts* (Wheaton, Ill.: Crossway, 1981); Noll, *Scandal of the Evangelical Mind*, 12.

40. Jeff Todd Titon, *Powerhouse for God: Speech, Chant, and Song in an Appalachian Baptist Church* (Austin: University of Texas Press, 1988), 246.

41. Chris Christian, *How to Get Started in Christian Music* (Dallas: Home Sweet Home, 1986), 9; Titon, *Powerhouse for God*, 246.

42. Stations that play southern gospel tend to transmit on comparatively low-wattage signals and to be owned by individuals, family businesses, or local religious organizations whose leaders portray these stations not primarily as financial concerns but as forms of ministerial outreach. Except at a comparatively small group of stations with corporate affiliation, airplay of southern gospel music is not tracked by any reliable reporting system (such as Broadcast Data Systems).

43. On evangelical apocalyptic fiction, see Amy Johnson Frykholm, *Rapture Culture: "Left Behind" in Evangelical America* (New York: Oxford University Press, 2004). On evangelical sermon rhetoric, see Harding, *Book of Jerry Falwell.*

44. Susan McClary, "Paradigm Dissonances: Music Theory, Cultural Studies, Feminist Criticism," *Perspectives of New Music* 32, no. 1 (1994): 77; Heidi Epstein, *Melting the Venusberg: A Feminist Theology of Music* (New York: Continuum, 2004), 5; Robert Fink, "Elvis Everywhere: Musicology and Popular Music Studies at the Twilight of the Canon," *American Music* 16, no. 2 (1998): 156–58.

45. McClary, "Paradigm Dissonances," 70.

46. "This World Is Not My Home," in *Homecoming Souvenir Songbook* (Alexandria, Ind.: Gaither, 1993), 2.

47. Del Shores, *Southern Baptist Sissies* (New York: Samuel French, 2001); Susan McClary, "A Musical Dialectic from the Enlightenment: Mozart's Piano Concerto in G Major, K.453, Movement 2," *Cultural Critique* 4, no. 4 (1986): 132.

48. In 2008 Jeff Steele told a BBC producer of *The World of White Gospel* that he regretted the song's use of what he called a "mean-spirited," "heavy-handed," and "rabble-rousing" approach, though he also claimed he still would have said "99 percent" of the same things if he were to do it over again. One does wonder about that 1 percent.

49. Raymond Williams, *Culture and Society, 1780–1950* (New York: Columbia University Press, 1983), xviii.

50. Douglas Harrison, "Scholarly Voice and Professional Identity in the Internet Age," *Thought and Action* 24 (Fall 2008): 23–33.

51. Harold Bloom, *How to Read and Why* (New York: Simon and Schuster, 2000), 29; Lauren Berlant, *The Queen of America Goes to Washington: Essays on Sex and Citizenship* (Durham: Duke University Press, 1997), 12. More recently, Stanley Fish has used his

New York Times blog to critique the rise of culture studies in departments of English and what he sees as their tendency to scatter the force and hasten the decline of the literary critical enterprise as he imagines it.

52. Epstein, *Melting the Venusberg*, 3.

53. See Fink, "Elvis Everywhere," 135–79.

54. Judith (now Jake) Halberstam, "Between Butches," in *Butch/Femme: Inside Lesbian Gender*, ed. Sally Munt (Washington, D.C.: Cassell Academic, 1998), 63; Michael Gilmour, "Radios in Religious Studies Departments: Preliminary Reflections on the Study of Religion in Popular Music," in *Call Me the Seeker: Listening to Religion in Popular Music*, ed. Michael Gilmour (New York: Continuum, 2005), viii.

55. Judith (now Jake) Halberstam, *Female Masculinities* (Durham: Duke University Press, 1998), 13; Adale Sholock, "Queer Theory in the First Person: Academic Autobiography and the Authoritative Contingencies of Visibility," *Cultural Critique* 66 (Spring 2007): 138; John Champagne, *The Ethics of Marginality: A New Approach to Gay Studies* (Minneapolis: University of Minnesota Press, 1995), 91.

56. Clifford Geertz, *The Interpretation of Cultures* (New York: Basic Books, 1973), 10.

Chapter 1. *Glory Bumps; or, The Psychodynamics of the Southern Gospel Experience*

1. Cusic, *Sound of Light* (see introduction, n. 13).

2. "I'll Fly Away," in *The American Country Hymn Book* (Nashville: Canaanland Music, 1975), 9.

3. Cecilia Tichi, *High Lonesome: The American Culture of Country Music* (Chapel Hill: University of North Carolina Press, 1994), ix; Fillingim, "Flight from Liminality," 80 (see introduction, n. 9).

4. Online response to author's query.

5. R. Williams, *Marxism and Literature*, 132 (see introduction, n. 24). All quotes from online responses to author's query.

6. For representative examples of Puritan captivity narratives, see William Andrews et al., *Journeys in New Worlds: Early American Women's Narratives* (Madison: University of Wisconsin Press, 1990). For a study of the Great Awakening in early America, see Frank Lambert, *Inventing the Great Awakening* (Princeton: Princeton University Press, 2001). For a literary critical analysis of antebellum women's fiction in America, see Susan Harris, *Nineteenth-Century American Women's Novels: Interpretive Strategies* (Cambridge: Cambridge University Press, 1990).

7. "Till the Storm Passes By," in *Homecoming Souvenir Songbook*, 108–9 (see introduction, n. 46). Lyrics and music by Mosie Lister. © 1973 Mosie Lister Songs (admin. by Music Services) / Southern Faith Songs (admin. by Music Services). All rights reserved. Used by permission.

8. "We'll Understand It Better By and By," on *Homecoming Souvenir Songbook*, vol. 2 (Alexandria, Ind.: Gaither, 1994), 154–55.

9. David Gibson, "Ted Haggard Is Back," *Politics Daily*, June 5, 2010, http://www.politicsdaily.com/2010/06/02/ted-haggard-is-back-gay-sex-and-drug-scandal-cant-keep-evangel/.

10. The Perrys, "Oh That Wonderful Promise," on *This Is the Day* (Daywind, 2003, DAY-1321D). Words and music by Kyla Rowland. Copyright © 2003 Christian Taylor Music (BMI). Rights in the United States and Canada for Christian Taylor Music Administered by BMG Chrysalis. All rights reserved. Used by permission. Reprinted by permission of Hal Leonard Corporation.

11. Robert McManus, "Southern Gospel Music vs. Contemporary Christian Music: Competing for the Soul of Evangelicalism," in *More than Precious Memories*, ed. Graves and Fillingim, 73 (see introduction, n. 13).

12. Kip Lornell, liner notes to *White Gospel* (Collectables, 1990, COL-5316).

13. Online response to author's query.

14. Craig Werner, *Playing the Changes: From Afro-Modernism to the Jazz Impulse* (Urbana: University of Illinois Press, 1994), xvii.

15. Andrae Crouch, "Can't Nobody," in *The Best of Andrae Crouch* (Milwaukee: Hal Leonard), 6–8. Lyrics and music by Andrae Crouch © 1982 Bud John Songs (ASCAP) (admin. at EMICMGPublishing.com). All rights reserved. Used by permission.

16. Werner, *Playing the Changes*, 108.

17. Online response to author's query.

18. Here, I am adapting a version of Maxine Grossman's formulation in "Jesus, Mama, and the Constraints of Salvific Love in Contemporary Country Music," in *Call Me the Seeker*, ed. Gilmour, 82 (see introduction, n. 54).

19. Online response to author's query.

20. The McKameys, "God on the Mountain," on *Gone to Meetin'* (Morning Star, 1989, CDC-4089). Lyrics and music by Tracy Dartt © Copyright 1988. Gaviota Music, Inc. / BMI (admin. By ClearBox Rights). All rights reserved. Used by permission.

21. Janice Rushing, "Gospel Music Rhetoric," *Religious Communication Today* 1, no. 1 (1978): 29.

22. Tracy Dartt, comments in *The God on the Mountain Legacy*, http://www.godonthemountainlegacy.com/ (accessed June 28, 2010); I. A. Richards, *Practical Criticism* (New York: Harcourt, Brace, and World, 1963), 254–74; Robert Milder, *Exiled Royalties: Melville and the Life We Imagine* (New York: Oxford University Press, 2005), 83.

23. Jerry Kirksey (then editor in chief of *Singing News*), in conversation with the author, September 2009.

24. "Truth Is Marching On," on *Gold City, Revival* (New Haven, 2006, CD-8064).

25. The Steeles, "We Want America Back," on *We Want America Back* (Daywind, 1996, CD-1117); Kelly Nelon Thompson and the Nelons, "We've Got to Get America Back to God," on *Kelly Nelon Thompson and the Nelons* (Riversong, 1993, CD-02086). Perhaps the Nelons' most famous politically polemical song was the 1986 hit "Famine in Their Land," about the former Soviet Union's spiritual impoverishment under communism: "There's a famine in their land," the chorus goes, "not of bread, not a water." On *Journeys* (Canaan, 1986, CAS-9951).

26. John Dougan, review of *Close Harmony*, *Virginia Magazine of History and Biography* 110, no. 2 (2002): 279–80 (emphasis added).

27. For lyrics and further discussion, see Goff, *Close Harmony*, 278–79 (see introduction, n. 13).

28. "Obama May Be the 'AntiChrist,'" *DailyKos*, March 23, 2010, http://www.dailykos.com/story/2010/3/23/144529/874.

29. Kenneth Burke, *The Philosophy of Literary Form* (New York: Vintage, 1957), 262.

30. Andrew Sullivan, "My Problem with Christianism," *Time*, May 7, 2006, http://www.time.com/time/printout/0,8816,1191826,00.html.

31. Burke, *Philosophy of Literary Form*, viii; "Sheltered in the Arms of God," in *Homecoming Souvenir Songbook*, 40. Lyrics and music by Dottie Rambo and Jimmie Davis. Copyright © 1969 by Peermusic LTD. Copyright renewed. All rights reserved. Used by permission.

32. Ralph Waldo Emerson, *The Complete Sermons of Ralph Waldo Emerson*, ed. Albert J. von Frank, 4 vols. (Columbia: University of Missouri Press, 1989–1992), 2:194; Emily Dickinson, "In Many and Reportless Places," in *Complete Poems of Emily Dickinson*, ed. Thomas Johnson (Boston: Little, Brown, 1961), 593–94.

33. Stephen Tucker, "Pentecostalism and Popular Culture in the South: A Study of Four Musicians," *Journal of Popular Culture* 16, no. 3 (1982): 68.

34. The Hinsons, "That I Could Still Go Free," on *Touch of Hinson, Glimpse of Glory* (Calvary Records, 1974, STAV-5110).

35. "I Will Glory in the Cross," in *Dottie Rambo Collection*, 6–7 (see introduction, n. 33).

36. The Bowling Family, "I Still Glory in the Cross," on *Shine* (Big Ten House of Music, 2010, [no album identification number]).

37. Greenes, "When I Knelt, the Blood Fell," on *Tenth Anniversary Live* (self-produced, 1989, ACA-007).

38. Jonathan Edwards, *Religious Affections*, ed. John Smith (New Haven: Yale University Press, 1959), 125–91; Bertram Wyatt-Brown, *The Shaping of Southern Culture: Honor, Grace, and War, 1760s–1880s* (Chapel Hill: University of North Carolina Press, 2000), 14–15.

39. John Milton, "Paradise Lost," in *Complete Poems and Major Prose*, ed. Merritt Hughes (New York: Macmillan, 1957), 212.

40. The Crabb Family, "Through the Fire," on *Driven* (Daywind, 2004, CD-871383). Words and music by Gerald Crabb. Copyright © 1999 MPCA Lehsem Songs. Administered by MPCA Music, LLC. International copyright secured. All rights reserved. Reprinted by permission of Hal Leonard Corporation.

41. Fillingim, "Oft Made to Wonder," 54 (see introduction, n. 14).

42. Thomas Shepard, *The Sincere Convert and the Sound Believer* (New York: AMS Press, 1967), 219; Perry Miller, *New England Mind: From Colony to Province* (Cambridge: Harvard University Press, 1953), 24.

43. Sacvan Bercovitch, *The Puritan Origins of the American Self* (New Haven: Yale University Press, 1975), 19; Miller, *New England Mind*, 70, 68.

44. For more on contemporary evangelical notions of exceptionalism, see Clifford Longley, *Chosen People: The Big Idea That Shaped England and America* (London: Hodder & Stoughton, 2003).

45. William James, *The Varieties of Religious Experience* (New York: Touchstone, 2004), 60–95; Joyce Meyer, *Battlefield in Your Mind: Winning the Battle in Your Mind* (New York:

Warner Books, 2000); Rick Warren, *The Purpose Driven Life* (Grand Rapids: Zondervan, 2002); Joel Osteen, *It's Your Time: Activate Your Faith, Achieve Your Dreams, and Increase in God's Favor* (New York: Free Press, 2009).

Chapter 2. Nostalgia, Modernity, and the Reconstruction Roots of Southern Gospel

1. Charles Edwin Morrison, "Aldine S. Kieffer and Ephraim Ruebush: Ideals Reflected in Post–Civil War Ruebush-Kieffer Company Music Publications" (Ph.D. diss., Arizona State University, 1992), 69.

2. Lonnie Speer, *Portals to Hell: Military Prisons of the Civil War* (Lincoln: Bison Books, 2005), 228.

3. Morrison, "Kieffer and Ruebush," 71.

4. Charles Wolfe claims that Kieffer and Ruebush first "met at a Union prisoner-of-war camp" (*Classic Country: Legends of Country Music* [New York: Routledge, 2000], 221), but in fact Kieffer's autobiographical writings in the *Musical Million* clearly indicate that the two met in Mountain Valley (later Singers Glen) in 1853. Aldine Kieffer, "Reminiscences," *Musical Million* (July 1890): 104.

5. Morrison, "Kieffer and Ruebush," 71.

6. Ibid., 41. What exactly Ruebush did during the war remains somewhat uncertain. Stephen Shearon suggests that Ruebush may have sat out all or part of the war in West Virginia. Shearon, "Ephraim Ruebush," in *Encyclopedia of American Gospel Music*, 325–36 (see introduction, n. 4).

7. Ibid., 72.

8. In the first half of the twentieth century, this romanticized notion of southern pastoralism resurfaced as the animating idea of the agrarian school of southern writers and intellectuals associated with Vanderbilt University. For the agrarians, modern capitalist society and its commodity-driven culture had blighted the South and severed the essential connection between the salt-of-the-earth yeomanry and the southern landscape. In the words of Andrew Lytle, who emerged as one of the movement's most eloquent spokesmen, capitalism "presents an awful spectacle: men, run mad by their inventions, supplanting themselves with inanimate objects." Lytle, "The Hind Tit," in *I'll Take My Stand: The South and the Agrarian Tradition* (Baton Rouge: Louisiana State University Press, 1977), 202–3. Lytle was, among other things, mentor to the novelist Harry Crews—author of *The Gospel Singer,* about an Elvisesque white gospel megastar caught in the vortex of violence, sex, and the religious ecstasy of gospel singing in the white-trash town of Enigma, Georgia. As a descendant of a response to the agrarian movement, Crews's fiction is notable for what Jeff Abernathy has called his "dark vision" of agrarianism, one that shared none of Lytle's fervent belief in the rejuvenating capacity of the land to repair the damage capitalism had done. Abernathy, "Agrarian Nightmare: Harry Crews' Dark Vision in *Naked in Garden Hills,*" *Southern Literary Journal* 34, no. 1 (Fall 2001): 68–78. Indeed, *The Gospel Singer,* Crews's first novel, uses the midcentury world of commercialized southern gospel music to critique the unrealistic sentimentality of the agrarian ethos and dramatize the totalizing, nihilistic effects of mass-market technologies and cultures on rural southern life.

9. Morrison, "Kieffer and Ruebush," 71–72.

10. Stephen Shearon, "Aldine S. Kieffer," in *Encyclopedia of American Gospel Music*, 216.

11. Marini, *Sacred Song in America*, 79–81.

12. For the development of shape-note music, see Eskew and Downey, "Shape-Note Hymnody" (see introduction, n. 5). For more on shape-note music in the development of professional southern gospel, see Goff, *Close Harmony*, 35–58 (see introduction, n. 13).

13. William Brooks, "Music in America: An Overview (Part 1)," in *Cambridge History of American Music*, ed. David Nichols (Cambridge: Cambridge University Press, 1998), 36.

14. George Pullen Jackson, *White Spirituals of the Southern Uplands: The Story of the Fasola Folk, Their Songs, Singings, and "Buckwheat Notes"* (Chapel Hill: University of North Carolina Press, 1933), 349.

15. See Bob Terrell, *The Music Men: The Story of Professional Gospel Music Singing* (Alexander, N.C.: Mountain Church, 1990), 14–16; Goff, *Close Harmony*, 44–51; and Cusic, *Sound of Light*, 154–55 (see introduction, n. 13).

16. Goff, *Close Harmony*, 4; Shearon, "Aldine S. Kieffer," 215. Cusic, *Sound of Light*, more than implicitly takes the origins of southern gospel back to Kieffer, but as part of a much more ambitious history of Christian music *sensu lato*, Cusic's treatment is necessarily cursory and, so, historiographically unobtrusive.

17. Morrison, "Kieffer and Ruebush," 72.

18. Drew Gilpin Faust, *This Republic of Suffering: Death and the American Civil War* (New York: Vintage, 2008), 137.

19. Morrison, "Kieffer and Ruebush," 48.

20. J. Wayne Flynt, *Dixie's Forgotten People: The South's Poor Whites* (Bloomington: Indiana University Press, 1979), 34.

21. Morrison, "Kieffer and Ruebush," 79, 54.

22. Ibid., 72.

23. See, for instance, Gavin James Campbell, "'Old Can Be Used Instead of New': Shape Note Singing and the Crisis of Modernity in the New South, 1880–1920," *Journal of American Folklore* 110, no. 436 (1997): 169–88. Campbell is one of the most astute historians of southern shape-note music, and his work insightfully contextualizes the emergence of shape-note white gospel music as a constitutive feature of the New South's rise in general. My point here is not to take issue with this type of reading so much as to note that while these developments ultimately contributed to the modernization of the New South, as Campbell shows, they had value for their proponents primarily as vehicles of social reform that reinforced populist ideals anchored in the past of southern pastoral romanticism, ideals that often put them at odds ideologically or psychosocially with the main currents of urban New Southernism.

24. "Twilight Whispers," in *The Temple Star*, ed. Aldine Kieffer (Dayton, Va.: Ruebush-Kieffer, 1886), 16; "Evergreen Shore" and "Jesus Will Let You In," in *Hours of Fancy; or, Vigil and Vision*, by Aldine Kieffer (Dayton, Va.: Ruebush-Kieffer, 1881), 208, 215.

25. Edward Ayers, *The Promise of the New South: Life after Reconstruction* (New York: Oxford University Press, 2007), 118.

26. Campbell, "'Old Can Be Used,'" 173.

27. Morrison, "Kieffer and Ruebush," 71. Kieffer is most likely mistaken in attributing the rank of captain to Ruebush. The latter appears to have been offered a lieutenancy in the Union army, a position he may have turned down because he wished not to fight family and friends serving in the Confederacy. Shearon, "Ephraim Ruebush," 326.

28. Wyatt-Brown, *Shaping of Southern Culture*, 233 (see chap. 1, n. 38).

29. Jackson, *White Spirituals*, 215.

30. For evolving attitudes and beliefs surrounding Protestant conversion, individual agency, and American freedom, see Nathan Hatch, *The Democratization of American Christianity* (New Haven: Yale University Press, 1991). For a reconsideration of American religious formation that implicitly revises Hatch's thesis, see David Sehat, *The Myth of American Religious Freedom* (New York: Oxford University Press, 2010).

31. Steven Cornelius, *Music of the Civil War Era* (Santa Barbara: Greenwood Press, 2004), 4–5, 17.

32. Ibid., 105–7.

33. Gilpin-Faust (*Republic of Suffering*, 171–210) traces forward the ontological fallout from the Civil War as it eroded traditional bases for American religious belief.

34. Morrison, "Kieffer and Ruebush," 67. For a broad survey of this epistolary tradition, see Cornelius, *Civil War Era*.

35. Morrison, "Kieffer and Ruebush," 69.

36. Cornelius, *Civil War*, 148.

37. Marini, *Sacred Song*, 81.

38. Kieffer, *The Temple Star*, 121, 130.

39. "Grave on the Green Hillside," in *The Royal Proclamation* (Dayton, Va.: Ruebush-Kieffer, 1886), 112–13.

40. Though published in 1886, "Grave" exhibits most of the key characteristics that would come to define early-twentieth-century shape-note gospel music as described by Jackson (*White Spirituals*, 380) and more recently Eskew and Downey ("Shape-Note Hymnody"). According to these scholars, early twentieth-century gospel music is based on diatonic scales; dotted rhythms; melodies in the major mode; progressions using tonic, dominant, and subdominant chords; and relatively large intervals. "Grave" anticipates most of these features. The melody is set in the major mode and based on a diatonic scale, rather than the pentatonic scales that were more common in late-nineteenth-century shape-note gospel. The chorus relies semiregularly on dotted rhythms, and the verses contain at least one dotted figure roughly every third or fourth measure. The tonal range is small in the melody, but other parts jump as much as a major sixth. The tune uses popular progressions, and the harmony includes dominant sevenths in the verse and sixths in the chorus. As for the sounds of the past that influence the song, the most likely predecessors for "Grave" are not primarily indigenous southern traditions but instead are probably the antebellum hymns and Sunday-school songs being published in places like New York, Boston, Philadelphia, Cincinnati, and Chicago. That different style dates back to the 1790s and followed a reform movement in the Northeast that began to shun the New England psalmody of William Billings and similar writers as primitive and instead embraced the music theory of the contemporaneous European masters. The hymns of Lowell Mason exemplify this trend. This is the same movement that caused the American music community to adopt the continental seven-syllable solfege system

and led them to turn away from tunes and hymns written in North America, to the point that some compilations of this era were almost exclusively European in origin. For more on these trends in antebellum music, see Richard Crawford, "'Ancient Music' and the Europeanizing of American Psalmody, 1800–1810," in *A Celebration of American Music: Words and Music in Honor of H. Wiley Hitchcock*, ed. Richard Crawford et al. (Ann Arbor: University of Michigan Press, 1990), 225–55.

41. Morrison, "Kieffer and Ruebush," 76.

42. Eugene McCammon, commenting in *I'll Keep on Singing: The Southern Gospel Convention Tradition*, DVD, dir. Stephen Shearon and Mary Nichols (Murfreesboro: Middle Tennessee State University, 2010). The emergence of modern southern gospel is a study of paradoxes: among them, the use of pastoral nostalgia to energize modern modes of music making commoditized in mass-market gospel music publishing, the commercialization of antebellum shape-note music pedagogy and notation to mobilize postbellum songbook culture, and "newness" as an indicator of "tradition." These paradoxes are consistent with what Leon Trotsky described as the combined and uneven development of capitalist cultures. According to Trotsky, when weaker middle- and laboring-class societies are coercively absorbed by more powerful forces (the experience of poor whites in the South from Reconstruction into the early twentieth century), the dominated groups often fall back on ideas and practices of an earlier era as a way to (try to) arrest the loss of indigenous identity. But by virtue of their obsolescence, those outdated modes of expression receive new articulation and meaning in the changed circumstances of postconflict domination. Thus, "the very process of assimilation acquires a self-contradictory character." Trotsky, *The History of the Russian Revolution*, trans. Max Eastman (Ann Arbor: University of Michigan Press, 1932), 5.

43. Eskew and Downey, "Shape-Note Hymnody." I am grateful to Nikos Pappas and Stephen Shearon for insights on the multimodality of Ruebush-Kieffer songbooks.

44. Charlie D. Tillman, ed., *The Revival No. 2* (Atlanta: Charlie D. Tillman, 1896), 210, 234, 242, 243.

45. See W. J. Cash, *The Mind of the South* (New York: Vintage, 1991); Wyatt-Brown, *Shaping of Southern Culture*; and Ted Ownby, *Subduing Satan: Religion, Recreation, and Manhood in the Rural South, 1865–1920* (Chapel Hill: University of North Carolina Press, 1990).

46. Gregory Eiselein, "Sentimental Discourse and the Bisexual Erotics of 'Work,'" *Texas Studies in Literature and Language* 41, no. 3 (1999): 203–33; Cusic, *Sound of Light*, 94; Flynt, *Dixie's Forgotten People*, 1; Laura Lovett, *Conceiving the Future: Pronatalism, Reproduction, and the Family in the United States, 1890–1938* (Chapel Hill: University of North Carolina Press, 2007), 11; Aldine Kieffer, ed., *Crowning Day No. 3* (Dayton, Va.: Ruebush-Kieffer, 1894).

47. Campbell, "'Old Can Be Used,'" 170, 173.

48. Charles Tillman, "Life's Railway to Heaven," in *American Country Hymn Book*, 110–11 (see chap. 1, n. 2). For more on the railroad in nineteenth-century popular song, see Jon Finson, *The Voices That Are Gone* (New York: Oxford University Press, 1994), 122–46.

49. Eric Foner, *Reconstruction: America's Unfinished Revolution, 1863–1877* (New York: Harper & Row, 1988), 382.

50. Albert E. Brumley, "Turn Your Radio On," in *Homecoming Souvenir Songbook*, 6–7 (see introduction, n. 46). For popular views of technology in turn-of-the-century American music, see Finson, *Voices That Are Gone*, 146–56. For radio's role in the emergence of the contemporary evangelical movement, see Philip Goff, "'We Have Heard the Joyful Sound': Charles E. Fuller's Radio Broadcast and the Rise of Modern Evangelicalism," *Religion and American Culture* 9, no. 1 (1999): 67–95.

51. Tillman grew up the son of itinerant evangelists and hoped to make it big in the entertainment business. But he spent the early years of adulthood bouncing around among the kinds of low-paying odd jobs available to a young man of his class, experience, and (minimal) education: a house painter, an organ salesman, a medicine-show performer, a minstrel-show entrepreneur. Only when he turned to gospel music songwriting in his late twenties did Tillman find vocational purpose. See "Charlie D. Tillman (1861–1943)," *New Georgia Encyclopedia*, http://www.georgiaencyclopedia.org/nge/Article.jsp?id=h-888 (accessed July 15, 2010). Brumley was born on a cotton farm in Oklahoma and had received only a grade school education before attending a singing school and starting to write songs. Of his most famous composition, he said, "Actually, I was dreaming of flying away from that cotton field when I wrote 'I'll Fly Away'." See "Albert E. Brumley," BrumleyMusic.com, http://www.brumleymusic.com/Bio_-_Albert.html (accessed July 14, 2010); "Albert E. Brumley," Nashville Songwriters Association, http://www.nashvillesongwritersfoundation.com/a-c/albert-e-brumley.aspx (accessed July 14, 2010).

52. Preface to *Dortch's Gospel Voices No. 1* (Charlotte: C. H. Robinson, 1895).

53. On the ecumenical dimension of early white gospel, see Ayers, *Promise of the New South*, 397–98.

54. Chad Seales, "Cultivating the Desolate Meadows: Industry, Religion, and Social Differentiation in Siler City, North Carolina, 1884–1932," *North Carolina Historical Review* 85, no. 1 (2008): 57.

55. Preface to W. E. Penn, *Harvest Bells 1, 2, and 3 Combined* (St. Louis: W. E. Penn, 1892) (emphasis in the original).

56. Ownby, *Subduing Satan*, 141.

57. Robert Toll, *Blacking Up: The Minstrel Show in Nineteenth Century America* (New York: Oxford University Press, 1974), 17–18. See also Gavin James Campbell, *Music and the Making of the New South* (Chapel Hill: University of North Carolina Press, 2004).

58. Jackson, *White Spirituals*. For helpful sociohistorical contexts surrounding Jackson's scholarship and its limitations, see Kiri Miller, *Traveling Home: Sacred Harp and American Pluralism* (Urbana: University of Illinois Press, 2008), 9–13.

59. Malone, *Southern Music, American Music* (see introduction, n. 6).

60. All references to shape-note songbooks and sheet music here and elsewhere refer to holdings at the Center for Popular Music at Middle Tennessee State University (MTSU).

61. Preface to *Dortch's Gospel Voices*; Penn, *Harvest Bells*.

62. Ayers, *Promise of the New South*, 112.

63. Preface to *Happy Voices No. 1* (Waco, Tex.: Kyger, 1898).

64. Penn, *Harvest Bells*.

65. Christina D. Romer, "Spurious Volatility in Historical Unemployment Data," *Journal of Political Economy* 94, no. 1 (1986): 31.

66. Richard Mason, "Singing People Are Happy People: A Brief Look at Convention Gospel Music," in *Corners of Texas*, ed. Francis Edward Abernethy (Denton: University of North Texas Press, 1993), 272.

67. Cusic, *Sound of Light*, 157; editorial in *Vaughan's Family Visitor* 12, no. 9 (1923): 7.

68. Morrison, "Kieffer and Ruebush," 55.

69. Foner, *Reconstruction*, 380–82.

70. Max Weber, *The Protestant Ethic and the Spirit of Capitalism* (New York: Penguin, 2002). I invoke Weber here inasmuch as his thesis identified deep structures of feeling and action linking the Puritan-Calvinist imagination and the rise of American capitalism; subsequent scholarship has helpfully corrected and complicated many of the finer points of Weber's thesis. See, for instance, James Henretta, *The Origins of American Capitalism* (Boston: Northeastern University Press, 1991).

71. Morrison, "Kieffer and Ruebush," 96.

72. Glen Payne and George Younce, *The Cathedrals: The Story of America's Best-Loved Gospel Quartet* (Nashville: Zondervan, 1998), 33, 111 (emphasis in the original); Michael English, *The Prodigal Comes Home: My Story of Failure and God's Story of Redemption* (Nashville: Thomas Nelson, 2007), 82, 2.

73. Payne and Younce, *Cathedrals*, 149. See also Gerald Williams, *Mighty Lot of Singin'* (Little Rock: TMBQ, 1999); and Russ Cheatham, *Bad Boy of Gospel Music: The Calvin Newton Story* (Jackson: University of Mississippi Press, 2003).

74. Payne and Younce, *Cathedrals*, 112–13. Certainly, other forms of American popular music—particularly country (southern gospel's closets secular kin)—have long served a pseudometaphysical function and been a means of cultural distinction for many people from similar socioeconomic backgrounds. What I wish to draw attention to here is the way southern gospel's ready access to the discourse of grace and its musicalization of divine omnipotence notionally subsumes the celebrity ego present in all mass-market forms of popular music (secular or religious) beneath a providential scheme. In the process, lyrical narratives of individual struggle are transformed into more than vernacular dramas of social self-embattlement or evocative stories about the working (wo)man's survival against tough odds (common themes of country music). By being both intensely pietistic and unreservedly sentimental, southern gospel is uncommonly good at supporting the weight placed upon it by those who find in it not just individual validation but a framework within which to cultivate a transformative sense of self as, say, soul-saving evangelists or blood-bought ministers to the Christian spirit in Christ's kingdom on earth.

75. Weldon Myers, "Aldine S. Kieffer, the Valley Poet, and His Work," in *Two Notable Shape-Note Leaders* (1908; reprint, Wytheville, Va.: Bookworm & Silverfish, 1994), 24. Kieffer himself boasted in 1890 of having led an effort that "equipped" and "armed" the "cause of music in behalf of the millions" (Morrison, "Kieffer and Ruebush," 14; Shearon, "Aldine S. Kieffer," 216), but this was mostly likely a wishful or figurative use of "millions," playing off the title of the *Musical Million*.

76. For a discussion of the link between music education and economics in Mason's life and work, see Richard Crawford, *American Musical Life: A History* (New York: W. W.

Norton, 2001), 139–41. For a general treatment of Mason's career and influence, see Carol Pemberton, *Lowell Mason* (Ann Arbor: University of Michigan Press, 1985).

77. For more on Sankey and the gospel hymn phenomenon, see Leonard Ellinwood, *The History of American Church Music* (New York: Morehouse Gorham, 1953); and Arthur Stevenson, *The Story of Southern Hymnology* (Roanoke, Va.: Stone Printing, 1931). Goff notes that Sankey's influence was most profound in linking "religious tunes with the specific message of the gospel" in the "popular religious music" of the nineteenth century among both blacks and whites. Not least of all, Sankey is widely credited with popularizing the term *gospel* to describe this type of song. However, Goff goes on to observe that "it is likely that too much has been made of the term 'gospel,' given that the music would have flourished regardless of the name." *Close Harmony*, 25, 299. In this light, it is important to recognize the degree to which Sankey inevitably shaped the gestalt of gospel music—North and South, urban and rural, white and black—at the end of the nineteenth century (in addition to his collaborations with Moody, Sankey went on to work for Biglow and Main, perhaps the most important publisher of American sacred music in the 1800s). At the same time, Goff's caution reminds us to take care not to overextend the reach of Sankey's influence in the various forms of gospel that emerged from this era. In the case of Ruebush-Kieffer and in addition to the individual examples of Mason and Sankey, some of the other models the company may have been drawing from are suggested in a retrospective Kieffer wrote in 1890 (around the time of the twentieth anniversary of the *Musical Million*). There, Kieffer names some of the publishers who, thanks to his efforts and the *Million*, were now using seven-shape notation, at least in part, in their publications. They are "the Methodist publishing houses in the South, notably those of the Southern Methodist Publishing House, Nashville, Tenn.; J. W. Burke & Co., Macon, Ga.; A. J. Showalter & Co., Dalton, Ga., and J. B. Vaughan, Elberton, Ga." Kieffer goes on to write, "Going north we find such houses as The John Church Co., Cincinnati; Oliver Ditson & Co., Boston; Biglow & Main, New York; Mennonite Publishing Co., Elkhart, Ind.; The Brethren Publishing Co., Waterloo, Iowa, and the Christian Publishing House, Cincinnati, and such evangelists as Rev. W. E. Penn and Rev. W. T. Dale." While some of these firms surely are those Ruebush-Kieffer emulated, this list also hints at the significance and originality of the Ruebush-Kieffer shape-note musical and lyrical style. The first three of the northern companies Kieffer lists (in Cincinnati, Boston, and New York) were significant establishments in the world of nineteenth-century music publishing and, like most of the other companies listed, were almost certainly bowing to the demands of some of their markets and providing certain of their publications in both round notation and seven-shape notation in the Ruebush-Kieffer style. Aldine Kieffer, "A Retrospect," *Musical Million* (April 1890): 56.

78. Cusic, *Sound of Light*, 107.

79. Myers, "Aldine S. Kieffer," 22.

80. Reproductions of extant Ruebush-Kieffer financial documents are housed at MTSU's Center for Popular Music. For analysis of company finances and historical context for understanding the accounting records that survive, see Morrison, "Kieffer and Ruebush," 111–14.

81. Shearon ("Aldine S. Kieffer," 215) suggests that rifts may have developed in the relationship between Kieffer and Ruebush in the 1890s as Ruebush and his heirs began

attempting to move the company away from shape-note publishing. See also Morrison, "Kieffer and Ruebush," 88.

82. Goff, *Close Harmony*, 64.

83. Mary Kern, "Poets of the Shenandoah Valley in the Nineteenth Century" (master's thesis, Duke University, 1949), 43.

84. James Peacock, *Grounded Globalism: How the U.S. South Embraces the World* (Athens: University of Georgia Press, 2007), 258.

85. Burke, *Philosophy of Literary Form*, 256 (see chap. 1, n. 29).

Chapter 3. The Rise of "Southern" Gospel Music and the Compensations of History

1. Charles Wolfe, "Gospel Goes Uptown: White Gospel Music, 1945–1955," in *Folk Music and Modern Sound*, ed. William Ferris and Mary Hart (Jackson: University Press of Mississippi, 1982), 81. Goff puts the number at just over six million. *Close Harmony*, 79 (see introduction, n. 13).

2. Goff, *Close Harmony*, 61–62; Terrell, *Music Men*, 14 (see chap. 2, n. 15); Lois Blackwell, *The Wings of the Dove: The Story of Gospel Music in America* (Norfolk, Va.: Donning, 1978), 45; Fanny Flagg, *Standing in the Rainbow* (New York: Ballantine, 2002), 77.

3. In this Vaughan echoes the nineteenth-century gospel hymn writer and publisher Rigdon McCoy McIntosh. The back cover of McIntosh's 1881 song collection, *New Life*, describes him as "the Most Eminent Composer of Music in the South." Eskew and Downey, "Shape-Note Hymnody" (see introduction, n. 5).

4. Southern Gospel Music Association, http://www.sgma.org/ (accessed June 24, 2010); James D. Vaughan Museum, "Introduction," http://www.members.tripod.com/vaughanmuseum/id15.htm (accessed June 24, 2010).

5. J. R. (Ma) Baxter and Videt Polk, *Gospel Song Writers Biography* (Dallas: Stamps-Baxter, 1971), 13–15; Cusic, *Sound of Light*, 127 (see introduction, n. 13).

6. Goff, *Close Harmony*, 67, xii.

7. Ibid., 62–63; Kirksey conversation (see chap. 1, n. 23).

8. The Vaughan insignia ran in *Singing News* through April 2006, which coincided with the sale of the magazine by owner Maurice Templeton to Salem Communications.

9. See Van Wyck Brooks, "On Creating a Useable Past," *Dial* (April 11, 1918): 337–41.

10. Robert Milder, *Exiled Royalties: Melville and the Life We Imagine* (New York: Oxford University Press, 2006), 96.

11. Michael McKeon, *The Origins of the English Novel, 1600–1740* (New York: Oxford University Press, 2002), 141.

12. Cusic, *Sound of Light*, 130–31, 159.

13. Vaughan himself formed a family quartet at least as early 1882. Ibid., 156.

14. Goff, *Close Harmony*, 69. For a discussion of the social impact of other quartet traditions in nineteenth- and twentieth-century American music, see, for instance, Gage Averill, *Four Parts, No Waiting: A Social History of the Barbershop Quartet in America* (New York: Oxford University Press, 2003).

15. Goff, *Close Harmony*, 36–38.

16. Ibid., 39.

17. Wolfe, "Gospel Goes Uptown," 86.

18. Goff, *Close Harmony*, 266–67.

19. Cusic, *Sound of Light*, 159.

20. Wolfe, "Gospel Goes Uptown," 81.

21. By the early 1950s, Stamps-Baxter and Blackwood Brothers songbooks regularly featured cover images or full-page inside photographs of performers, in contrast with the standard practice in southern shape-note music publishing theretofore of covers adorned with ornate drawings of stylized religious scenes, settings, and iconography. For a typical cover photo from the midcentury era, see Blackwood Brothers, *Songs in the Air* (Memphis: Blackwood Brothers, ca. 1953). For an example of full-page inside photos, see Stamps Quartet, *Favorite Specials* (Dallas: Stamps Quartet Music, 1953). These types of self-promotional practices took various other forms as well. For instance, in another early 1950s songbook, the Blackwood Brothers included six pages of full-page photos—one group photo and a full-page portrait for each singer and the pianist—with biographical captions beneath each. *Radio Song Album* (Memphis: Blackwood Brothers, ca. 1950).

22. Payne and Younce, *Cathedrals*, 36–40, 99–105 (see chap. 2, n. 72); Bill Gaither, *It's More than Music: Life Lessons for Loving God* (New York: Faithway, 2003), 29, 39–40; G. Williams, *Mighty Lot of Singin,'* 20–28 (see chap. 2, n. 73).

23. "Stamps-Baxter," in *Encyclopedia of American Gospel Music*, 371 (see introduction, n. 4).

24. "How Gospel Music Has Grown," *Vaughan's Family Visitor* 27, no. 4 (1938): 8; Eskew and Downey, "Shape-Note Hymnody."

25. Publication of the magazine was revived under the Church of God's ownership and continued until 1986. A version of the press resumed under the Church of God's publishing arm, Tennessee Music and Printing Company, now a division of Pathway Press. See ibid.

26. "How Gospel Music Has Grown," 8.

27. The following exchange took place at "Farther Along: A Conference on the Southern Gospel Singing-Convention Tradition," hosted by the Center for Popular Music at Middle Tennessee State University, April 4–5, 2008.

28. Eskew and Downey, "Shape-Note Hymnody."

29. For American migration patterns in the twentieth century, see Donald Meinig, *The Shaping of America: Global America, 1915–2000* (New Haven: Yale University Press, 2006), 118–19. In addition to the cultural effects of migration on the development of southern gospel, Eskew and Downey ("Shape-Note Hymnody") note that the "introduction of traditional notation in the music programmes of public and private schools contributed to a decline in shape-note singing." Wolfe ("Gospel Goes Uptown," 96) further discusses the sociocultural implications of participatory and spectatorial modes of musical entertainment.

30. William Martin, "At the Corner of Glory Avenue and Hallelujah Street," *Harper's*, January 1972, 98.

31. A. D. Horsley, "The Spatial Impact of White Gospel Quartets in the United States," *John Edwards Memorial Foundation Quarterly* 15 (1979): 91–98 (quote on 91).

32. Wolfe, "Gospel Goes Uptown," 87.

33. Ibid., 87, 97.

34. Goff, *Close Harmony*, 201, 233.

35. Ibid., 235.

36. *Singing News*, September 1971, 23.

37. I borrow this concept as first encountered in David Bruce Murray's review of *Come Thirsty*, by the Perrys, Musicscribe blog, June 6, 2006, http://www.musicscribe .com/2006/06/cd-review-perrys-come-thirsty.html.

38. The Happy Goodman Family, "When Morning Sweeps the Sky," on *Good and Happy* (Canaan, 1966, CANAAN-9636). The song is rereleased under the correct title, "When Morning Sweeps the Eastern Sky," on *The Very Best of the Happy Goodman Family* (Crown Music Group, n.d., CCD-77721).

39. In conversation with the author, September 2009.

40. I include the 1970s here in light of recent scholarly rethinkings of the 1970s and the important realignments in politics, society, and globalism afoot in this often overlooked or misunderstood decade. See Niall Ferguson, Erez Manela, and Charles Maier, *The Shock of the Global: The 1970s in Perspective* (Cambridge: Harvard University Press, 2010).

41. Cusic, *Sound of Light*, 237–50; *Encyclopedia of Christian Music* (Peabody, Mass.: Hendrickson, 2002), 217. For more on the rise of early Christian rock, see John J. Thompson, *Raised by Wolves: The Story of Christian Rock & Roll* (Toronto: ECW, 2000). For Christian pop music and its relationship to evangelicalism, see David Stowe, *No Sympathy for the Devil: Christian Pop Music and the Transformation of American Evangelicalism* (Chapel Hill: University of North Carolina Press, 2011).

42. Goff, *Close Harmony*, 4.

43. Goff, "Rise of Southern Gospel Music," 725 (see introduction, n. 12). In *Close Harmony*, the intensity of this claim is moderated considerably.

44. Suzanne Lee, email to H-Southern Music Network mailing list, March 11, 2009.

45. "I Knows Bettah Now," in *The Modern Singer* (Lawrenceburg, Tenn.: James D. Vaughan Music, 1917), 101.

46. Walter Seale and Adger Pace, "Wake Up, America and Kluck, Kluck, Kluck" (Lawrenceburg, Tenn.: James D. Vaughan, 1924). "Wake Up, America" was recorded by the Vaughan Quartet on April 8, 1924 (recordings accessed at Middle Tennessee State University's Center for Popular Music). Records that included the song were advertised in the Klan's *Fiery Cross* magazine at Klan rallies. Cynthia Carr, *Our Town: A Heartland Lynching, a Haunted Town, and the Hidden History of White America* (New York: Crown, 2006), 62.

47. J. D. Sumner, "Sad Sam Jones," on *Blackwood Brothers* (Blackwood Brothers, 1956, BBL-1189); The Statesmen, *God, Family & Country with Gov. Lester Maddox* (LeFevre Sound, 1971, LS-3485); Dan Carter, *The Politics of Rage: George Wallace, the Origins of the New Conservatism, and the Transformation of American Politics* (Baton Rouge: Louisiana State University Press, 2000), 314; Gold City, *Gold City Quartet: Live* (HeartWarming, ca. 1982, HW-3817S).

48. Hovie Lister, Statesmen concert in Dallas, Tex., unreleased, May 10, 1959; "George Wallace," comment in *The American Experience: George Wallace: Settin' the Woods on Fire* (PBS, 2000).

49. The Statesmen, *Live at the Joyful Noise* (Skylite, 1979, SLP-6225); David Vest, "Elvis, Lester Maddox, and Peter Guralnick," Kaliyuga Highway, August 14, 2007, http://

davidvest.blogspot.com/2007/08/elvis-lester-maddox-and-peter-guralnick.html. Most available evidence suggests Lister saw himself as a friend to black gospel groups struggling to tour and earn a living under Jim Crow segregation. In 1966, for instance, a *Billboard* editorial singled Lister out for praise for having vocalized support for admitting black gospel singers and groups into the Gospel Music Association at a GMA board meeting:

> One of the most interesting aspects of the meeting, assuredly, was the quiet and rapid approval of a list of new members. These included several Negroes, including gospel composer Thomas A. Dorsey and Edna Mae Rittenhouse, an evangelistic singer.
>
> As a guide for passing upon new members, Hovie Lister, noted gospel singer, stated simply and flatly: 'We are only interested in a person's character and dedication to the field.' It was clear that was applicable to both white and black.
>
> Well said, Hovie. And well done, GMA!
>
> Let us hope other trade organizations follow this example.

"Answer to Bigotry," editorial, *Billboard*, August 27, 1966, 3.

Perhaps Lister felt that this kind of support for black gospel in the GMA made up for the racist stories he told onstage, but more likely, he simply saw no contradiction between his behavior onstage and his words in the GMA board meeting. In any event, though black gospel performers were eligible for GMA membership from 1966 forward, black performers were not included in the Dove Awards until well into the 1970s.

50. There are notable moments of exception to the rule of whiteness as normative in southern gospel. After she recorded a Grammy-winning album with a black gospel choir in 1968 (*It's the Soul of Me* [Heartwarming, no album identification number]), songwriter and singer Dottie Rambo famously defied Ku Klux Klan death threats and appeared onstage in the Jackson (Mississippi) County Auditorium. Rambo is said to have taken the stage, "opened up her arms," and directly addressed the KKK: "Here I stand. If you want to shoot me for singing with twenty spiritual people who know God [referring to the black gospel choir on *It's the Soul of Me*], here I am; go ahead and shoot." The audience is reported to have "responded with a standing ovation in praise to the Lord." Buck Rambo, *The Legacy of Buck and Dottie Rambo: The Inspiring Story of the Family That Changed the Direction of Gospel Music*, as told to Bob Terrell (Nashville: Star Song, 1992), 104.

51. See the opening of the introduction. In my experience, overt racism is no longer a part of ordinary southern gospel performance. But I have had uncomfortably close encounters with the psychosocial residue of racism that persists today. At the National Quartet Convention in 2007, Reggie Sadler—a black gospel singer whose family regularly headlines the NQC—was standing offstage, waiting to be brought on by the emcee, Gerald Wolfe, a popular white gospel vocalist. Squinting through the spotlights, Wolfe at first seemed not to have seen Sadler waiting to come on and started stalling, evidently thinking Sadler needed time to get to the stage. When Sadler started good-naturedly waving and yelling to get Wolfe's attention, Wolfe pretended to speak only to the house manager and said into his microphone, "Y'all put the spotlight on Reggie—we can't see him in the dark!" The crowd laughed heartily. The southern gospel blogosphere quickly picked up on the comment and started discussing its various racial overtones. Live blogging from the event that night, I called it a "fairly innocuous" remark, and I

still think this is true insofar as Wolfe did not seem to be acting out of overtly racist motives. Later, though, it became clear to me that my own initial reaction reflected my immersion in a part of southern white culture where, as I wrote in a follow-up mea culpa on my blog, it is acceptable and even hilarious for "a white man [to make] a joke about a black man's race in a room full of 15,000 white people in the South." "NQC 07: Black and White," Averyfineline, September 14, 2007, http://averyfineline.com/2007/09/14/nqc-07-black-and-white/.

52. For four-shape song styles and African American music, see K. Miller, *Traveling Home*, 10–12 (see chap. 2, n. 58). For informal mixed-race congregational worship experiences, see Allan Moore, "Surveying the Field: Our Knowledge of Blues and Gospel Music," in *Cambridge Companion to Blues and Gospel*, 6 (see introduction, n. 4). For "Gospel Boogie," see Wolfe, "Gospel Goes Uptown," 90. For Thomas A. Dorsey and southern gospel, see Elizabeth Desnoyers-Colas and Stephanie Howard [Asabi], "Bridge over Troubled Gospel Waters: The Cross-Cultural Appeal of Thomas A. Dorsey's Signature Songs," in *More than Precious Memories*, ed. Graves and Fillingim, 131–52 (see introduction, n. 13).

53. W. E. B. DuBois, *The Souls of Black Folk* (New York: NuVision, 2007), 108; Lornell, liner notes to *White Gospel* (see chap. 1, n. 12); Oak Ridge Boys, *Our Story* (Chicago: Contemporary, 1987), 22, 81; "Go Out to the Programs," on *Oak Ridge Boys in Toronto* (Canada, unreleased, April 30, 1972).

54. Stephen Shearon, email to H-Southern Music Network mailing list, March 27, 2009.

55. In addition to the various black gospel performers who have succeeded in southern white gospel, at least as notable Native American families of singers have made names for themselves in southern gospel as well, most notably the Klaudt Indian Family, who traveled for nearly sixty years in the twentieth century, and, more recently, the Jody Brown Indian Family. As their professional group names suggest, each family intentionally foregrounded their racial difference as part of their appeal. The Klaudts went so far as to perform in full tribal regalia as well. That these groups went out of their way to announce their racial difference in an overwhelmingly white industry suggests the degree to which "southern" gospel has rendered whiteness falsely normative, thereby reifying nonwhiteness as a marketable difference.

56. Kirksey conversation.

57. R. Williams, *Marxism and Literature*, 120–23 (see introduction, n. 24). Scholarly accounts of white gospel that focus on its northern, urban origins tend to see George Beverly Shea, Billy Graham's lead vocalist, as representing the dominant culture of white gospel in the mid–twentieth century and point to Shea's place as the heir to Sankey and Rodeheaver (Eskew et al., "Gospel Music" [see introduction, n. 5]), or to his international acclaim and record sales (Cusic, *Sound of Light*, 182) for proof of his dominance (see also introduction, n. 5). But this view holds true only by assuming mass American revival music occupied the same place in evangelical popular culture in the 1950s as it had a half century before. There is reason to doubt this assumption. In the earlier Sankey-Rodeheaver era, revival hymnody inarguably dominated white gospel because revivals were *the* way evangelical mass audiences cultivated popular religious music culture (indeed, the word *gospel* became a shorthand in this era for sacred music

introduced and popularized outside the church, though many "gospels"—such as "Love Lifted Me" and "Power in the Blood"—became popular enough to wend their way into the church-hymn canon). Like the music it made popular, this revivalism succeeded largely on the basis of its flamboyant departure from the expressively conservative norms of most Protestant worship experiences. But by the time of the Billy Graham crusades, American revivalism resembled nothing so much as a giant traveling Baptist church service—Graham himself the evangelical preacher par excellence. Shea's musical style, unlike his predecessors Sankey and Rodeheaver, reflected this new parachurch dynamic at work within Graham revivals: Shea sang "with reserved emotion" and "a controlled passion" typical of the singing in most midcentury evangelical churches, as opposed to the more emotionally demonstrative and charismatically expressive style associated with gospel singing of earlier eras, northern and southern. Shea was without doubt a major radio personality even before he joined forces with Graham, but as Cusic demonstrates (*Sound of Light*, 186), Shea's music always primarily had the church and church culture as its "focal point" (this aspect of Shea's oeuvre gets at part of what Eskew seems to mean in dismissing Shea's style of midcentury revival music as largely derivative). To the extent, then, that it is useful to speak of northern, urban (i.e., not southern) white gospel music in the mid-twentieth-century Billy Graham era, this music was, in effect, not so much gospel as it was church music writ large, with a big toe in the waters of commercial broadcast and record sales. Contrastingly, midcentury professional southern gospel emerged largely beyond the expressive confines of denominational worship experience and so became a fully formed mode of Christian entertainment in the gospel tradition that succeeded not despite its (comparative) distance from the church but because of it. In other words, midcentury professional southern gospel occupied roughly the same dominant pop-culture position as Sankey-Rodeheaver music in its time, while the Graham revival music was aligned with mainstream church culture. So while Shea in many ways became the voice of the mainstream Protestant gospel-hymn tradition in the mid–twentieth century, his music existed on the periphery of the dominant popular religious music entertainment industry emerging in Nashville and other pan-southern environs. For an alternative account of the history of gospel music's evolution in the first half of the twentieth century, see Mark Ward, *The Music in the Air: The Golden Age of Gospel Radio* (Belfast: Emerald House, 2004).

58. Brooks, "Creating a Useable Past," 337–41.

59. Kirksey conversation.

60. Bruce Feintuch, "Musical Revival as Musical Transformation," in *Transforming Tradition: Folk Music Revivals Examined*, ed. Neil Rosenburg (Urbana: University of Illinois Press, 1993), 191–92. Feintuch's influential paradigm applies to revivals within traditional folk music cultures, whereas professional southern gospel is a commercialized music industry. But many aspects of southern gospel—particularly its eschewal of notated music, its increasing reliance on amateurs, and its "unusual" distribution (see the introduction's discussion of the economic structure and distribution of southern gospel)—overlap with key features of folk music, as described in Philip Tagg, "Musicology and the Semiotics of Popular Music," *Semiotica* 66 (1987): 279–98.

61. To some extent, this decline can be seen as fallout from the larger decline of the recording industry in general, but the record executives and other industry insiders with

whom I spoke confirm that no other genre of Christian music has declined as rapidly and as dramatically as southern gospel in the past two decades.

62. Homi Bhabha, *The Location of Culture* (New York: Routledge, 1994), 90.

63. Daniel Walker Howe, "Politics, Secularization, and the Public Square" (presentation at the First Biennial Religion and American Culture Conference, Indianapolis, June 6, 2009).

64. Anthony Badger, *New Deal/New South: An Anthony J. Badger Reader* (Fayetteville: University of Arkansas Press, 2007).

65. On secularization and resacrilization, see, among others, N. J. Demerath III, "Secularization Deconstructed and Reconstructed," in *Sage Handbook of the Sociology of Religion*, ed. James Beckford and N. J. Demerath III (Los Angeles: Sage, 2007), 57–80. The career of "secularization" in the study of religion and American culture is varied and contentious. As Kathryn Lofton has pithily observed, "'Secularization' did not happen, precisely, but it also did not *not* happen" either. Lofton, review of *Culture and Redemption: Religion, the Secular, and American Literature*, by Tracy Fessenden, *Journal of the American Academy of Religion* 76, no. 2 (2008): 218. It is beyond the scope of this work to engage in a debate about or study of secularization. For my purposes, and following David Sehat, among others, I take "secularization" in America to describe a multimodal process by which religion as an institutional presence was displaced from the seat of cultural authority, independent of personal religious commitment. Sehat, *Myth of American Religious Freedom* (see chap. 2, n. 30). As this state of affairs pertains to southern gospel, I wish here to emphasize that the popular religious culture of mid-century evangelicals from the South or of southern extraction emerged from within a dynamic in which they perceived themselves to be in the midst of a cultural process of humanist secularization and impious devaluation of American piety. In turn, this perception intensified investment in personal and collective modes of expression for religious belief and experience.

Chapter 4. The Gaitherization of Contemporary Southern Gospel

1. See *Homecoming Video Album*, VHS (Nashville: StarSong, 1991).

2. Goff, *Close Harmony*, 292 (see introduction, n. 13).

3. Powell, "There's Just Something about That Man" (see introduction, n. 11).

4. Online responses to author's query.

5. On Gaither's vision of himself as a "putter together of talent," see Bill Gaither, *I Almost Missed the Sunset: My Perspectives on Life and Music* (Nashville: Thomas Nelson, 1992), 20, 200.

6. Gaither Vocal Band/Ernie Haase and Signature Sound, "I Then Shall Live," on *Together* (Gaither, 2007, SHD-2729).

7. Gaither, *It's More than Music*, 69–71 (see chap. 3, n. 22). My point here is meant to highlight the way the Homecoming series invites fans to identify primarily with Bill Gaither's personality and autobiography (namely, his personal relationships with a host of Christian music celebrities). A more sustained examination of the division of labor in the Gaithers' relationship would reward further investigation. Such a study would,

I suspect, reveal Gloria Gaither as a much greater influence on the Gaither style and brand than is suggested by her comparatively diminished roles in the Gaithers' various onstage endeavors together.

8. For one of the more influential theoretical explorations of nostalgia and history, see Frederic Jameson, *Postmodernism: The Cultural Logic of Late Capitalism* (Durham: Duke University Press, 1991). See the discussion of sentiment in chapter 2.

9. For Vestal Goodman's own account of her addiction to painkillers, see Vestal Goodman, *Vestal!* (Colorado Springs: Water Brook, 1998), 190–91. For more on the breakup of the Happy Goodman Family, see David Bruce Murray, *Murray's Encyclopedia of Southern Gospel Music* (n.p.: Musicscribe, 2005), 50.

10. *Bill and Gloria Gaither Present the Journey: The Goodman Family*, VHS (Nashville: StarSong, 1994); Sean Scanlan, "Introduction: Nostalgia," *Iowa Journal of Cultural Studies* 5 (2008): 3.

11. See *Feelin' at Home*, DVD (VHS, 1997) (Alexandria, Ind.: Gaither Gospel Series, 2006); *Homecoming Texas Style*, VHS (Alexandria, Ind.: Gaither Gospel Series, 1996); *O Happy Day: Old-Time Southern Singing Convention Hall of Honor*, vol. 4, VHS (Alexandria, Ind.: Gaither Gospel Series, 1994); *Turn Your Radio On*, VHS (Alexandria, Ind.: Gaither Gospel Series, 1998); *Old Friends*, DVD (Alexandria, Ind.: Gaither Gospel Series, 2008); *Precious Memories*, VHS (Alexandria, Ind.: Gaither Gospel Series, 1994).

12. Scanlan, "Introduction: Nostalgia," 4. For a sustained examination of nostalgia's place in contemporary history, see also Margaret McMillan, *Dangerous Games: The Uses and Abuses of History* (New York: Modern Library, 2009).

13. Anderson, *Imagined Communities* (see introduction, n. 23).

14. Elsewhere I have traced Homecoming's influence on markets and cultures beyond its own and those immediately adjacent to it. See Douglas Harrison, "Gaither Homecomings, College Football Reunions, and the Consecration of Cultural History," *Journal of Religion and Popular Culture* 22, no. 1 (2010), http://www.usask.ca/relst/jrpc/art22(3)-homecomings.html.

15. Gaither, *It's More than Music*, 14.

16. "Where Could I Go?" in *New Songs of Inspiration: No. 9* (Nashville: John T. Benson), 113.

17. Michael Graves, "The Gaither Homecoming Videos and the Ceremonial Reinstatement of Southern Gospel Music Performers," in *More than Precious Memories*, ed. Graves and Fillingim, 153 (see introduction, n. 13).

18. For English's own account of his ordeal, see English, *Prodigal Comes Home* (see chap. 2, n. 72). For more on Calvin Newton, see Cheatham, *Bad Boy of Gospel Music* (see chap. 2, n. 73).

19. Gaither, *It's More than Music*, 305.

20. Ibid., 178–88.

21. "Southern and Country Artists Featured at Bill Gaither's Celebration Theater," *Singing News*, June 1992, 39–41.

22. This reverence may help explain why so many artists are willing to appear on Homecoming recordings under contractual terms that by all accounts financially redound lopsidedly to Gaither's benefit. Gospel music business executives and artists are

reluctant to talk openly about the details of contracts required of those who appear on the Homecoming tour. But numerous discussions I have had with industry professionals confirm that artists who appear on Homecoming videos must relinquish many remunerative rights to their appearance, which include most of the kinds of royalties that would typically be generated for each artist by the sales of the video or televised broadcasts of a concert.

23. See Michael Nelson, "Church on Saturday Night: Garrison Keillor's *A Prairie Home Companion*," *Virginia Quarterly Review* 77, no. 1 (2001): 1–18; and Sonja K. Foss and Karen A. Foss, "The Construction of Feminine Spectatorship in Garrison Keillor's Radio Monologues," *Quarterly Journal of Speech* 80 (1994): 410–26.

24. Gaither, *I Almost Missed the Sunset*, 91. See also Mark Lowry's comedy skit about all the humorous imperfections and foibles that the "famous" Bill Gaither reveals to Lowry as they travel on a tour bus together, on *Bill & Gloria Gaither Present: Ryman Gospel Reunion with Their Homecoming Friends*, DVD (Alexandria, Ind.: Gaither, 1996).

25. "His Eye Is on the Sparrow," in *Homecoming Souvenir Songbook*, 2:34–45 (see chap. 1, n. 8).

26. The unorthodox gendering of the Homecoming aesthetic, like Gaither's own peculiar brand of masculinity, seems to share some symmetries with W. Bradford Wilcox's "new man" paradigm for thinking through shifts in ideas about gender roles in evangelical patriarchy at the end of the twentieth century. Wilcox, *Soft Patriarchs: How Christianity Shapes Fathers and Husbands* (Chicago: University of Chicago Press, 2004). In particular, Wilcox stresses the way that the "new man" thinking of postmodern evangelicalism emphasizes more egalitarian modes of interaction with family and community and a more highly developed range of emotional registers with which to imagine the self and respond to the world.

27. Gaither, *It's More than Music*, 1.

28. Gaither, *I Almost Missed the Sunset*, 54.

29. Ibid., 76.

30. Ibid., 79–82. See also Gaither, *It's More than Music*, 138–39; "Because He Lives," in *Homecoming Souvenir Songbook*, 81–82 (see introduction, n. 46).

31. Gaither, *I Almost Missed the Sunset*, 1–2.

32. T. J. Jackson Lears, *No Place of Grace: Antimodernism and the Transformation of American Culture, 1880–1920* (Chicago: University of Chicago Press, 1994); Gaither, *It's More than Music*, 2–5.

33. "Shallow Water," on *Touched by an Angel* (CBS, May 20, 2001).

34. Gaither, *It's More than Music*, 115.

35. It has only been in the past decade that *Singing News* has stopped rigidly insisting that males featured on the magazine's cover have hair cropped above the collar.

36. *Joy in My Heart*, DVD (Alexandria, Ind.: Gaither Gospel Series, 2009).

37. David Taylor, *Happy Rhythm: A Biography of Hovie Lister and the Statesmen Quartet* (Lexington, Ind.: TaylorMade, 1994), 156–57.

38. Gaither, *It's More than Music*, 238–39.

39. Goff, *Close Harmony*, 278.

40. Murray, *Murray's Encyclopedia*, 46.

41. *Grand Ole Gospel Reunion*, VHS (Greenville, S.C.: Reel to Reel, 1989).

42. *Grand Ole Gospel Reunion*, VHS (Greenville, S.C.: Reel to Reel, 1991). Of course, it should not go without saying that there is a long "homecoming" tradition within rural evangelical churches stretching back at least a century. Usually annual events, these homecomings are times for former church members or family of current and former church members to gather for a day of celebration, memorials, food, and religious fellowship honoring the local church's legacy and influence in the community and efforts in advancement of the kingdom of heaven. This type of homecoming celebration is a central theme in Jeff Todd Titon's ethnographic study of southern Freewill Baptists, *Powerhouse for God* (see introduction, n. 40), and a documentary film of the same title.

43. To some extent, this debate is a proxy fight between conflicting factions in southern gospel. GOGR tends to be aligned with devotees of the so-called classic quartet style of southern gospel music that dates from the music's midcentury heyday. Consequently, GOGR has a throwback look and feel, echoing the preferences of fans who prize classic-quartet music above all else. Male quartets predominate, and standard tunes arranged in a traditional manner—acoustic performances of piano and vocals (no digital accompaniment tracks), homophonic verses, polyphonic courses, and staggered endings—are the norm. In contrast, Gaither partisans typically emphasize the way Homecoming rehabilitated the hillbilly image of southern gospel and raised its profile within the wider world of Christian entertainment at a moment when contemporary Christian music was eclipsing traditional white gospel.

44. Gaither, *It's More than Music*, 141–44.

45. See Greater Vision, "Well Done, My Child," on *Live at First Baptist Church Atlanta* (Daywind, 2001, DAY-1267D).

46. Gaither, *It's More than Music*, 29, 39–41.

47. Montell, *Singing the Glory Down*, 32 (see introduction, n. 29).

48. Kammen, *Mystic Chords of Memory* (see introduction, n. 17).

49. Montell, *Singing the Glory Down*, 49.

50. Ibid., 45.

51. To see the kinds of rustic, rural churches where singing conventions are often held, see *I'll Keep on Singing*, DVD (Murfreesboro: Middle Tennessee State University, 2010).

52. Wolfe, "Gospel Goes Uptown," 91 (see chap. 3, n. 1).

53. Hayden White, "Manifesto Time," in *Manifestos for History*, ed. Keith Jenkins et al. (London: Routledge, 2007), 224. This is not to say that Homecoming fans never engage in more traditional forms of participation. In addition to fans' singing along at home with the videos, audiences not irregularly join in at live concerts with those singing onstage, as one fan of the Homecoming concerts told me: "During a Gaither Homecoming concert a couple of years ago, the people seated behind us especially seemed to feel at home. They commented and sang along (both loudly) throughout the concert, as though they were at home, watching a video on TV."

54. Anderson, *Imagined Communities*, 5–8.

55. For the psychological function of nostalgia in song lyrics, see Krystine Irene Batcho, "Nostalgia and the Emotional Tone and Content of Song Lyrics," *American Journal of Psychology* 120, no. 3 (2007): 361–81.

Chapter 5. Southern Gospel in the Key of Queer

1. D. A. Miller, *Place for Us: Essay on the Broadway Musical* (Cambridge: Harvard University Press, 1998), 94.

2. For a similar treatment of homosexuality and opera, see Wayne Koestenbaum, *The Queen's Throat: Opera, Homosexuality, and the Mystery of Desire* (New York: Da Capo, 1993).

3. Adrienne Rich, "Compulsory Heterosexuality and Lesbian Experience," in *Blood, Bread, and Poetry* (New York: W. W. Norton, 1986), 26; Allison Glock, "Out of the Lord's Closet," GQ, August 2005, 168.

4. Nadine Hubbs, *The Queer Composition of America's Sound: Gay Modernists, American Music, and National Identity* (Berkeley and Los Angeles: University of California Press, 2004), 5; "Gay Singer's Blackmailer Gets Prison," Rainbow Network News, August 6, 2004, http://www.rainbownetwork.com/UserPortal/Article/Print.aspx?ID=14441&sid=27; Greg Linscot, "Gaither Addresses Lesbian Endorsement Allegations," Sharper Iron, May 7, 2006, http://www.sharperiron.org/gaither-addresses-lesbian-singer-endorsement-allegations; Kirk Talley, "Testamony [*sic*] of Kirk Talley," Restorationnet.com, http://www.restorationnet.org/12.html (accessed March 24, 2009); Glock, "Lord's Closet," 171–72; Bill Gaither, "Bill Gaither Issues Statement Regarding Misrepresentation," *Singing News*, May 2006, http://www.singingnews.com/southern-gospel-news/11592497.

5. For this reason, the utility of human-subject studies of the sort Gerald Walton has productively conducted within more progressive sectors of Protestant Christianity is severely limited in fundamentalist evangelicalism. See Gerald Walton, "'Fag Church': Men Who Integrate Gay and Christian Identities," *Journal of Homosexuality* 51, no. 2 (2006): 1–17.

6. Terry Lee Derrick, "Thinking Out Loud: The Gospel Truth," *Inside Out Nashville*, April 10, 2006, 5.

7. Judith Peraino, *Listening to the Sirens: Musical Technologies of Queer Identity from Homer to Hedwig* (Berkeley and Los Angeles: University of California Press, 2006), 6.

8. Judith (now Jake) Halberstam, *Female Masculinities* (Durham: Duke University Press, 1998); Adale Sholock, "Queer Theory in the First Person: Academic Autobiography and the Authoritative Contingencies of Visibility," *Cultural Critique* 66 (Spring 2007): 127–52; Champagne, *Ethics of Marginality*, 90 (see introduction, n. 55).

9. Murray, *Murray's Encyclopedia*, 41 (see chap. 4, n. 9).

10. This signature Vestal Goodman behavior—the clutching and waving of the white hankie for emphasis onstage—is well known and rehearsed among gay men in the southern urban bars, where her music is a fixture of gospel drag shows. When Vestal songs are featured, audiences will often flourish cocktail napkins in a participatory memorial to her fabulousness and to the fact that her style of costuming and makeup combined with her body type to eerily evoke the self-conscious artificiality and conscious bulk of many female impersonators. Edward Gray and Scott Thumma describe having witnessed this hankie-waving phenomenon in their ethnographic study of gospel hour at a southern urban gay bar during a performance of "Looking for a City," one of Vestal Goodman's most famous songs. But because they admittedly "[did] not know the choreographic

origins . . . of the hankie waving," it is inadvertently portrayed as a kind of indigenous folk mystery rather than what it really is: a gesture of camp homage. Gray and Thumma, "The Gospel Hour: Liminality, Identity, and Religion in a Gay Bar," in *Gay Religion*, ed. Gray and Thumma (Walnut Creek, Calif.: AltaMira, 2004), 291.

11. Anthony Heilbut, *Gospel Sound* (New York: Simon and Schuster, 1985), 182, 185. Heilbut also propounds a series of related explanations for homosexuality in black gospel, including a quasi-psychoanalytic claim about gospel's "enshrinement of the Mother" and the (unsubstantiated) assertion that rates of bisexuality are higher among poor blacks and Puerto Ricans.

12. Philip Brett and Elizabeth Wood, "Lesbian and Gay Music," *Revista Eletrônica de Musicologia* 7 (2002): 5.

13. Gray and Thumma, "Gospel Hour," 286.

14. Jeffrey Bennett and Isaac West, "'United We Stand, Divided We Fall': AIDS, Armorettes, and the Tactical Repertoires of Drag," *Southern Communication Journal* 74, no. 3 (2009): 307.

15. Judith Butler, "Imitation and Gender Insubordination," in *The Lesbian and Gay Studies Reader*, ed. Henry Abelove, Michele Aina Barale, and David Halperin (New York: Routledge, 1993), 314–15.

16. Bennett and West, "'United We Stand,'" 307; Gray and Thumma, "Gospel Hour," 286.

17. Joe Wlodarz, "Love Letter to Jane," *Camera Obscura* 67, no. 23 (2009): 160.

18. The McKameys, "God Will Make This Trial a Blessing," on *Sing Praises* (Morningstar, 1989, MS-4103).

19. Richard Hofstadter discusses the general dynamic of resentment and grievance animating American history in *The Paranoid Style in American Politics* (1964; reprint, New York: Vintage, 2008).

20. Surveys of American evangelicals consistently find high incidences of anxiety about negative perceptions of their religion among outsiders, accompanied by a widespread belief that evangelicals are "under attack" by secular American society. These beliefs occur at much higher rates among evangelicals than among nonbelievers. See Anna Greenberg and Jennifer Berktold, *Evangelicals in America* (Washington, D.C.: Greenberg Quinlan Rosner Research, 2004), http://www.pbs.org/wnet/religionandethics/week733/results.pdf; "Poll: Americans Believe Religion Is 'under Attack'—Majority Says Religion Is 'Losing Influence' in American Life," Anti-Defamation League, November 1, 2005, http://www.adl.org/PresRele/RelChStSep_90/4830_90.htm. These reports are reinforced by self-portrayals from within evangelical media. See "Evangelicals under Attack: Al Mohler & Franklin Graham on Secular Oppression," Big Daddy Weave: News and Commentary about All Things Baptist, May 6, 2010, http://www.thebigdaddyweave.com/2010/05/evangelicals-under-attack-al-mohler-franklin-graham-on-secular-oppression.html.

21. Tirdad Derakhshani, "Our Celebrity Madness: A Reflection of Consumerism," *Philadelphia Inquirer*, August 19, 2007, 29–32.

22. Erin Myers, "'Can You Handle My Truth?': Authenticity and the Celebrity Star Image," *Journal of Popular Culture* 42 (2009): 895.

23. See the discussion of the Reconstruction roots of southern gospel in chapter 2.

24. This dynamic holds true in politics as well, accounting for the appeal of George W. Bush and Sarah Palin in ways that most mainstream observers of American political culture have never seemed able to understand.

25. Bennett and West have identified a subset of southern drag queens who rely on "tactical repertoires" that strategically deviate from mimetic imitations of females common in so-called "glamour drag queen shows." Bennett and West, "'United We Stand,'" 307. For Tammy Faye Bakker as gospel drag queen, see Stephen Tropiano, "The Woman behind the Mascara," review of *The Eyes of Tammy Faye*, dir. Randy Barbato and Fenton Bailey, Pop Matters, http://www.popmatters.com/film/reviews/e/eyes-of-tammy-faye .shtml (accessed June 9, 2010).

26. I do not mean to suggest that these two subject positions—American evangelical and gay male—are experientially equivalent, exactly, and I will return to the (in)comparability of these two statuses in the epilogue. For now, it is enough to note that the imagined position of the "persecuted Christian majority" is no less experientially meaningful for largely being a construct of the evangelical imagination.

27. Michael Joseph Gross, "The Queen Is Dead," *Atlantic Monthly*, August 2000, http://www.theatlantic.com/past/docs/issues/2000/08/gross.htm.

28. Kelefah Sanneh, "Revelations: A Gospel Singer Comes Out," *New Yorker*, February 8, 2010, 52. Flunder's comment was made in the context of discussing black gospel music and the black church, which are much more closely aligned than southern gospel music and the white evangelical church. This chapter's primary focus is on queer identity and experience within southern gospel, an approach that reflects the sociohistorically distinct trajectories along which southern white and black gospel developed in the twentieth century. However, there are enough stylistic and experiential overlaps in the two traditions—not to mention literary depictions from James Baldwin (*Just above My Head*) and Langston Hughes's gospel plays—to strongly suggest that some black gay men find psychosexual affirmation of variant sexuality through black gospel in ways not wholly dissimilar from the white gospel dynamics I am interested in exploring here. In any event, further research is clearly needed into the extent to which race variously mediates the experience of gay men in gospel music among the black and white gospel traditions. For a preliminary discussion of race and gay male sexuality, see Charles Nero, "Black Gay Men and White Gay Men: A Less than Perfect Union," in *Out in the South*, ed. Carlos Dews and Carolyn Leste Law (Philadelphia: Temple University Press, 2001), 115–36. For a case study of scholarly lacunae in the scholarship of black gospel and African American literature, see Robert Reid-Pharr, *Once You Go Black: Choice, Desire, and the Black American Intellectual* (New York: New York University Press, 2007), 96–120.

29. Jerry Kirksey, "Sin Is Not News," *Singing News*, March 2004, 52.

30. Beginning on January 14, 2004, Kirk Talley copiously documented these and other aspects of the professional—and much of the personal—fallout he experienced after he was outed by the FBI case. These posts continued through March 5, 2004, when the conclusion of his "treatment" with the Restoration Team was announced in a post by the team's leader, Phil Hoskins. Talley has since removed all these posts from his Web site, kirk-talley.com, though I have retained page captures of these Web journal entries for research purposes.

31. Douglas Harrison, "NQC 2004," Averyfineline.com, September 6, 2004, http://averyfineline.com/2004/09/06/nqc-coverage-2004/.

32. Email message to author, October 6, 2004. Names of email correspondents withheld for privacy.

33. Eve Kosofsky Sedgwick, *Between Men: English Literature and Male Homosocial Desire* (New York: Columbia University Press, 1985), 89.

34. Michael Warner, "Tongues Untied: Memoirs of a Pentecostal Boyhood," in *Que(e)rying Religion: A Critical Anthology,* ed. Gary Comstock and Susan Henking (New York: Continuum, 1997), 228.

35. Though this linkage emerges from my own experience and analysis, I am not the first to see a general connection between conversion and coming out. For different takes on this connection, see Frank Browning, *A Queer Geography* (New York: Continuum, 1996); and Randy Shilts, *The Mayor of Castro Street* (New York: St. Martin's, 1982).

36. Warner, "Tongues Untied," 229 (emphasis in the original).

37. Email message to author, November 5, 2004.

38. Though hymnody and white gospel are largely distinct traditions with separately distinguishing stylistic and cultural functions, they share many features, especially in fundamentalist Protestant religious communities. In referring to hymns in the gospel tradition here, I mean to designate the way the lyrics and musical style of certain classic hymns used in the play borrow more heavily from and rely primarily on conventions of southern gospel than traditional hymnody.

39. Shores, *Southern Baptist Sissies,* 60 (see introduction, n. 47).

40. Ibid., 60–61.

41. All personal statements in this paragraph selected from online responses to author's query.

42. Dorothy Allison, *Bastard Out of Carolina* (New York: Plume, 1992), 136.

43. Augustine, *Confessions* (New York: Penguin, 1986), 177, 178. For an incisive (and queer) reading of music's function in Augustine's writings, see Peraino, *Listening to the Sirens.*

44. Shores, *Southern Baptist Sissies,* 16–17.

45. Ethnographers have observed a version of this effect at work in the popularity of gay gospel drag shows. In their study of Gospel Hour at an Atlanta gay bar, Gray and Thumma write about "Gary, a tall, handsome son of a famous Pentecostal preacher" who says of himself: "'I really missed gospel music [after I came out].' . . . 'There is a part of me that likes to sing,' Gary continued, 'so now I sing gospel music in a gay bar.'" Gray and Thumma conclude that "like so many at the Gospel Hour, Gary loves to sing, and he loves to sing these songs" ("Gospel Hour," 290).

46. K. Miller, *Traveling Home,* 128–29 (see chap. 2, n. 58); Brett and Wood, "Lesbian and Gay Music," 5.

47. See the discussions of "Oh, What a Savior" and "That I Could Still Go Free" in chapter 1.

48. Brett and Wood, "Lesbian and Gay Music," 43.

49. The radically shifting and highly contingent meanings of homosocial interactions in evangelicalism is part of what makes ex-gay responses to homosexuality so

problematic from a practical standpoint. As part of many ex-gay "treatment" regimes, men with same-sex attractions are commonly put into notionally therapeutic situations that involve sharing deeply intimate thoughts and feelings with other men in similar situations. This sharing encourages men to bond and express such bonds in ways that can in turn easily lead to physical encounters (shoulder pats, embraces, hands clasped in communal prayer) that strain the rational distinction between Christian brotherhood and the felt reality of homoerotic attraction. For more on ex-gay reparative therapy, see Tanya Erzen, *Straight to Jesus: Sexual and Christian Conversions in the Ex-Gay Movement* (Berkeley and Los Angeles: University of California Press, 2006).

50. William James, *The Varieties of Religious Experience* (New York: Touchstone, 2004), 191; Sedgwick, *Between Men*, 89.

51. Mitchell Morris, "Stories Coming Out," *Journal of Popular Music Studies* 18, no. 2 (2006): 223; "Jonathan Wilburn Celebrates 10 Years with Gold City," Sogospelnews.com, June 14, 2006, http://sogospelnews.com/index/content/articles/jonathan-wilburn-celebrates-10-years-with-gold-city/.

52. Kirk Talley, "Intimacy with Jesus," on *Live at the River: My Story, My Song* (Springside, 2005, IR-37086).

53. Kirk Talley, interview with Pamela Furr, Loyalears.com, August 4, 2005, http://podcast.loyalears.com/midwest.php.

54. Arguably, Talley's infusion of religious imagery with same-sex erotic possibility continues a long-standing tradition of gospel hymns suffused with queer potential. In an unpublished essay from 1925, composer and music critic Virgil Thomson reads gospel hymns as surreptitious vehicles for homosexual erotics, going so far as to tally up the number of songs in the 1917 hymnal *Treasury of Song*—ninety-one, by Thomson's count—that "confess erotic feeling for the person of Jesus." In Thomson's view, the preoccupation with sexualized rhetoric about Christ manifests a Freudian "fixation of the libido upon an unattainable object." The eroticized Jesus of gospel hymns transforms taboo homosexual desires into a more acceptable religious "yearning" for the Savior that does not run afoul of the "imaginary social code which is such a terror to Americans." Carol Oju, *Making Music Modern: New York in the 1920s* (New York: Oxford University Press, 2000), 252–63.

55. Bob Whitehead, review of *Live at the River: My Story, My Song*, by Kirk Talley. *Absolutely Gospel*, August 31, 2005, http://susan.sogospelnews.com/index/content/articles/4465/.

56. Talley interview.

Epilogue

1. Laurence R. Iannoccone, "Why Strict Churches Are Strong," *American Journal of Sociology* 99, no. 5 (1994): 1181–82; Shayne Lee and Phillip Luke Sinitiere, *Holy Mavericks: Evangelical Innovators and the Spiritual Marketplace* (New York: New York University Press, 2010), 7. See also Timothy Beal, "Among the Evangelicals," *Chronicle Review*, December 12, 2010.

2. Robert Orsi, "Everyday Miracles: The Study of Lived Religion," in *Lived Religion in America: Toward a History of Practice*, ed. David D. Hall (Princeton: Princeton University

Press, 1998), 7; James Bielo, *Words upon the Word: An Ethnography of Evangelical Group Bible Study* (New York: New York University Press, 2009), 3. Bielo's work is representative of some of the best recent ethnographic and sociological studies of American evangelicalism (see also, for instance, Frykholm, *Rapture Culture* [see introduction, n. 43]). This work is particularly powerful in its careful mapping of how evangelicals cultivate a shared vision of cultural identity and simultaneously negotiate the shoals of internal dissent through religious activities explicitly or implicitly organized around the church community.

3. This is particularly true in the study of evangelical music, which is often always already assumed to be synonymous with hymnody. For an example of studies that de-center the church as the focal point for the study of evangelicalism in ways similar to my own approach, see Goff, "'We Have Heard the Joyful Sound,'" 67–95 (see chap. 2, n. 50). For an exploration of music and agency in American systems of belief, see Philip V. Bohlman, "Prayer on the Panorama: Music and Individualism in American Religious Experience," in *Music in the American Religious Experience*, ed. Philip Bohlman, Edith Blumhofer, and Maria Chow (New York: Oxford University Press, 2006), 233–54. For treatments of music and evangelicalism in particular, see Stowe, *No Sympathy for the Devil* (see chap. 3, n. 41).

4. Here I have in mind my own somewhat queer version of what Robert Orsi has called an "erotics of religious studies." Orsi, "Snakes Alive: Resituating the Moral in the Study of Religion," in *Women, Gender, Religion: A Reader*, ed. Elizabeth A. Castelli and Rosamond C. Rodman (New York: Palgrave, 2001), 99.

5. Brumley, "Turn Your Radio On," 6–7 (see chap. 2, n. 50).

6. Online responses to author's query.

7. I emphasize the effort to take southern gospel "seriously" with no little awareness of the critique of scholarly "seriousness" in religious studies that Elizabeth Pritchard has rightly made. Pritchard draws attention to the risks of what she calls "the heroics of seriousness," a scholarly approach that uses the rhetoric of liberal secularism to mask "a tacit discomfort with, and ritualistic management of, difference and conflict." Pritchard, "Seriously, What Does 'Taking Religion Seriously' Mean?" *Journal of the American Academy of Religion* 78, no. 4 (2010): 1087–111. I cannot guarantee my own work does not at times inadvertently fall into this trap, only that I have rigorously attempted to balance scholarly analysis with a healthy respect for the incommensurability of academic and absolutist habits of mind and experience at some level.

8. Jonathan Edwards, *Religious Affections*, in *Jonathan Edwards: Representative Selections*, ed. Thomas Johnson and Clarence Faust (New York: American, 1962), 243.

9. See Harry Crews, *The Gospel Singer*; James Baldwin, *Just above My Head*; Harold Frederic, *Damnation of Theron Ware*; Sinclair Lewis, *Elmer Gantry*; Fanny Flagg, *Standing in the Rainbow*; Dorothy Allison, *Bastard Out of Carolina*; and Del Shores, *Southern Gospel Sissies*.

10. Mark Hulsether, *Religion, Culture, and Politics in the Twentieth-Century United States* (New York: Columbia University Press, 2007), 16–17.

11. Allison Durham Speer, "I'm Bound for That City," on *This Old House* (Crossroads, 2006, CD-0746).

Appendix B

1. This breakdown contrasts with other attempts to describe the gender distribution in southern gospel. Readership demographics provided by *Singing News* estimate the proportion of men and women in southern gospel more evenly (48 percent men and 52 percent women). "*Singing News* Media Kit," *Singing News* (2006), 1.

2. I am grateful for the work of Maryann Batlle, Elizabeth Weatherford, and Kimberly Lojewski in this process. Robert Higginbotham also provided research assistant in the early stages of working this data. I am grateful to the Department of Language and Literature (particularly Myra Mendible) and the College of Arts and Sciences at Florida Gulf Coast University for their financial support of this research project.

3. On latent coding, see G. Shapiro and J. Markoff, "A Matter of Definition," in *Text Analysis for the Social Sciences: Methods for Drawing Statistical Inferences from Texts and Transcripts*, ed. C. W. Roberts (Mahwah, N.J.: Lawrence Erlbaum Associates, 1997).

4. On analyst-constructed typologies and indigenous categories, see Michael Q. Patton, *Qualitative Evaluation and Research Methods* (Thousand Oaks, Calif.: Sage, 1990).

Index

DOUGLAS HARRISON is an associate professor of English at Florida Gulf Coast University.

Music in American Life

Carl Ruggles: Composer, Painter, and Storyteller   *Marilyn Ziffrin*
Never without a Song: The Years and Songs of Jennie Devlin, 1865–1952
   Katharine D. Newman
The Hank Snow Story   *Hank Snow, with Jack Ownbey and Bob Burris*
Milton Brown and the Founding of Western Swing   *Cary Ginell, with special
   assistance from Roy Lee Brown*
Santiago de Murcia's "Códice Saldívar No. 4": A Treasury of Secular Guitar
   Music from Baroque Mexico   *Craig H. Russell*
The Sound of the Dove: Singing in Appalachian Primitive Baptist Churches
   Beverly Bush Patterson
Heartland Excursions: Ethnomusicological Reflections on Schools of Music
   Bruno Nettl
Doowop: The Chicago Scene   *Robert Pruter*
Blue Rhythms: Six Lives in Rhythm and Blues   *Chip Deffaa*
Shoshone Ghost Dance Religion: Poetry Songs and Great Basin Context
   Judith Vander
Go Cat Go! Rockabilly Music and Its Makers   *Craig Morrison*
'Twas Only an Irishman's Dream: The Image of Ireland and the Irish in
   American Popular Song Lyrics, 1800–1920   *William H. A. Williams*
Democracy at the Opera: Music, Theater, and Culture in New York City, 1815–60
   Karen Ahlquist
Fred Waring and the Pennsylvanians   *Virginia Waring*
Woody, Cisco, and Me: Seamen Three in the Merchant Marine   *Jim Longhi*
Behind the Burnt Cork Mask: Early Blackface Minstrelsy and Antebellum
   American Popular Culture   *William J. Mahar*
Going to Cincinnati: A History of the Blues in the Queen City   *Steven C. Tracy*
Pistol Packin' Mama: Aunt Molly Jackson and the Politics of Folksong
   Shelly Romalis
Sixties Rock: Garage, Psychedelic, and Other Satisfactions   *Michael Hicks*
The Late Great Johnny Ace and the Transition from R&B to Rock 'n' Roll
   James M. Salem
Tito Puente and the Making of Latin Music   *Steven Loza*
Juilliard: A History   *Andrea Olmstead*
Understanding Charles Seeger, Pioneer in American Musicology
   Edited by Bell Yung and Helen Rees
Mountains of Music: West Virginia Traditional Music from *Goldenseal*
   Edited by John Lilly
Alice Tully: An Intimate Portrait   *Albert Fuller*
A Blues Life   *Henry Townsend, as told to Bill Greensmith*
Long Steel Rail: The Railroad in American Folksong (2d ed.)   *Norm Cohen*
The Golden Age of Gospel   *Text by Horace Clarence Boyer; photography by
   Lloyd Yearwood*
Aaron Copland: The Life and Work of an Uncommon Man   *Howard Pollack*
Louis Moreau Gottschalk   *S. Frederick Starr*
Race, Rock, and Elvis   *Michael T. Bertrand*

Theremin: Ether Music and Espionage *Albert Glinsky*
Poetry and Violence: The Ballad Tradition of Mexico's Costa Chica
    John H. McDowell
The Bill Monroe Reader *Edited by Tom Ewing*
Music in Lubavitcher Life *Ellen Koskoff*
Zarzuela: Spanish Operetta, American Stage *Janet L. Sturman*
Bluegrass Odyssey: A Documentary in Pictures and Words, 1966–86
    Carl Fleischhauer and Neil V. Rosenberg
That Old-Time Rock & Roll: A Chronicle of an Era, 1954–63 *Richard Aquila*
Labor's Troubadour *Joe Glazer*
American Opera *Elise K. Kirk*
Don't Get above Your Raisin': Country Music and the Southern Working Class
    Bill C. Malone
John Alden Carpenter: A Chicago Composer *Howard Pollack*
Heartbeat of the People: Music and Dance of the Northern Pow-wow *Tara Browner*
My Lord, What a Morning: An Autobiography *Marian Anderson*
Marian Anderson: A Singer's Journey *Allan Keiler*
Charles Ives Remembered: An Oral History *Vivian Perlis*
Henry Cowell, Bohemian *Michael Hicks*
Rap Music and Street Consciousness *Cheryl L. Keyes*
Louis Prima *Garry Boulard*
Marian McPartland's Jazz World: All in Good Time *Marian McPartland*
Robert Johnson: Lost and Found *Barry Lee Pearson and Bill McCulloch*
Bound for America: Three British Composers *Nicholas Temperley*
Lost Sounds: Blacks and the Birth of the Recording Industry, 1890–1919 *Tim Brooks*
Burn, Baby! BURN! The Autobiography of Magnificent Montague
    Magnificent Montague with Bob Baker
Way Up North in Dixie: A Black Family's Claim to the Confederate Anthem
    Howard L. Sacks and Judith Rose Sacks
The Bluegrass Reader *Edited by Thomas Goldsmith*
Colin McPhee: Composer in Two Worlds *Carol J. Oja*
Robert Johnson, Mythmaking, and Contemporary American Culture
    Patricia R. Schroeder
Composing a World: Lou Harrison, Musical Wayfarer *Leta E. Miller*
    and Fredric Lieberman
Fritz Reiner, Maestro and Martinet *Kenneth Morgan*
That Toddlin' Town: Chicago's White Dance Bands and Orchestras, 1900–1950
    Charles A. Sengstock Jr.
Dewey and Elvis: The Life and Times of a Rock 'n' Roll Deejay *Louis Cantor*
Come Hither to Go Yonder: Playing Bluegrass with Bill Monroe *Bob Black*
Chicago Blues: Portraits and Stories *David Whiteis*
The Incredible Band of John Philip Sousa *Paul E. Bierley*
"Maximum Clarity" and Other Writings on Music *Ben Johnston,*
    edited by Bob Gilmore
Staging Tradition: John Lair and Sarah Gertrude Knott *Michael Ann Williams*